National Parks

EXPLORE AMERICA

National Parks

Reader's Digest

THE READER'S DIGEST ASSOCIATION, INC.
Pleasantville, New York / Montreal

NATIONAL PARKS was created and produced by St. Remy Multimedia.

PRESIDENT: Pierre Léveillé
PUBLISHER: Kenneth Winchester

STAFF FOR NATIONAL PARKS
Series Editor: Carolyn Jackson
Series Art Director: Diane Denoncourt
Senior Editor: Elizabeth Cameron
Art Director: Odette Sévigny
Picture Editor: Christopher Jackson
Assistant Editors: Margaret Caldbick,
Alfred Lemaitre, Christopher Little
Researcher: Rory Gilsenan
Contributing Researchers: Olga Dzatko,
Joanne Miller
Designer: Hélène Dion
Index: Christine Jacobs

Writers: Rita Ariyoshi—Hawaii
Bob Devine—Yosemite
Kim Heacox—Denali, Everglades
Jim Henderson—Big Bend
Rose Houk—Great Smoky Mountains
Rick Marsi—Acadia, Yellowstone
Tim McNulty—Olympic
Jeremy Schmidt—Grand Canyon

Contributing Writers: Susan Purcell,
Lynne Roberts, Stanley Whyte

Administrator: Natalie Watanabe
Production Manager: Michelle Turbide
Systems Coordinator: Jean-Luc Roy

READER'S DIGEST STAFF
Editor: James Cassidy
Art Director: Evelyn Bauer
Art Associate: Martha Grossman

READER'S DIGEST GENERAL BOOKS
Editor in Chief: John A. Pope, Jr.
Managing Editor: Jane Polley
Executive Editor: Susan J. Wernert
Art Director: David Trooper
Group Editors: Will Bradbury, Sally French,
Norman B. Mack, Kaari Ward
Group Art Editors: Evelyn Bauer,
Robert M. Grant, Joel Musler
Chief of Research: Laurel A. Gilbride
Copy Chief: Edward W. Atkinson
Picture Editor: Richard Pasqual
Rights and Permissions: Pat Colomban
Head Librarian: Jo Manning

Opening photographs
Cover: Brahma Temple, Grand Canyon National Park
Page 2: Redwood trees, Redwood National Park
Page 5: Herd of elk, Yellowstone National Park

The credits and acknowledgments that appear on page 144 are hereby made a part of this copyright page.

Library of Congress Cataloging in Publication Data

National parks.
       p.   cm.—(Explore America)
    ISBN 0-89577-447-X
    1. National parks and reserves—United States—Guidebooks.
  I. Reader's Digest Association. II. Series
  E160.N247 1993
  917.3'04928—dc20   92-35785

Printed in the United States of America
Third Printing, July 1996

CONTENTS

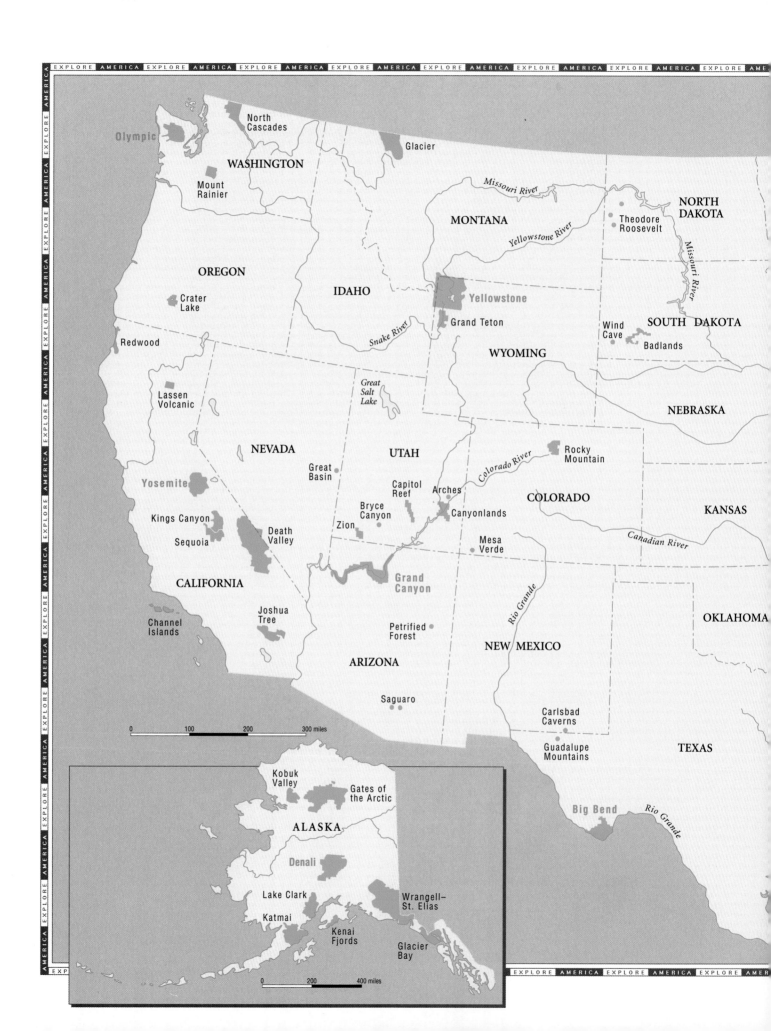

Olympic

North
Cascades

Glacier

WASHINGTON

Mount
Rainier

Missouri River

MONTANA

Yellowstone River

Theodore
Roosevelt

NORTH
DAKOTA

Missouri River

OREGON

IDAHO

Crater
Lake

Yellowstone

Snake River

Grand Teton

SOUTH DAKOTA

Wind
Cave

Badlands

Redwood

WYOMING

Lassen
Volcanic

Great
Salt
Lake

NEBRASKA

NEVADA

UTAH

Great
Basin

Capitol
Reef

Arches

Colorado River

Rocky
Mountain

Yosemite

Bryce
Canyon

Canyonlands

COLORADO

KANSAS

Kings Canyon

Zion

Death
Valley

Mesa
Verde

Canadian River

Sequoia

CALIFORNIA

Grand
Canyon

Channel
Islands

Joshua
Tree

Petrified
Forest

Rio Grande

OKLAHOMA

NEW MEXICO

ARIZONA

Saguaro

Carlsbad
Caverns

TEXAS

Guadalupe
Mountains

Big Bend

Rio Grande

0   100   200   300 miles

Kobuk
Valley

Gates of
the Arctic

ALASKA

Denali

Lake Clark

Wrangell–
St. Elias

Katmai

Kenai
Fjords

Glacier
Bay

0   200   400 miles

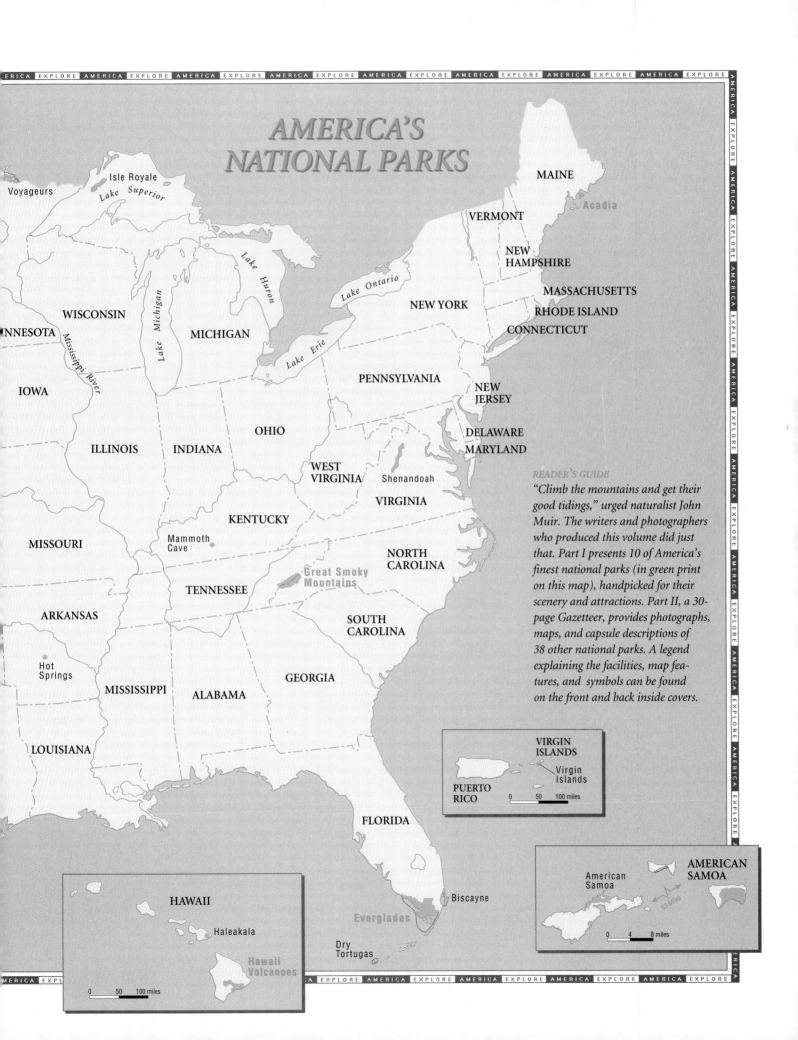

AMERICA'S NATIONAL PARKS

Voyageurs

Isle Royale
Lake Superior

MAINE

Acadia

VERMONT

NEW
HAMPSHIRE

Lake Huron

Lake Ontario

MASSACHUSETTS

RHODE ISLAND

CONNECTICUT

NEW YORK

MINNESOTA

WISCONSIN

Lake Michigan

MICHIGAN

Lake Erie

IOWA

Mississippi River

PENNSYLVANIA

NEW
JERSEY

ILLINOIS

INDIANA

OHIO

DELAWARE
MARYLAND

WEST
VIRGINIA

Shenandoah

VIRGINIA

MISSOURI

KENTUCKY

Mammoth
Cave

NORTH
CAROLINA

Great Smoky
Mountains

ARKANSAS

TENNESSEE

SOUTH
CAROLINA

Hot
Springs

MISSISSIPPI

ALABAMA

GEORGIA

LOUISIANA

READER'S GUIDE

"Climb the mountains and get their good tidings," urged naturalist John Muir. The writers and photographers who produced this volume did just that. Part I presents 10 of America's finest national parks (in green print on this map), handpicked for their scenery and attractions. Part II, a 30-page Gazetteer, provides photographs, maps, and capsule descriptions of 38 other national parks. A legend explaining the facilities, map features, and symbols can be found on the front and back inside covers.

VIRGIN ISLANDS

PUERTO
RICO

Virgin
Islands

0   50   100 miles

FLORIDA

AMERICAN SAMOA

American
Samoa

63 Miles

0   4   8 miles

Biscayne

Everglades

HAWAII

Haleakala

Dry
Tortugas

Hawaii
Volcanoes

0   50   100 miles

ACADIA

*With the rugged coast of Maine
as their arena, two giants do battle
in a perpetual struggle.*

The adversaries are ocean versus granite, sea against shoreline, time and erosion in combat with rocks that seem tougher than any on earth. And the battleground is Mount Desert Island, the largest rock island on the Atlantic coast of the United States.

Roughly half the island—about 30,000 acres—comprises the largest section of Acadia National Park, a stunning combination of cliffs, pounding waves and the round, lichen-covered peaks of worn granite mountains.

Surrounding the park—swaying, lapping or slamming like thunder—is the sea, tireless grinder, reducer of boulders to sand. Admirers of Acadia claim no other place on America's eastern seaboard bears such beautiful witness to the interaction of ocean and shore. Standing on the crest of a Mount Desert Island headland that plows like the bow of a great granite ship through the surf, a first-time visitor would find this claim borne out by vistas of virtual perfection.

Rising from the Atlantic less than a quarter of a mile from the mainland, and connected to it by a modern causeway, Mount Desert Island owes

as much of its beauty to the nearby coastline as it does to its own rugged features.

Shedding islands into the sea like fragments of tattered fabric, the Maine coast near Acadia features a seemingly endless procession of ragged peninsulas, each one a bastion of rock against wave, where spruces edge down from dense forested headlands to the line of the surf's longest reach.

One such headland, Schoodic Peninsula, houses Acadia National Park's only mainland component: a scenic section of coast, including Schoodic Point, where the sea hammers granite ledges with breakers that shoot up like geysers. Fifty miles from Acadia's main entrance on Mount Desert Island, the Schoodic Peninsula section of Acadia is joined by the tiny islands of Baker and Isle au Haut in rounding out the park's holdings.

Lying about six miles east of Mount Desert Island's southern tip, uninhabited Baker Island and its lighthouse welcome day visitors on cruises led by National Park Service naturalists during the summer. Fifteen miles southwest of Mount Desert, 4,500-acre Isle au Haut also hosts a small but steady number of visitors. More than half of this island—some 2,800 acres—belongs to the National Park Service. A network of trails allows hikers access to Isle au Haut's boulder-strewn beaches, where tidal pools brim with marine organisms. Other trails lead them up to windswept promontories, where every direction offers views of the ocean, sighing or crashing, bright blue or black as a thunderhead.

But the spot in Acadia people visit most is Mount Desert Island, the jewel in this park's salt-sprayed crown. Home to more than a dozen ancient gray mountains, Mount Desert Island is the ultimate stage for the drama of earth versus ocean.

Nowhere in the park is this clash more impressive—and more easily viewed—than along Acadia's 27-mile Park Loop Road. Beginning at the Hulls Cove Visitor Center near the island's northeastern shore, the road first skirts the ocean before heading inland through glacier-carved valleys and past lakes fringed with conifer stands.

Near the end of this loop, a spur route starts climbing Cadillac Mountain. At 1,530 feet, its summit on the island's northeastern shoulder is the highest point on the Atlantic coast. Depending on the time of year, the first sunlight to touch the U.S. each morning strikes either this mountain or the village of Eastport, farther up the Maine coast.

From Cadillac's summit, the island's surroundings unfold: below, to the east and rolling out toward the coast, rise the bare rock summits of Dorr and Champlain mountains; beyond them lies wind-whipped Frenchman Bay, studded by small granite humps called the Porcupine Islands. Away from the sea, to the west, a new vista unfolds. Eagle Lake lies below, a two-mile-long hollow scooped out of granite by glaciers. Summer sometimes finds loons knifing through its cool waters, their spear-shaped bills skewering fish.

These vistas from Cadillac Mountain are diverse and breathtaking, but slightly removed from the action. To feel the salt spray, visitors must drive the Loop Road, getting out at its frequent pull-off points and walking the wave-battered shore. However, it's best not to leave Cadillac Mountain without pondering Acadia's roots. Here, on the summit, it is easy to envision how this beautiful island was formed. Observers need only gaze out at the Porcupine Islands, those worn granite blocks rising up from Frenchman Bay. The Porcupines weren't always separated from the Maine coast. Neither was Mount Desert Island. Not until glaciers covered this land, then receded, did Mount Desert's highlands become isolated by ocean waters.

About one million years ago, during a time called the Pleistocene Epoch, a thick sheet of ice began building up over most of eastern and southern Canada. Slowly, inexorably, it crept southeastward and smothered New England. Several times during the Pleistocene, it advanced, melted back, then advanced once again.

Coming and going, this debris-laden ice covered and scoured the Maine coastal region. On what is now Mount Desert Island, it pushed over a formidable east-west granite ridge, slicing it into numerous individual mountains. The glacier ground their peaks smooth, rounded them off and grooved them with deep striations. Below the peaks, glacial ice

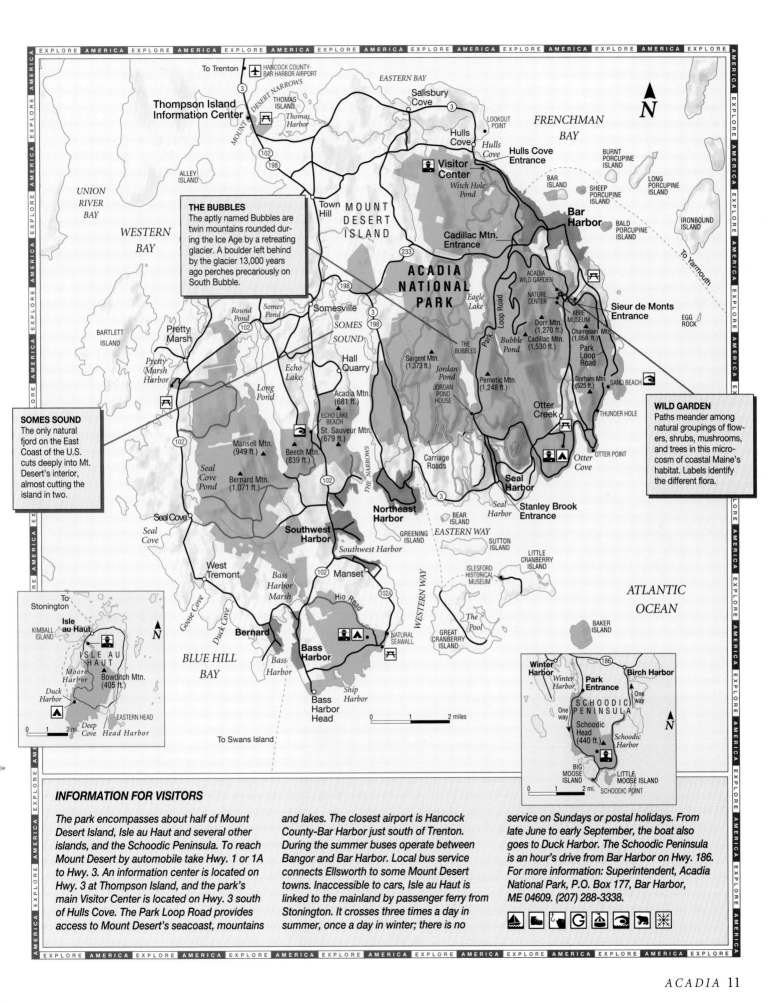

To Trenton

HANCOCK COUNTY-
BAR HARBOR AIRPORT

**Thompson Island
Information Center**

THOMAS
ISLAND

Thomas Harbor

MOUNT DESERT NARROWS

EASTERN BAY

Salisbury
Cove

3

LOOKOUT
POINT

*FRENCHMAN
BAY*

Hulls
Cove

*Hulls
Cove*

**Hulls Cove
Entrance**

BURNT
PORCUPINE
ISLAND

N

ALLEY
ISLAND

102

198

Town
Hill

M O U N T
D E S E R T
I S L A N D

233

**Visitor
Center**

*Witch Hole
Pond*

**Cadillac Mtn.
Entrance**

BAR
ISLAND

SHEEP
PORCUPINE
ISLAND

LONG
PORCUPINE
ISLAND

**Bar
Harbor**

BALD
PORCUPINE
ISLAND

IRONBOUND
ISLAND

To Yarmouth

*UNION
RIVER
BAY*

*WESTERN
BAY*

BARTLETT
ISLAND

THE BUBBLES
The aptly named Bubbles are
twin mountains rounded during the Ice Age by a retreating
glacier. A boulder left behind
by the glacier 13,000 years
ago perches precariously on
South Bubble.

*Round
Pond*

*Somes
Pond*

Pretty
Marsh

*Pretty
Marsh
Harbor*

102

Somesville

*SOMES
SOUND*

198

3

198

A C A D I A
N A T I O N A L
P A R K

*Eagle
Lake*

ACADIA
WILD GARDEN

NATURE
CENTER

ABBE
MUSEUM

**Sieur de Monts
Entrance**

EGG
ROCK

*Dorr Mtn.
(1,270 ft.)*

*Champlain Mtn.
(1,058 ft.)*

SOMES SOUND
The only natural
fjord on the East
Coast of the U.S.
cuts deeply into Mt.
Desert's interior,
almost cutting the
island in two.

*Long
Pond*

*Echo
Lake*

Hall
Quarry

ECHO LAKE
BEACH

*Acadia Mtn.
(681 ft.)*

*St. Sauveur Mtn.
(679 ft.)*

*Sargent Mtn.
(1,373 ft.)*

THE
BUBBLES

*Bubble
Pond*

*Cadillac Mtn.
(1,530 ft.)*

*Jordan
Pond*

JORDAN
POND
HOUSE

*Pemetic Mtn.
(1,248 ft.)*

Park Loop Road

Park
Loop
Road

*Gorham Mtn.
(525 ft.)*

SAND BEACH

WILD GARDEN
Paths meander among
natural groupings of flowers, shrubs, mushrooms,
and trees in this micro-
cosm of coastal Maine's
habitat. Labels identify
the different flora.

*Mansell Mtn.
(949 ft.)*

*Beech Mtn.
(839 ft.)*

Carriage
Roads

THE NARROWS

THUNDER HOLE

**Otter
Creek**

OTTER POINT

*Otter
Cove*

*Seal
Cove
Pond*

*Bernard Mtn.
(1,071 ft.)*

Seal Cove

*Seal
Cove*

**Northeast
Harbor**

BEAR
ISLAND

GREENING
ISLAND

EASTERN WAY

SUTTON
ISLAND

**Seal
Harbor**

*Seal
Harbor*

**Stanley Brook
Entrance**

**Southwest
Harbor**

Southwest Harbor

West
Tremont

102

Manset

102A

*Bass
Harbor
Marsh*

Hio Road

ISLESFORD
HISTORICAL
MUSEUM

LITTLE
CRANBERRY
ISLAND

WESTERN WAY

*ATLANTIC
OCEAN*

Goose Cove

Duck Cove

Bernard

*Bass
Harbor*

**Bass
Harbor**

NATURAL
SEAWALL

*BLUE HILL
BAY*

*Ship
Harbor*

Bass
Harbor
Head

*The
Pool*

GREAT
CRANBERRY
ISLAND

BAKER
ISLAND

To Swans Island

0 1 2 miles

Isle au Haut inset:

To
Stonington

KIMBALL
ISLAND

**Isle
au Haut**

I S L E A U
H A U T

*Moore
Harbor*

*Bowditch Mtn.
(405 ft.)*

*Duck
Harbor*

EASTERN HEAD

*Deep
Cove*

Head Harbor

N

0 1 2 mi.

Schoodic Peninsula inset:

**Winter
Harbor**

186

Birch Harbor

*Winter
Harbor*

**Park
Entrance**

One
way

S C H O O D I C
P E N I N S U L A

One way

One
way

*Schoodic Head
(440 ft.)*

*Schoodic
Harbor*

BIG
MOOSE
ISLAND

LITTLE
MOOSE ISLAND

SCHOODIC POINT

N

0 1 2 mi.

INFORMATION FOR VISITORS

The park encompasses about half of Mount
Desert Island, Isle au Haut and several other
islands, and the Schoodic Peninsula. To reach
Mount Desert by automobile take Hwy. 1 or 1A
to Hwy. 3. An information center is located on
Hwy. 3 at Thompson Island, and the park's
main Visitor Center is located on Hwy. 3 south
of Hulls Cove. The Park Loop Road provides
access to Mount Desert's seacoast, mountains
and lakes. The closest airport is Hancock
County-Bar Harbor just south of Trenton.
During the summer buses operate between
Bangor and Bar Harbor. Local bus service
connects Ellsworth to some Mount Desert
towns. Inaccessible to cars, Isle au Haut is
linked to the mainland by passenger ferry from
Stonington. It crosses three times a day in
summer, once a day in winter; there is no
service on Sundays or postal holidays. From
late June to early September, the boat also
goes to Duck Harbor. The Schoodic Peninsula
is an hour's drive from Bar Harbor on Hwy. 186.
For more information: Superintendent, Acadia
National Park, P.O. Box 177, Bar Harbor,
ME 04609. (207) 288-3338.

Dinghies are moored to the dock at Bass Harbor after a day of fishing. The quiet village is located just outside park boundaries on Highway 102. It is a pleasant sidetrip for visitors with the urge to explore a traditional Maine working harbor and fishing village.

SEAFOOD LOVERS

Inquisitive but cautious harbor seals lounge at sunset on one of Acadia's offshore islands. The animals are remarkable swimmers, slipping from their rocky sun-bathing perches into the open sea for a meal of fish or crustaceans.

gouged and deepened river-carved valleys. It ripped boulders from steep slopes, then scattered them over miles. Pressed down by the weight of this glacier, the coast slowly warped downward, setting the stage for great floods at the end of the Ice Age.

When the earth warmed and the glacier finally began receding, its melting ice drained into the ocean. Augmented by this tremendous influx of water, seas rose and flooded Maine's sunken and glacier-gouged coastline. Lowlands were inundated. Valleys filled with water. Mountains became islands, their summits besieged by the ocean.

This was the way in which water cut off Mount Desert Island, the Porcupines, Isle au Haut and other high points along the coast. Looking down from Cadillac Mountain, one can picture a time when they all called the mainland their home.

place. He christened it "L'Isle des Monts Deserts"—the island of bare mountains.

Nearly four centuries have passed, and those mountains still thwart efforts by trees to claim their summits. But the island has not turned back efforts by humans to put down their roots.

By the mid-19th century word about Mount Desert Island had spread down the northeastern coast. Painter Thomas Cole, of the Hudson River School, discovered its beauty in 1844. After steamship connections to the island were established in 1870, a steady stream of Bostonians and other travelers eagerly booked passage to this newly discovered vacation spot. As the number of visitors grew, so did the status of the island village of Bar Harbor as a bustling summer resort. America's wealthy and prominent families began spending summers there. Name almost any tycoon from the turn of the century—someone with a last name like Morgan or Astor—and chances are his yacht could be found bobbing somewhere off the island.

DISCARDED ARMOR

Empty mussel shells and the dried shell of a sea urchin, called a test, blend with multicolored pebbles on one of Acadia's rocky shorelines. Mussels are common inhabitants of Maine coasts, anchoring themselves in massive clusters to rocks and other underwater surfaces by means of thin filaments planted in the mussel's foot.

A GIFT FROM CITIZENS

In 1901, something wondrous happened: a small group of Mount Desert admirers decided to set aside land on the island for all of the nation's enjoyment. John D. Rockefeller, Jr. spearheaded the effort, donating more than 11,000 acres. His gift represented approximately one-third of the park's eventual total of 35,000 acres. In 1919, the donated land was dedicated as Lafayette National Park, and in 1929, it received its current name.

The park's creation was significant on two fronts: not only did Acadia become the first national park east of the Mississippi River, but it also became the first in the nation created by citizens who gave their land to the government.

What did these early admirers see in Mount Desert Island that made them so keen to preserve it? They saw what today's nearly five million annual visitors to Acadia can enjoy on a short tour along the Loop Road. They saw forests of spruce and fir, shady and moist, sometimes swaddled in fog, always perfectly suited for mushrooms and mosses. They saw hardwood stands showing off autumnal colors: bright yellow on birches; red maple leaves painted with scarlet.

Acadia's forests today still enchant those who see them. Gaining access to forest surroundings is easy for park visitors. The park boasts more than 120

That mainland, in concert with the myriad rock islands and hidden ledges that clutter its coastal waters, has always lain in wait for sailors and ships in the fog. In September, 1604, the ship of French explorer Samuel de Champlain struck a shoal near present-day Mount Desert Island. On a mapping mission for the French government, Champlain decided to investigate his surroundings while his ship received needed repairs.

Approaching an island where granite bluffs plunged in steep steps to the sea, he made note of its numerous mountains, their bare summits resisting the colonizing efforts of trees and other vegetation. Coming ashore, Champlain met native Americans—the Abnaki—who lived on the island. "Pemetic" they called it: the sloping land. Champlain had his own thoughts about this harsh

miles of hiking trails, plus a 50-mile network of wooded carriage roads, built by John D. Rockefeller, Jr. between 1915 and 1933. Free of motor vehicles, these beautiful byways (made even more attractive by their scenic stone bridges) host bicyclists, horseback riders and even horse-drawn carriages, which visitors can hire for summer rides.

Acadia's early admirers also saw small fishing villages, tucked into snug harbors, their docks stacked with colorful buoys in tangled profusion. Here, the gulls cried and the air smelled of freshly caught fish. Weathered men piled their boats high with slatted wood traps and set out for lobsters.

Such craft still ply coastal waters off Mount Desert Island. Climbers who hike the steep trail to the top of Gorham Mountain can look down and watch them in the ocean, bobbing like tiny toy boats.

At day's end the lobster boats return to havens such as Bass Harbor and Bernard, two typical down east fishing villages that share a long protected harbor near the island's southern tip. As they enter, the boats pass Bass Harbor Head, with its spruce-framed lighthouse atop a high cliff.

Quaint fishing villages, fog-shrouded forests, the worn peaks of old granite mountains—sights such as these made the island's earliest devotees know it

was well worth preserving. But more than these features, it was the sea that won them over.

It still dominates at Acadia, whether smooth like a mirror or battering cliffs in a storm. The park's ocean attractions point up how diverse and intense ocean action can be as it ceaselessly grinds at the island. Every turn in the Loop Road reveals new examples of sea and shoreline interacting. The frequent overlooks, trails and picnic areas make enjoying these sights safe and easy.

SOUND AND FURY	At Thunder Hole, waves hurtle through a narrow 55-foot canyon before slamming into the chasm's back wall with a

deep resonating boom. A brief hesitation ensues as each spent wave holds its ground momentarily, swaying like a staggered boxer before draining back toward the sea. This hiatus is peaceful but brief. Seconds later a new wave surges down the ocean-carved corridor, only to see granite slap back its rush with a roar.

Walls in the Thunder Hole chasm are curtained in seaweed nearly to the high water line. Twice a day tides rise and fall in this canyon. Low tide reveals clearly delineated tidal zones, each one offer-

ing optimal conditions for specific marine organisms. These zones span the spectrum of tidal existence; from a continuously submerged world of jellyfish and kelp strands to rocks that receive only spray when the waves crash below them. In between lie the middle zones, teeming with barnacles, mussels and snails.

Walkers along Mount Desert's rugged shoreline can watch as the tides drain away from the rocks, leaving myriad isolated pools, their water-filled cups and bowls brimming with stranded sea life.

Looking up from these pools, beyond the breakers toward open water, sharp-eyed observers may spy a flock of eider ducks, or watch as streamlined birds called black guillemots dive near the shore catching fish. A pair of ravens may sweep overhead, their black wings assisted by updrafts that rise from the cliffs. As the ravens grapple and tumble, their croaks bounce off the cliff walls.

And all along the jagged shore, the sea gnaws at Mount Desert Island. Pounding the rocks, it leaps high in a foamy eruption. Then it drains back wildly to regroup, marshaling fresh waves that will, in time, reduce rocks to rubble and sand. This is Acadia National Park at its finest. This is why people come back: to watch ocean and island collide.

SIGNATURE OF THE TIDES

The restless tides lap against Mount Desert's rockbound coast (left), continuously sculpting and resculpting its countless harbors and coves. During storms, the massive granite rocks at Schoodic Point on Schoodic Peninsula (above) take a beating from the thundering surf.

NEARBY SITES & ATTRACTIONS

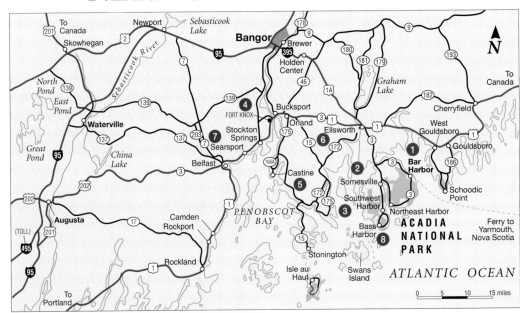

A humpback whale frolics off the coast of Maine. These waters are excellent feeding grounds for finback, humpback and minke whales. Whale watching excursions usually include professional naturalists who identify the whales and point out the other varieties of animals encountered, including dolphins, porpoises, seals, sea birds and bald eagles.

① BAR HARBOR

The town started as a fishing and shipbuilding center before becoming fashionable with the rich and famous in the 1850's. Its grand homes stand as proud reminders of this period, and along with the Bar Harbor Historical Society Museum afford visitors a glimpse at the town's gilded past. Sightseeing boat cruises that leave from Bar Harbor treat passengers to a seabound view of Acadia's snug coves and surf-scoured cliffs. Whale watching, sunset viewing and three-masted schooner cruises also are available. Two divisions of the Mount Desert Oceanarium—the Lobster Hatchery and the Marine Educational Center at Thomas Bay—offer exhibits at Bar Harbor's Southwest Harbor Oceanarium. Located on Mount Desert Island on Hwy. 3, 20 miles southeast of Ellsworth.

② SOMESVILLE

The oldest settlement on Mount Desert Island, Somesville is a carefully preserved fishing village. Situated at the head of Somes Sound—the only true fjord on the East Coast—it is one of a string of small towns on the island's "quiet" west side. The town's Victorian white-clapboard houses skirted by cheerful flower gardens are irresistible to photographers. A picturesque pond, created in 1763, graces the center of the village. The Somesville Historical Society Museum traces the site's arduous and sometimes turbulent history. Located just outside the park on Hwy. 102.

③ WENDELL GILLEY MUSEUM, SOUTHWEST HARBOR

Founded in 1981, the museum bears the name of one of the finest wood carvers of his time, Wendell Gilley, and houses one of the world's best collections of bird carvings. Anchoring the collection are Gilley's own masterpieces. A native of Southwest Harbor, Gilley worked as a master plumber until his skills as a bird carver turned a hobby into a career. A full-scale replica of his workshop serves as a school where a resident carver teaches the craft. Located in Southwest Harbor at the intersection of Herrick Road and Main Street.

The picturesque town of Castine was founded in the 1670's by Baron Castin, a French Canadian. Because of its strategic location on Penobscot Bay, the town was the site of many skirmishes between the British and the Revolutionaries.

4 FORT KNOX

Strategically situated on the Penobscot River, Fort Knox was built to protect the river valley and the town of Bangor, then lumber capital of the world, from possible attack by the British navy. Manned for battle again during the Civil and Spanish American Wars, the fort is now designated as a National Historic Landmark and is considered to be a remarkable example of military architecture. Visitors are welcome to tour the soldiers' quarters, the granite spiral staircases and the parade ground, as well as to examine the 10- and 15-inch Rodman cannons. Located on Hwy. 174 just west of the Waldo-Hancock Bridge.

5 CASTINE

Castine is one of Maine's most picturesque coastal towns. A short stroll across town to the common leads past 19th-century clapboard houses, as well as stately Greek and Federal revival homes and churches. Perkins House, constructed in 1763, is the only prerevolutionary home still standing; it has been fully restored and furnished with period items. The house is now a part of the Wilson Museum, the site of a fine collection of prehistoric to Victorian artifacts that trace the development and use of tools. Just outside the town are the ruins of Fort George, a former British stronghold; off its shores was one of the worst military defeats in American naval history: the loss of a fleet of 44 ships to the British in 1779. Located on Hwys. 166A and 175.

6 ELLSWORTH

This town of gracious homes, set on a hill overlooking the Union River, is a commercial center and the gateway to Mount Desert Island. One of its outstanding features is the Ellsworth First Congregational Church, considered to be the best example of Greek revival ecclesiastical architecture in Maine. Another of the town's landmarks is the Colonel Black Mansion, a Georgian building constructed by the extravagant John Black, who imported the red bricks for it from Philadelphia. The house is filled with fine furnishings. The Stanwood Wildlife Sanctuary includes a bird sanctuary and a Cape Cod-style house that was built by sea captain Roswell Stanwood. Located southeast of Bangor on Hwys. 1, 1A and 3.

7 SEARSPORT

Maine's second-largest deepwater port keeps alive its seafaring tradition at the Penobscot Marine Museum, a complex of seven buildings that houses an outstanding collection of maritime artifacts. The museum is noted for its fine paintings, including many examples of 19th-century Chinese and European ship portraits, all done by commission in different ports of call around the world. The town is also the self-appointed antiques capital of Maine, hosting a seasonal flea market along its stretch of Route 1, as well as being the home of dozens of shops, barns and other markets. On Hwys. 1 and 3, north of Belfast.

8 SOUTHWEST HARBOR OCEANARIUM

Here visitors are treated to a close-up look at the remarkable creatures that make their home along Maine's shoreline. More than 20 tanks are stocked with live sea animals, the smallest of which can be examined through magnifying glasses or microscopes. There is a touch-tank full of starfish and shells, as well as displays on lobstering and weather forecasting. Located in Southwest Harbor on Clark Point Road, just off Hwy. 102.

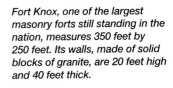

A ruffed grouse by master carver Wendell Gilley seems ready to step off its perch. Gilley, who died in 1983, lived and worked in Southwest Harbor before gaining an international reputation as a bird carver. Today, a museum named for him displays 300 of his works and gives workshops in the art.

Fort Knox, one of the largest masonry forts still standing in the nation, measures 350 feet by 250 feet. Its walls, made of solid blocks of granite, are 20 feet high and 40 feet thick.

GREAT SMOKY MOUNTAINS

*Moisture works magic here,
creating the jewel in the crown of
this mountainous land.*

The air is diffused with gray-green light. Velvet mosses soak up the moisture and swell until the rocks and logs they cover are no longer gray or brown, but a glowing iridescent green. It is a typical day in Great Smoky Mountains National Park where the rain feeds everything from the lowliest mosses to record-sized trees, and where—only a 15 minute drive from the glitter of Gatlinburg, Tennessee—it feeds the eyes and the soul, too.

Here, at the trail head of the steep, four-mile-long Ramsay Cascade Trail, the hardiest visitors can make the 2,375-foot climb to a breathtaking waterfall at trail's end. But the less athletically inclined will derive as much pleasure from the small details, the constant surprises and discoveries that are just as much a part of the Great Smokies.

People flock to these comforting old mountains and deep forests for solace and renewal. Within a day-and-a-half's drive of 50 percent of the U.S. population, Great Smoky Mountains National Park receives nearly nine million visits each year. Of those millions, perhaps only a handful of visitors may see the eastern narrowmouth

HYDROTHERAPY

The sound of moving water permeates the park. Roaring Fork is just one of the many mountain creeks nourished by the park's abundant rainfall—an average of more than 55 inches of annual precipitation. Trout fishing is a popular activity in the fast-water streams of the Smokies.

SHADOWY SILHOUETTES

Overleaf: The contour of these ancient mountains, some of the oldest on earth, is softened by the thick haze enveloping them. The "smoke," for which both the mountains and the park are named, is created by the phenomenal amount of water vapor exhaled by the thick mantle of forests draping the slopes.

toad or the southern bog lemming. Most may also miss the marbled salamander and the whorled pogonia. But in a park containing 1,570 species of flowering plants—including almost 130 native trees—2,000 different fungi, more than 200 bird species, 48 freshwater fishes, 60 mammals, 78 kinds of reptiles and amphibians, including 27 salamander species, missing a few things is not surprising. It was in recognition of this fantastically diverse biological heritage that the park was designated an International Biosphere Reserve in 1976.

Some visitors come to the Smokies to fish. Others set off on foot or horseback along some portion of the park's 800 miles of trails. But the majority see the sights in private vehicles. Beautiful drives, such as the Little River Road, wind through the park. Only one drive, the Newfound Gap Road, enters the heart of the park's half-million acres. In 26 miles, this highway climbs from 1,436 feet elevation at the Sugarlands Visitor Center in Tennessee to 5,048 feet at Newfound Gap, then down to about 2,000 feet at Oconaluftee near Cherokee, North Carolina. A spur road off the Newfound Gap Road leads to Clingmans Dome, at 6,643 feet the highest peak in the Smokies. A half-mile-long paved trail leads to an observation tower atop the Dome. On clear days it affords sweeping views of the entire range.

Newfound Gap is an especially significant part of Great Smoky Mountains National Park because it was here, in September 1940, that President Franklin D. Roosevelt dedicated the park that had taken two decades to create. And it is here that you

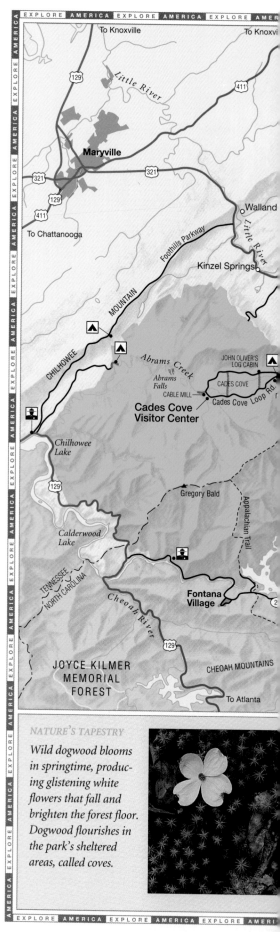

NATURE'S TAPESTRY

Wild dogwood blooms in springtime, producing glistening white flowers that fall and brighten the forest floor. Dogwood flourishes in the park's sheltered areas, called coves.

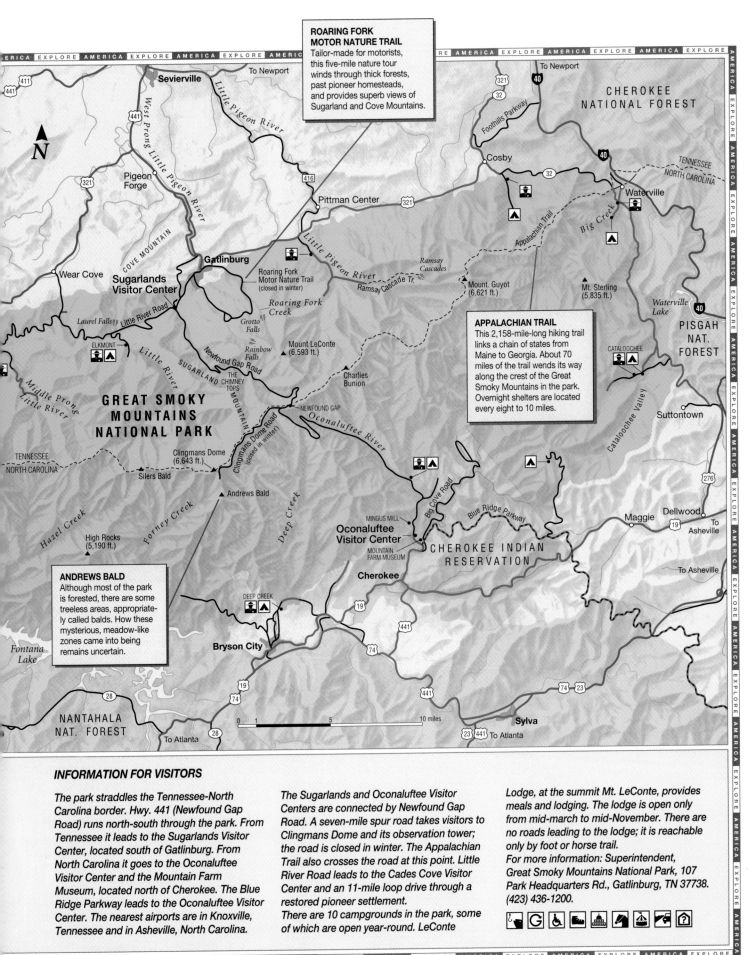

ROARING FORK MOTOR NATURE TRAIL
Tailor-made for motorists, this five-mile nature tour winds through thick forests, past pioneer homesteads, and provides superb views of Sugarland and Cove Mountains.

To Newport

Sevierville

To Newport

CHEROKEE NATIONAL FOREST

Foothills Parkway

Cosby

Waterville

TENNESSEE
NORTH CAROLINA

Pigeon Forge

Pittman Center

Little Pigeon River

Big Creek

Appalachian Trail

Wear Cove

Gatlinburg

Roaring Fork Motor Nature Trail (closed in winter)

Ramsay Cascades

Mount. Guyot (6,621 ft.)

Mt. Sterling (5,835 ft.)

Waterville Lake

PISGAH NAT. FOREST

Sugarlands Visitor Center

Little River Road

Roaring Fork Creek

Ramsay Cascade Tr.

Laurel Falls

Grotto Falls

APPALACHIAN TRAIL
This 2,158-mile-long hiking trail links a chain of states from Maine to Georgia. About 70 miles of the trail wends its way along the crest of the Great Smoky Mountains in the park. Overnight shelters are located every eight to 10 miles.

CATALOOCHEE

ELKMONT

Rainbow Falls

Mount LeConte (6,593 ft.)

THE CHIMNEY TOPS

Charlies Bunion

Middle Prong Little River

GREAT SMOKY MOUNTAINS NATIONAL PARK

Newfound Gap Road

Cataloochee Valley

Suttontown

Little River

NEWFOUND GAP

Oconaluftee River

TENNESSEE
NORTH CAROLINA

Clingmans Dome (6,643 ft.)

Clingmans Dome Road (closed in winter)

Silers Bald

Blue Ridge Parkway

Maggie

Dellwood

To Asheville

Andrews Bald

Forney Creek

Deep Creek

Big Cove Road

MINGUS MILL

Oconaluftee Visitor Center

MOUNTAIN FARM MUSEUM

CHEROKEE INDIAN RESERVATION

To Asheville

Hazel Creek

High Rocks (5,190 ft.)

ANDREWS BALD
Although most of the park is forested, there are some treeless areas, appropriately called balds. How these mysterious, meadow-like zones came into being remains uncertain.

DEEP CREEK

Cherokee

Fontana Lake

Bryson City

NANTAHALA NAT. FOREST

To Atlanta

0 1 5 10 miles

Sylva

To Atlanta

INFORMATION FOR VISITORS

The park straddles the Tennessee-North Carolina border. Hwy. 441 (Newfound Gap Road) runs north-south through the park. From Tennessee it leads to the Sugarlands Visitor Center, located south of Gatlinburg. From North Carolina it goes to the Oconaluftee Visitor Center and the Mountain Farm Museum, located north of Cherokee. The Blue Ridge Parkway leads to the Oconaluftee Visitor Center. The nearest airports are in Knoxville, Tennessee and in Asheville, North Carolina.

The Sugarlands and Oconaluftee Visitor Centers are connected by Newfound Gap Road. A seven-mile spur road takes visitors to Clingmans Dome and its observation tower; the road is closed in winter. The Appalachian Trail also crosses the road at this point. Little River Road leads to the Cades Cove Visitor Center and an 11-mile loop drive through a restored pioneer settlement.
There are 10 campgrounds in the park, some of which are open year-round. LeConte

Lodge, at the summit Mt. LeConte, provides meals and lodging. The lodge is open only from mid-march to mid-November. There are no roads leading to the lodge; it is reachable only by foot or horse trail.
For more information: Superintendent, Great Smoky Mountains National Park, 107 Park Headquarters Rd., Gatlinburg, TN 37738. (423) 436-1200.

The gristmill above was the center of activity for the agricultural community of Cades Cove. Today park employees in period costumes demonstrate the farming techniques of those Smokies pioneers. The crested dwarf iris (right) is just one of the more than 1,500 species of flowering plants that live in the park. Heavy rainfall combined with rich soil and a gentle climate make the forest floor an ideal habitat for wildflowers of every color and description. The annual Wildflower Pilgrimage—three days of wild-flower viewing—takes place at the end of April when the flowers are at their peak.

can stand with a foot in each of the two states that helped fund that creation. Contributions from Tennessee and North Carolina—along with the federal government, the Laura Spellman Rockefeller Memorial Fund, and pennies from school children—purchased the thousands of private land parcels from which the national park was created.

The Smoky Mountains sit like a knotted fist on the border separating Tennessee from North Carolina. They are the highest mountains in the eastern United States, with a mainline crest punctuated by 16 peaks rising more than 6,000 feet above sea level. At Newfound Gap, where the wind always seems to blow, the mountains swell into the distance, separated by dizzyingly deep valleys. Their rugged profile is softened by the bluish haze that gave the Smokies their name, a haze produced by fog, clouds, and the voluminous moisture transpired from the leaves of all the greenery. Mesmerizing wisps of fog thread up from the val-

leys like smoke from a log cabin, to join masses of clouds rolling over the mountain tops.

The Smokies are part of the southern Appalachian Mountains, uplifted for the first time some 300 million years ago—a time span that is impressive even by geological standards. Many scientists believe the southern Appalachians were created by the collision of two of the earth's great crustal plates. The compression that resulted from this massive pileup brought to the surface deeply buried rock, some a billion years old. So old is this nondescript gray to reddish rock that no sign of fossil life can be detected in it. Outcrops of it can best be seen in winter, when they are not obscured by foliage.

Once the mountains were raised, at one time perhaps as high as 20,000 feet, extensive faulting turned them heels over head until their true history became extremely difficult to decipher. Water then went to work on the mountains, dispatching whale-sized boulders down hillsides and sculpting narrow valleys between tall, steep slopes. The sound of water is never far away in the Smokies. Some

A white-tailed deer stands silently amid the lush vegetation that lines one of the park's more than 800 miles of hiking trails. The deer became scarce because of excessive hunting. Today they are protected within the park boundaries and are a common sight as they graze the open meadows in Cataloochee Valley and Cades Cove. Dawn and dusk are the best times to spot them.

2,000 miles of clear, cold streams, born in the highest reaches of the mountains, flow through the park, interrupted as they tumble into falls along their course.

MOUNTAINS MAKE WEATHER

The simple fact of the mountains' existence determines the life of the Smokies. Their height creates what is called an "orographic effect," which means, in essence, that mountains make weather. At Gatlinburg, for example, annual rainfall is about 50 inches a year. On Clingmans Dome precipitation totals more than 80 inches a year, some of it in the form of snow.

Plant communities directly reflect the increased moisture and cooler temperatures found at higher elevations. Above 4,500 feet in the Smokies grows a forest of red spruce and Fraser fir distinctly Canadian in character. Adjoining the spruce-fir forest are northern hardwoods, predominantly yellow birch and American beech that are more common to Indiana and Michigan.

The Smokies are not high enough to have a true timberline. Yet there are treeless places—sometimes 12 to 15 acres—in the upper elevations of the southern Appalachians called balds. Hikers value them for the rare open vistas they permit, while botanists puzzle over their enigmatic existence. Many people suppose the grassy balds were caused by cattle grazing in pre-park days. In the 60 years since grazing has ceased, trees have begun to encroach upon them. The shrubby heath balds, called "slicks" or "hells" by the early mountaineers, consist primarily of wind-pruned rhododendron, mountain laurel and sand myrtle. Though the conditions that created them are also uncertain, they seem to be self-maintaining, perhaps due to natural fires.

On the drier west- and south-facing slopes, scarlet and black oaks coexist with white, pitch, shortleaf and Table Mountain pines. Below 4,000 feet eastern hemlocks, some of them awe-inspiring giants, cast dark shade in ravines. With an estimated 100,000 acres of trees that have never felt the logger's saw, the Smokies contain the largest expanse of old-growth forest in the eastern U.S.

Magnificent hemlocks, 300-year-old oaks, tulip trees five feet in diameter—these are trees that command respect.

In moist, sheltered, deep-soiled valleys grow the Smokies' famed cove hardwood forests. These unique associations of deciduous trees often include Carolina silverbell, yellow buckeye, basswood, white ash and sugar maple, with 20 other possible tree species in various combinations. In the cove hardwood forests, wildflowers—another Smokies specialty—put on extravagant displays in March and April. White trilliums brighten hillsides, fringed phacelia covers acres, and an occasional bloodroot briefly shows delicate petals. Hepatica, rue anemone, squirrel corn, trout lily, Solomon's seal, bellwort and a host of other vernal lovelies bloom before the leafy tree canopy closes out the light. During the annual Wildflower Pilgrimage on the last weekend in April, nature lovers descend upon the park, well-thumbed guidebooks in hand, reveling in this flower riot.

Animals, most notably birds, reflect the differences in plant communities. Carolina chickadees of the valley forests, for example, turn over their niche to black-capped chickadees in the higher elevations. Likewise, the barred owl that dwells in the closed forests at lower elevations is replaced by the northern saw-whet—heard and sometimes seen on clear moonlit nights—in the spruce-fir forest.

HUMAN HISTORY TOO

Wildlife is a major draw for visitors to Cades Cove, a large grassy meadow in the west end of the Smokies. White-tailed deer graze in misty fields; curious woodchucks poke their heads from their burrows; belted kingfishers perch in streamside sycamores; and an occasional flock of wild turkeys roams a churchyard. Sightings of black bears, whose nursery ground is the Smoky Mountains, create "bear-jams" on the 11-mile loop road that winds its way through the Cove.

In addition to natural history, Cades Cove is rich in human history, represented by one of the country's best collections of reconstructed historic buildings. At John Oliver's log cabin, dating from about the 1820's, the smell of kerosene and ripe apples permeates the simple space. Rooms are small and dim, wooden hinges creak, and bare plank floors dip and weave. Though the pioneers' homes are empty now and rather lonely, when the Olivers and Tiptons and Shields lived in them, the shrieks of children bounding off front porches would have filled the Cove.

Settlers entered the Smokies in the early 19th century, buying land that had once belonged to the Cherokees. Cades Cove was especially attractive for the large amount of that rare commodity in the mountains—flat land. Its limestone soil was good for raising corn and wheat, and the forest provided nearly all the settlers' needs. To clear the trees, farmers girdled entire groves in areas called "deadenings." A few large chestnut trees, hewn with a broad axe and notched into tight dovetail joints, made a small cabin. Cattle were grazed on the balds, and medicines came from the profusion of other plants. Year-round springs furnished pure water.

As a community, the settlers joined to build churches (Baptist and Methodist mostly) and roads. Milling day was a big occasion, when the people brought in bushels of corn and wheat, catching up on local gossip while they waited for the meal and flour to be ground. At the Cable Mill in Cades Cove, a water-powered gristmill still produces stone-ground cornmeal. Living history programs, with costumed interpreters, recreate pioneer life at Cades Cove and Oconaluftee.

The popularity of Cades Cove can rob it of its pastoral character. One way to escape the crowds is to rent a chartreuse, one-speed bicycle at the Cades Cove store and pedal the loop road in early morning. Cades Cove was made for mornings, when drops of dew still glisten in the spider webs and few people are about. On summer Saturday mornings the road is closed to vehicles, and cars give way to bicyclists and walkers. There is ample opportunity to linger—a side trip on a country lane, a quiet visit to an old cemetery, or a stroll out into a wet meadow. The air may be muggy, the ground spongy-soft. A coral-colored salamander with black spots may slither over a rock, or clumps of yellow trillium may dance like ballerinas in the breeze, tiny perfect surprises against the comforting green bulwarks that are the Smokies.

MASKED BANDIT
An innocent-looking raccoon rests its head on the branch of a pine tree. Its regular diet is small animals, plants and nuts, but this nocturnal creature prowls around campsites looking for food to steal.

BURST OF COLOR
Warm, sunny days, alternating with cool nights, produce the vivid reds, yellows and oranges of the Smokies' autumn art show. The park's deciduous forests, a mixture of oak, maple, hemlock, birch and beech, are found at the lower elevations. The colors are usually at their peak from mid-October to the end of the month.

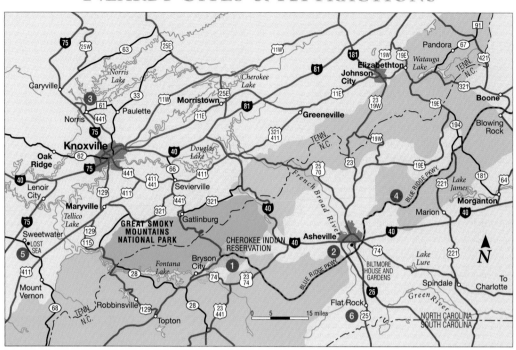

Widely regarded as one of America's most scenic drives, the Blue Ridge Parkway offers spectacular views of the Appalachian Mountain chain.

① CHEROKEE INDIAN RESERVATION

Long before Europeans set foot in the New World, the Cherokees ruled over vast regions of land south of the Ohio River. Their legends, myths, language and crafts are kept alive by their descendants, who live on the reservation. Oconaluftee Indian Village, a replica of a 1750 Cherokee community, is staffed with costumed guides who carry on day-to-day life. Guided tours bring visitors inside the Ceremonial Grounds, where they learn about Cherokee ritual objects such as eagle wands and gourd rattles. The Arboretum and Nature Trail, located nearby, contains flowers and plants native to the region as well as an Indian herb garden. The Museum of the Cherokee Indian displays artifacts representing 10,000 years of Cherokee history. Summer visitors can see *Unto These Hills*, a historical drama, held outdoors, which reenacts the story of the Cherokee Nation from 1540 to their departure to the West along the infamous Trail of Tears in 1838. Located off Hwy. 441 on the North Carolina side of the park.

② BILTMORE HOUSE AND GARDENS

In the late 1880's, George Washington Vanderbilt, a young man of 25, began to purchase land near Asheville, eventually buying some 125,000 acres. He relied on the talents of his friend, architect Richard Morris Hunt, to help him design and build his 255-room French Renaissance chateau. The formal and informal gardens were designed by Frederick Law Olmsted, the landscape architect of Central Park in New York City. The house and gardens are open to the public. Among the priceless objects on display are 16th-century Flemish tapestries, paintings by Renoir, Sargent and Whistler, and a chess set that belonged to Napoleon Bonaparte. Self-guided tours lead through the chateau's many rooms,

including the Banquet Hall with its 70-foot-high arched ceiling, the Music Room and Library on the main floor, to the bedrooms, guest rooms, sitting rooms and bathrooms upstairs. There is a bowling alley, indoor swimming pool and gymnasium downstairs along with the servants' quarters, kitchens and pantries. The gardens surrounding the chateau are just as grandiose. Each spring, about 50,000 Dutch tulips bloom in the four-acre English Walled Garden. There is also a Rose Garden and an Azalea Garden. A tour of the Winery, housed in the original dairy buildings, steps visitors through the wine-making process and allows them to sample Biltmore Estate wines. Located near Asheville, North Carolina, on Hwy. 25.

③ MUSEUM OF APPALACHIA

This "living" museum is a reconstruction of a typical 18th-century mountain village. The 65-acre site contains more than 30 log buildings, including pioneer homesteads and barns, school, church, jail, gristmill, blacksmith shop and smokehouse. The Main Display Barn houses authentic pioneer relics and memorabilia, collected from the surrounding region. On display are everyday items such as barrels and baskets, spinning wheels, wooden toys and farming tools, as well as hundreds of handmade musical instruments and folk art carvings. Located in Norris, Tennessee, 16 miles north of Knoxville on Hwy. 75.

④ BLUE RIDGE PARKWAY

The parkway follows the backbone of the scenic Blue Ridge mountain range and links Great Smoky National Park in North Carolina and Tennessee to Shenandoah National Park in Virginia. The 470-

mile-long drive reaches elevations of more than 6,000 feet. Overlooks allow motorists to stop and admire the verdant mountain forests, rolling hillsides covered in rhododendron and azaleas, deep gorges, waterfalls and patchwork valleys of fields, farms and villages. Facilities include picnic areas, campsites, hiking trails, ranger-led tours and designated fishing areas.

5 LOST SEA

Located deep inside a series of caverns, this 4½-acre lake is considered to be North America's largest underground lake. Although it was not discovered until 1905, the caverns had been known for some time before that. Pioneer settlers had mixed red clay from the cavern walls with buttermilk to make red paint, and during the Civil War, Confederate soldiers had extracted saltpeter from the caverns for gunpowder. Visitors can explore the cave's numerous chambers as they descend to lake level. The Sand Room, for example, is a natural refrigerator with a constant temperature of 58°F; it was used by early settlers to preserve their food. The Cat Chamber takes its name from the Pleistocene jaguar skeleton found here. Glass-bottom boat tours are an excellent way to observe the transplanted trout that thrive in this predator-free environment. Located west of Great Smoky Mountains National Park in Sweetwater, Tennessee, on Hwy. 68.

6 CARL SANDBURG HOME

This white clapboard farmhouse, surrounded by pastures and woodlands overlooking the Blue Ridge Mountains, was home to the acclaimed poet and historian from 1945 until his death in 1967.

Biltmore House, set amid the splendor of the Blue Ridge Mountains, is the largest private residence in the United States. The house, which took five years to build, is made of Indiana limestone.

The 240-acre estate, known as Connemara, was run as a prize-winning goat farm by Sandburg's wife. Today, visitors can explore the grounds, farm buildings and the 22-room house, which looks as if the poet had just stepped out for a minute. Books line the bookshelves, the ashtrays are full of cigar butts, and Sandburg's slippers are under the bed. The tiny upstairs room where Carl Sandburg wrote contains his antique typewriter and research notes. Located in Flat Rock, 26 miles south of Asheville on Hwy. 25.

Mules and oxen plow the fields and sheep graze in the pastureland surrounding the homes in Museum of Appalachia. The goal of the museum's founder, John Rice Irwin, was to make the site "appear as though the family had just strolled down to the spring to fetch the daily supply of water."

EVERGLADES

---

*This is the old Florida, the Florida
that belongs to wild things in
a world half water and half land.*

Few events in Florida are filled with more promise than sunrise in the Everglades. Pink light leaks across the eastern horizon beneath Venus shining in an aquamarine, predawn sky. The air is windless and cool, the water calm, the darkness dying. Night herons stand motionless on the tide flat, or on the elevated, exposed roots of mangrove trees, their bright eyes returning your stare on the edge of land and sea. Nearby, a cloud of black skimmers wings over Florida Bay in fluid synchrony, then circles and lands on a sandy island in the ebbing tide. Brown pelicans flap by, break from formation and plummet into the bay with beaks wide open, surfacing with their mouths filled with seawater, and perhaps a fish or two. The sun arrives, Venus winks away, and the Everglades—sequestered at the southern end of that familiar limestone peninsula where temperate America reaches to within 75 miles of the tropics—begins another day.

But this is one of the rarest and most threatened ecosystems in North America. It survives today—though barely—as the largest designated wilderness area in the eastern United States.

A great jumble of exposed mangrove roots grapples for space in the 20-mile-wide strip of "mangle," or mangrove forest, that flourishes along the park's southwestern shore. A broad-leafed evergreen, the mangrove survives in an environment where the fresh water from the north drains into the salt water at the ocean's edge. The dense roots protect the coastline from erosion and act as land builders when sediment is trapped between them.

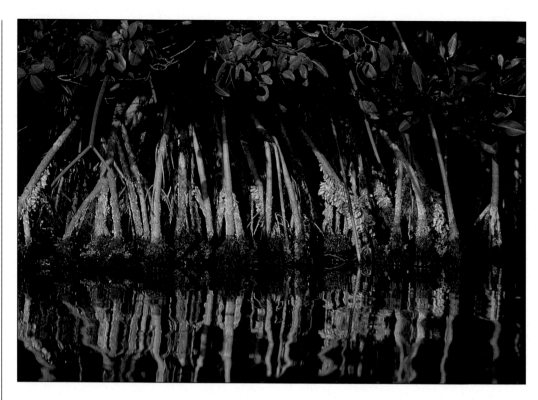

Overleaf: A shining expanse of sawgrass evokes the Indian name for the Everglades, Pa-hay-okee, "Grassy Water." The vast, thick river of grass stretches across the Everglades, drawing its life from the fresh water below it. Sawgrass is not really a grass at all but a sedge—one of earth's oldest plant species.

"There are no other Everglades in the world," wrote the conservationist Marjory Stoneman Douglas in 1947. "They are, they always have been, one of the most unique regions of the earth, remote, never wholly known. They are unique also in the simplicity, the diversity, the related harmony of the forms of life they enclose. The miracle of the light pours over the green and brown expanse of sawgrass and of water, shining and slow-moving below, the grass and water that is the meaning and the central fact of the Everglades of Florida. It is a river of grass."

Douglas' words attracted national attention and that same year, 1947, Everglades National Park was created, and President Harry S Truman proclaimed, "Here are no lofty peaks seeking the sky, no mighty glaciers or rushing streams wearing away the uplifted land. Here is land, tranquil in its quiet beauty, serving not as the source of water but as the last receiver of it. To its natural abundance we owe the spectacular plant and animal life that distinguishes this place from all others in our country."

Call it a Noah's Ark. The animal life consists of approximately 350 species of birds, 60 species of amphibians and reptiles, 25 species of mammals and countless species of insects. With such abundance, it is easy to overlook the vegetation. And that would be a mistake, for wildlife find habitat in the plant kingdom, and in the Everglades that kingdom is as rich and diverse as can be found almost anywhere. Sawgrass plains cover much of the park, but scattered throughout are freshwater sloughs, pine forests, broad-leafed hardwood forests

(called hammocks) and coastal mangrove forests. Then there is Florida Bay, part of the Gulf of Mexico, covering the southern third of the park.

Because the Everglades is flat, an elevation gain of only a few feet can have a significant effect. Sawgrass covers the watery low areas during the summer wet season. Where the land is slightly elevated and therefore substantially drier, pine forests and hammocks replace the sawgrass. Pine forests are open and generously bathed in sunlight; hammocks are shaded and cool. In fact, hammocks can even occur within pine forests, like islands within islands in a sea of sawgrass.

Step into a hammock and the Everglades becomes an inner sanctum of biological diversity. The canopy above shades a forest floor thick with leaf litter, called duff, and brightened by ferns and orchids. Strangler figs wrap around large host trees. Oaks, myrtles, laurels and gumbo-limbos—some of the more than 100 species of broad-leafed trees native to the Everglades—reach to the sky. After a summer rain, banded tree snails inch across the trunks of smooth-barked fig, wild tamarind and pigeon plum trees to feed on moist algae and lichen. Rosette-shaped air plants frequent the hammocks, as do ants, beetles, tree frogs, snakes, the three-inch bark mantis and the beautiful zebra butterfly. As darkness falls, cardinals and towhees call softly, barred owls hoot and crickets add their high notes to the forest music.

For centuries summer thunderstorms have thrown their lightning into the Everglades, and fires have burned a balance into the ecosystem,

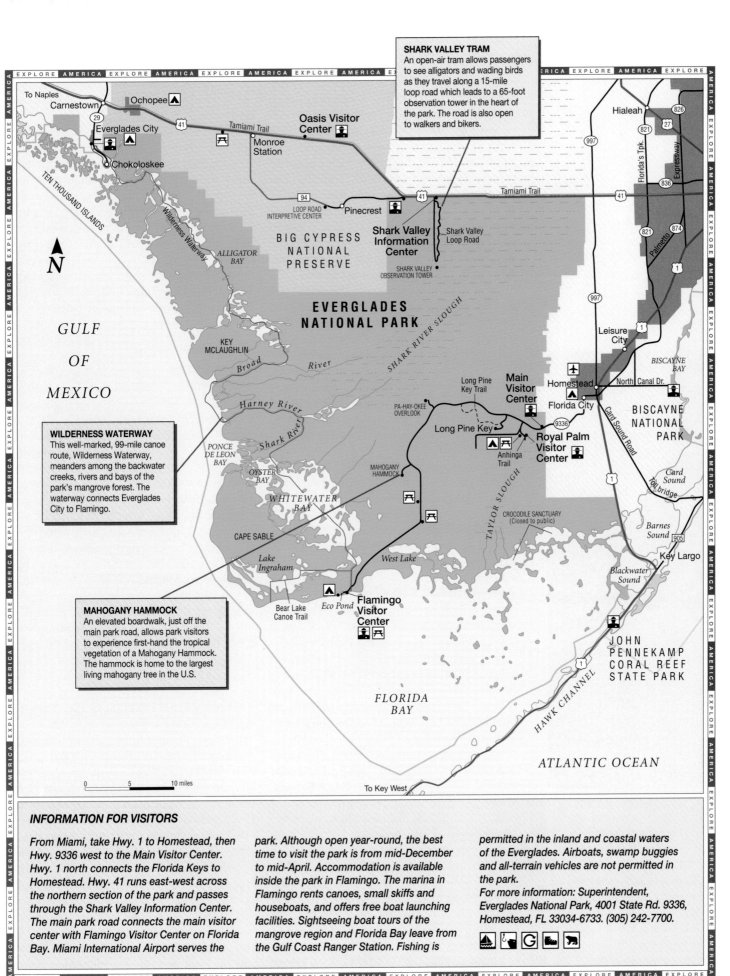

SHARK VALLEY TRAM

An open-air tram allows passengers to see alligators and wading birds as they travel along a 15-mile loop road which leads to a 65-foot observation tower in the heart of the park. The road is also open to walkers and bikers.

To Naples

Carnestown

Ochopee

Everglades City

Chokoloskee

TEN THOUSAND ISLANDS

Wilderness Waterway

Tamiami Trail

Monroe Station

Oasis Visitor Center

Loop Road Interpretive Center

Pinecrest

94

41

Tamiami Trail

Hialeah

826

27

821

997

836

Florida's Tpk.

Expressway

821

874

Palmetto

1

BIG CYPRESS NATIONAL PRESERVE

Shark Valley Information Center

Shark Valley Loop Road

SHARK VALLEY OBSERVATION TOWER

ALLIGATOR BAY

N

GULF
OF
MEXICO

KEY McLAUGHLIN

Broad   River

EVERGLADES NATIONAL PARK

SHARK RIVER SLOUGH

997

Leisure City

BISCAYNE BAY

Harney River

Shark River

PONCE DE LEON BAY

OYSTER BAY

WHITEWATER BAY

CAPE SABLE

Long Pine Key Trail

PA-HAY-OKEE OVERLOOK

Long Pine Key

Anhinga Trail

MAHOGANY HAMMOCK

Main Visitor Center

Homestead

Florida City

9336

Royal Palm Visitor Center

North Canal Dr.

BISCAYNE NATIONAL PARK

1

Card Sound Road

Card Sound Toll bridge

WILDERNESS WATERWAY

This well-marked, 99-mile canoe route, Wilderness Waterway, meanders among the backwater creeks, rivers and bays of the park's mangrove forest. The waterway connects Everglades City to Flamingo.

TAYLOR SLOUGH

CROCODILE SANCTUARY (Closed to public)

Barnes Sound

905

Key Largo

MAHOGANY HAMMOCK

An elevated boardwalk, just off the main park road, allows park visitors to experience first-hand the tropical vegetation of a Mahogany Hammock. The hammock is home to the largest living mahogany tree in the U.S.

Lake Ingraham

Bear Lake Canoe Trail

Eco Pond

Flamingo Visitor Center

West Lake

Blackwater Sound

JOHN PENNEKAMP CORAL REEF STATE PARK

FLORIDA BAY

HAWK CHANNEL

1

ATLANTIC OCEAN

0   5   10 miles

To Key West

INFORMATION FOR VISITORS

From Miami, take Hwy. 1 to Homestead, then Hwy. 9336 west to the Main Visitor Center. Hwy. 1 north connects the Florida Keys to Homestead. Hwy. 41 runs east-west across the northern section of the park and passes through the Shark Valley Information Center. The main park road connects the main visitor center with Flamingo Visitor Center on Florida Bay. Miami International Airport serves the

park. Although open year-round, the best time to visit the park is from mid-December to mid-April. Accommodation is available inside the park in Flamingo. The marina in Flamingo rents canoes, small skiffs and houseboats, and offers free boat launching facilities. Sightseeing boat tours of the mangrove region and Florida Bay leave from the Gulf Coast Ranger Station. Fishing is

permitted in the inland and coastal waters of the Everglades. Airboats, swamp buggies and all-terrain vehicles are not permitted in the park.

For more information: Superintendent, Everglades National Park, 4001 State Rd. 9336, Homestead, FL 33034-6733. (305) 242-7700.

maintaining the difference between hammocks and pine forests. Hammocks seldom go up in smoke, but pine forests do. The flames cut through palmettos and grasses on the forest floor, and crackle high into the crowns of South Florida pines, leaving charred remains that look desolate and sterile. But in a decade the area will be alive with new pines rising forth, and the young forest will be dappled with the blossoms of wildflowers and the flights of woodpeckers and red-shouldered hawks. Were a pine forest not to burn every so often, it would eventually be invaded by shade-tolerant broad-leafed trees, and develop into a hammock.

To the south, the mix of glades, hammocks and pine forests surrenders to the shallow waters of Florida Bay and a serpentine coast dominated by the tangled forests of mangrove trees. Here salt water and tides, not fire, play a regulatory role. Fresh water mixes with the sea to form a rich estuary where manatees sometimes dwell, where schools of silver fish called mullet eat detritus and are eaten by ospreys, where cormorants, pelicans, egrets and herons make their livings, and raccoons patrol the night.

Also abundant are mosquitoes. Forty-three species occur in the park, but on the bright side, only 12 species bite. People who live in the Everglades joke that the mosquitoes are so thick in the summer you can wave a pint jar through the air and catch a quart of them. A sign in the Flamingo Visitor Center shows a large caricature of a mosquito pointing its imposing proboscis at a chart showing current mosquito conditions. From best to worst the mosquito chart reads: Enjoyable, Bearable, Unpleasant, Horrible and Hysterical. If you want Enjoyable or Bearable, visit in winter.

The Everglades belongs not just to the plants and animals and the balance that binds them, but to the more than one million visitors who come here each year, some year after year, driving south out of Miami and Fort Myers. They ride bicycles or open-air trams along the Shark Valley Loop Road, or go tour boating from Everglades City into the area called Ten Thousand Islands. Those who are more adventurous canoe the 99-mile Wilderness Waterway along the coast. Many drive through the park on a single-lane highway, which ends at the seaside hamlet of Flamingo.

One of the most popular spots is the Anhinga Trail, a quarter-mile boardwalk and asphalt path in the heart of the park, next to the Royal Palm Visitor Center. As the sun rises here, so does a chorus of wildlife calls. Purple gallinules walk with long toes on aquatic, broad-leafed spatterdock, while moorhens—a similar species of wading bird—cluck and call incessantly. Green-backed herons chase each other through thick willows and some-

times land on the boardwalk handrail, astonishing nearby visitors, then fly away, scolding each other as they go.

Other species of herons—great blue, tricolored, little blue—wade along shore and stand still on the shore, waiting for fish. Patience is their virtue. At times they sway, grasslike, to imitate movement from the wind and lure their prey closer. Then suddenly one plunges its head into the water and comes up with a fish impaled on the end of its sharp beak. The anhinga—the bird for which the trail is named—also spears fish with its beak, but by swimming underwater rather than by wading on shore. The anhinga feeds primarily in freshwater ponds and sloughs; between feedings, it perches on limbs above the water and spreads its wings to dry.

MONARCH OF THE PARK

Wildlife stories drift up and down the Anhinga Trail, and sooner or later a commotion comes from somewhere that the most talked about animal of them all is on the prowl. It is the monarch of the Everglades—the alligator. Though common in the park, alligators are seldom taken for granted. They move in strange reptilian ways, punctuating long hours of motionlessness with an occasional twitch of the head or tail, a sliding into the water, a silent running submarine style with only the dark snout and eyes visible, a sudden burst of speed, a splash of water, and a flash of teeth. This is the alligator park visitors expect to see, and sometimes do; the alligator drifting up on a box turtle and waiting, waiting, then lunging and sinking out of sight with the turtle in its jaws. The turtle could also be an unsuspecting ibis or heron. It happens now and then along the Anhinga Trail, and at Shark Valley, Eco Pond and elsewhere in the Everglades, and people who see it spend hours talking about it.

Though alligators take life in the Everglades, they also give it. As the summer wet season surrenders to the winter dry season and the water table drops, the sloughs and glades in the river of grass go dry. This would be a time of serious ecological stress for many animals were it not for the alligator. Called a "natural hydraulic engineer," a big alligator will find depressions across the flat land, sense water below and roll in the soft earth to create a gator hole—a pond that fills with water a few feet deep and 6 to 8 yards across. Fish, frogs, snails and other animals can survive the dry season in these gator holes, and repopulate the glades when rain returns.

Water is the key to life in the Everglades; not just its abundance, but also its quality and seasonal fluctuations. The glades is not a swamp, but rather a sheet of water measuring 50 miles wide in some places, and yet only a few inches deep, moving

COLORFUL COHABITANTS
Clusters of common bromeliad cling to the bark of the bald cypress tree. Where soil is at a premium, air plants such as this have adapted by living piggyback on established trees. Air plants draw nothing from their host: instead, they absorb nutrients from the air and from decaying debris that builds up around their stalks.

slowly south from Lake Okeechobee, in the middle of the state, to Florida Bay at the bottom.

Nearly every serious ecological problem threatening the Everglades (and there are many of them—The Wilderness Society regards this park as the most endangered in the U.S. National Park System) deals directly or indirectly with water. And most of those problems originate from outside park boundaries. Even though Everglades National Park was created in 1947, and adjoining Big Cypress National Preserve in 1974, the two combined contain only the lower one-fifth of the original Everglades ecosystem.

The problems began early. Running for governor in 1904, Napoleon Bonaparte Broward announced his intentions to drain the Everglades. "Centuries ago," he said in an election speech, "the people of Holland...looked out over the adjacent salt and shallow reaches of the sea and said, 'Here is land in plenty which the sea does not need, we

HITCHHIKING PRODIGY
A baby alligator has little to fear while sunning aboard his mother's craggy nose. Female alligators are attentive mothers, protecting their young from hungry predators. The Everglades' most renowned inhabitant is also its preeminent engineer. The alligator's excavated winter water hole provides an oasis of fresh water, where smaller animals and plants can survive during the dry season.

NATURE'S SPUN SILK
Covering acres of an untouched sawgrass marsh, dew-covered spider webs glitter in the midmorning light. In the background, solitary dwarf cypresses rise above the marsh. The diverse animals and plants of the park live to the ancient rhythm of drought (mid-December through mid-April) and deluge (the rest of the year).

BIRDS OF DIFFERENT FEATHER
*A preening female anhinga (top)
primps its flight feathers. Anhingas'
necks have a special quick-release
mechanism so that they can pierce
passing fish with lightning speed.
A tricolored heron (above) scans the
marsh with a sharp eye. Herons also
use their bills as spears.*

will take it.' They built dikes, shut out the sea, pumped water and today the bottom of the sea has become the garden spot of Europe."

But the Everglades was not Holland, and Broward could not have been more wrongheaded. The people elected him, and over the decades one piece after another of the Everglades was ditched, diked and drained. Farms and highways replaced pine forests, glades and sloughs. The 103-mile meandering Kissimmee River, feeding Lake Okeechobee from the Kissimmee Lakes, was straitjacketed into a 50-mile channel; one biologist later said it was akin to performing heart surgery with a meat cleaver.

Alligators were no longer the chief engineers of the Everglades, man was. The clouds of birds that had once filled the sky, and had "astonished" John James Audubon in 1832, were gone. By 1990, only five percent of the original numbers of wading birds remained, many species of wildlife were endangered, or extinct, mercury and other toxins had leaked into the glades, and greater Miami, once a sleepy town of a couple of thousand people, had swelled to two million. One thousand people per day were moving to Florida, each of whom would use 200 gallons of fresh water every day. To describe the plight of the Everglades, biologists needed only two words: "Ecosystem collapse."

THE FIGHT TO PRESERVE

Soon the rallying cry became "Save the Everglades," and Marjory Stoneman Douglas, then in her hundredth year, never stopped fighting. People began to realize that this feisty lady had been right all along; the health of Florida depends on the health of the Everglades. Save one and you save the other.

CYCLES OF CHANGE
Great building thunderheads, drawing their vapor from the Gulf Stream, announce the approach of the spring rains. In summer, rivers overflow: in winter, the water shrinks below the grass roots.

PRESERVING THE WETLANDS
The Anhinga Trail (bottom), part boardwalk, part asphalt, threads through the protected habitat of alligators, snapping turtles and magnificent broad-winged wading birds. One heartening sight is the roseate spoonbill (below), its pink plumage mirrored in the water beneath it. Nearly extinct earlier in this century, the protected spoonbill is making a comeback.

Slowly, the political climate changed. In 1989, the Everglades National Park Protection and Expansion Act added 107,000 acres to the northeast corner of the park, and plans were drafted to put the river back into its original channel. The Everglades will never be what it once was, but with a growing enlightenment, corrected priorities and serious restoration, by the year 2000 Floridians intend to have an Everglades more like 1900 than 1980.

In a 1988 revision to *The Everglades: River of Grass*, Marjory Douglas and Randy Lee Loftis wrote: "A century after man first started to dominate the Everglades, that progress has stumbled. It is, perhaps, an opportunity. The great wet wilderness of South Florida need not be degraded to a permanent state of mediocrity. If the people enforce their will on the managers of Florida's future, the Everglades can be restored to nature's design."

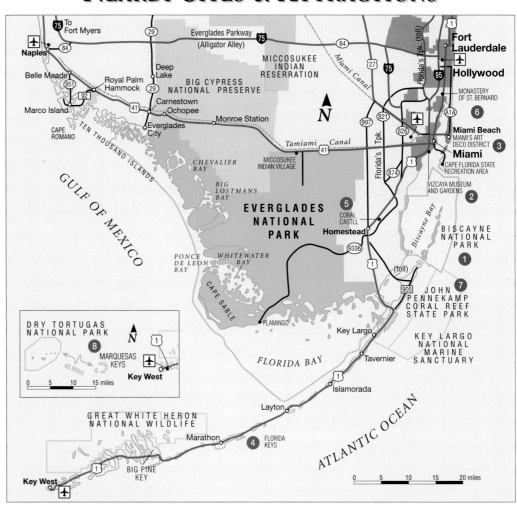

The Vizcaya Museum, once a private home, contains an opulent collection of furniture, paintings and decorative arts from Europe.

1 BISCAYNE NATIONAL PARK

Made up of a thin strip of the mainland and a chain of 45 small islands ringing Biscayne Bay, only four percent of this subtropical park is land. The rest of it lies submerged in aquamarine waters and protects the only living coral reef in the continental U.S. The reef's living polyps attract more than 200 kinds of fish, which can be seen from glass-bottom boats. There are also cruises for snorkelers and scuba divers. Mangrove forests grow along the western shoreline and forests of hardwood hammocks cover the interior of the larger islands. Hiking trails enable visitors to see the park's flora and fauna. Located 21 miles east of Everglades National Park on Hwy. 1.

2 VIZCAYA MUSEUM AND GARDENS, MIAMI

This impressive example of Italian Renaissance-style architecture, begun in 1914, took eight years to complete and cost $18 million. Constructed as a winter residence for International Harvester heir James Deering, the museum's 34 rooms house a vast collection of 15th- to 19th-century furniture, textiles and sculpture. The villa's 10 acres of formal gardens were designed as an extension of the villa and combine the elements of 16th- and 17th-century Italian hill gardens with 17th-century French gardens. An ornate stone barge, anchored in front of the mansion, serves as a decorative breakwater for Biscayne Bay. Located south of the Rickenbacker Causeway on Hwy. 95.

A cowfish, one of the more than 200 types of reef fish that live in Biscayne Bay, seems to pose for the camera. This distinctive creature is named for the tiny hornlike projections over its eyes.

③ ART DECO HISTORIC DISTRICT, MIAMI

In the 1930's, Miami turned its back on its former passion, Mediterranean Revival architectural styles, and adopted a more modern, streamlined look known now as Miami Art Deco. The district contains more than 800 buildings—hotels, shops and private homes—all of which feature pastel colors, rounded corners, porthole windows and glass-brick walls. The area stretches from Sixth to Twenty-third Streets and from Ocean Drive to Lennox Court.

④ FLORIDA KEYS

Forty-two bridges connect the 32 islands of the Keys, all linked by the 113-mile-long Hwy. 1. Nature enthusiasts can visit the Great White Heron National Wildlife Refuge, Big Pine Key's National Key Deer Refuge, and the Lignumvitae Key State Botanical Site. For bird lovers, there is the Key West National Wildlife Refuge, a protected sanctuary for terns, frigatebirds, ospreys and herons. History buffs can explore Indian Key State Historic Site and Key West's historic district, including Ernest Hemingway's house. Boaters can meander among the keys and go deep-sea fishing for blue marlin and tarpon. Located south of Miami on Hwy. 1.

⑤ CORAL CASTLE

Painstakingly carved out of more than 1,000 tons of coral, this remarkable structure was erected by Latvian-born Edward Leedskalnin as a symbol of his unrequited love; he devoted 25 years of his life to complete it. Among the castle's many fascinations are hand-made furniture, solar-heated bathtubs and a nine-ton swinging gate—all sculpted from coral. Claiming that he knew the secrets of the Egyptian pyramid-builders, the 100-pound Leedskalnin never divulged the means by which he himself transported the massive pieces of coral. Located on Hwy. 1, 15 miles south of Miami.

⑥ THE ANCIENT SPANISH MONASTERY, NORTH MIAMI BEACH

This transitional Romanesque-Gothic cloister and chapter house of the 12th century is the oldest structure from Europe in the U.S. Brought from Spain by newspaper magnate William Randolph Hearst for his mansion at San Simeon, California, the cloister was disassembled and shipped to New York; 10,751 packing crates were needed to hold its blocks of stone and columns, all wrapped in straw for protection. Upon arrival, U.S. Customs opened the crates and removed their contents to inspect the straw for hoof-and-mouth disease. Unfortunately for Hearst, the crates were numbered, but not their contents; reassembly became a giant jigsaw puzzle and he soon sold the disassembled pieces. In 1952 the cloister was reconstructed in Miami, and now houses an Episcopal church as well as art and antiques. Located in North Miami Beach, just off Hwy. 95.

⑦ JOHN PENNEKAMP CORAL REEF STATE PARK

Located offshore from Key Largo, the state park preserves a 75-square-mile area of the same living coral reef that extends up the coast to Biscayne National Park. About 178 nautical square miles of coral reefs, seagrass beds and mangrove swamps are protected within the state park and neighboring Key Largo Coral Reef National Marine Sanctuary. The park and sanctuary together are home to tropical vegetation and wading shore birds, along with more than 40 types of living coral and hundreds of species of fish. Glass-bottom boats are available for viewing the coral, or, for the more adventurous, the park offers guided scuba-diving and snorkeling excursions. A submerged nine-foot bronze statue in the sanctuary, called "Christ of the Deep," symbolizes peace for humankind, and is a popular venue for divers and snorkelers. Located north of Key Largo at Mile Marker 102.5.

⑧ DRY TORTUGAS NATIONAL PARK

Seven small islands make up Dry Tortugas National Park. The warm shallow waters surrounding the islands support living coral reefs, which in turn attract marine life ranging from lobsters, brightly colored reef fish such as amberjacks, groupers, wahoos and tarpons to sharks and barracudas. Endangered green, loggerhead, and hawksbill sea turtles dig nests on the islands' pristine beaches. Between March and September, about 100,000 sooty terns congregate on Bush Key to nest. Historic Fort Jefferson, under construction during the Civil War, dominates Garden Key. Located 70 miles west of Key West.

Two of Miami's buildings display the characteristic pastel pink and aquamarine colors of the Art Deco style. This architectural fashion grew out of the boom days of the 1930's when Miami real-estate developers, influenced by the Exposition des Arts Décoratifs in Paris, designed and built more than 800 buildings in Miami's Art Deco Historic District.

The lure of Florida's clear waters makes recreational boating one of the most popular ways of experiencing island life in the Keys. Boaters often visit Cape Sable, the southernmost point in the Keys and in the continental U.S.

BIG BEND

*Its moody landscape is a study
in extremes: drought and deluge;
deserts and forests of yucca.*

For a thousand miles, the Rio Grande snakes
down from the Colorado Plateau on a steady
course toward the Gulf of Mexico until it reaches a mysterious detour on the Chihuahuan Desert.
There, canyons and basins grab the river and fling
it on a great loop, taking from Mexico and giving
to Texas a desolate, triangular expanse of mountainous badlands known as the Big Bend.

It is a place of foreboding beauty, at once hos-
tile and alluring, barren and abundant, only lightly touched by time but possessing a lore as rich as
a quicksilver lode. To enter here is, seemingly, to
draw near to the end of the earth.

Somewhere south of the tiny Texan village of
Marathon, even the radio waves turn back, and
long before you reach Big Bend National Park,
the last and sturdiest signal—a Spanish language
broadcast from Eagle Pass—hisses and cracks
and fades into a static drone. Except for the whine
of an engine and the whisper of wind, an eerie
and all-consuming quiet settles like a delicate
sparrow on the ancient sea bed that is now a
bunch-grass plain. But soon, the grassland yields
to a nappy desert carpet of cacti and creosote and

CONTORTIONS IN STONE
Bizarrely shaped rocks line the Grapevine Hills Trail, a 2.2-mile round-trip hike through some of the park's most intriguing landscape. The weird rock formations were formed when columns of hardened lava were exposed and carved by erosion. Grapevine Hills Road, west of Basin Junction, leads to the area.

CHISOS TWILIGHT

Overleaf: The day's failing light brushes pads of purple-tinged prickly-pear cactus, the most abundant cactus in the park. In the background loom the glowing Chisos, washed lavender-rose by a classic Big Bend sunset.

then to oak, piñon, and junipers as the Chisos Mountains begin to take form. Hawks and falcons and turkey vultures lie on the wind, scanning the arid landscape for jack rabbits, reptiles and kangaroo rats. South of the park's Persimmon Gap entrance, there are signs warning hikers to clear their routes with park rangers, lest they trek into the path of migrating mountain lions.

Now, the Chisos—the name may be derived from the Spanish *hechizos*, meaning enchantments, or from an Indian term for ghosts—rise abruptly and sprawl under a dense overcast. Clouds cling to the mountainsides, leaving the peaks floating above, and lie across the mesas, spilling a thin haze down the dark cliffs to refract an occasional burst of sunlight into wisps of lavender and powder blue.

Around the mountains are the ruins of a violent struggle of nature: fields of gray and black boulders, white volcanic ash and red rock towers driven from the depths by primordial turbulence and eroded into intricate statuary. Indians who once hunted and gathered here believed that when the Great Spirit finished making the earth, he dumped the leftover rocks on Big Bend.

At certain times of the year, it is a land of botanical and zoological splendor and, if approached cautiously, a place for solitude, discovery and renewal. Taken lightly, it is unforgiving. The desert hides rattlesnakes and scorpions, and sudden rains can send flash floods roaring through the washes and draws. Conditions can be so harsh that men have ventured into the hills never to return.

Spanish explorers called it the "unknown land." One Texas writer, Carlton Stowers, described it as "the kind of country only those with the souls of poets or armadillos can appreciate." Author Ludwig Bemelmans was among the former. "Here, the mantle of God touches you," he wrote. "It is what Beethoven reached for in music."

Perhaps no poet verbalized the Big Bend's mystique more eloquently than did an old Mexican cowboy, giving directions to Anglo wanderers more than a century ago: "You go south until you come to the place where the rainbows wait for rain, and the big river is kept in a stone box, and the water runs uphill. And the mountains float in the air, except at night when they go away to play with the other mountains."

For most of its history, humankind has given the region a wide berth, except to rend it for its lodes of mercury, then called quicksilver, or to trespass it in search of wild game or to deliver cargoes of contraband drugs and liquor. But it is, perhaps, the Texas most firmly fixed in the American mind. It is the land of Pancho Villa and Judge Roy Bean, of ghost towns and buried treasure, Indian wars, banditos, desperadoes, lost mines and lost dreams.

This arching stretch of the Rio Grande was not explored by European Americans until 1852 and even then the most intimidating reaches were charted by mapmakers who looked down from the limestone cliffs that rise 1,200 to 1,500 feet above Boquillas and Santa Elena Canyons.

In 1881, a party led by the Texas Rangers floated through Santa Elena, but the captain went by horseback across Mesa de Anguila and met his boaters at the mouth of the canyon. It was not until 1899 that a team from the U.S. Geological Survey dared to enter, and conquer, Boquillas Canyon.

Today, rafting and canoeing through the canyons are among Big Bend's main attractions. The river, a gritty soup of silt and sand, normally moves at a safe and languid pace, hurried infrequently by rapids no more menacing than an amusement park ride. Float trips take from one day to a week, which allows time for bird watching, studying fossils lodged in the canyon walls or more sporting pursuits, such as fishing. Thirty-eight-pound catfish have been pulled from the Rio Grande.

Like the river, the desert and the mountains have been conquered, if not tamed, by familiarity and use. Though still no place for the timid or the sedentary, the Big Bend National Park, established in 1944, draws close to 300,000 visitors each year. Even at its most crowded, the 1,252-square-mile park, like the immense badlands surrounding it, seems as deserted as an asteroid.

One does not visit the park on an impulse. The nearest commercial airport is 230 miles north, in

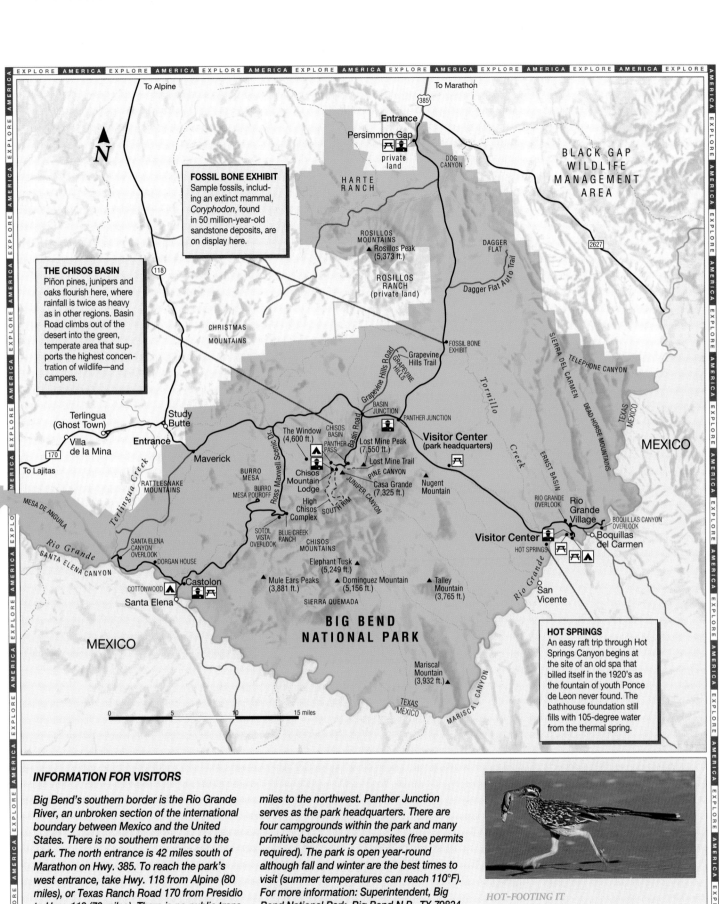

To Alpine

To Marathon

385

Entrance

Persimmon Gap

private land

BLACK GAP WILDLIFE MANAGEMENT AREA

HARTE RANCH

DOG CANYON

2627

FOSSIL BONE EXHIBIT
Sample fossils, including an extinct mammal, *Coryphodon*, found in 50 million-year-old sandstone deposits, are on display here.

ROSILLOS MOUNTAINS
▲ Rosillos Peak (5,373 ft.)

DAGGER FLAT

Dagger Flat Auto Trail

ROSILLOS RANCH (private land)

118

THE CHISOS BASIN
Piñon pines, junipers and oaks flourish here, where rainfall is twice as heavy as in other regions. Basin Road climbs out of the desert into the green, temperate area that supports the highest concentration of wildlife—and campers.

CHRISTMAS MOUNTAINS

FOSSIL BONE EXHIBIT

SIERRA DEL CARMEN

TELEPHONE CANYON

Grapevine Hills Road

Grapevine Hills Trail

GRAPEVINE HILLS

Tornillo Creek

DEAD HORSE MOUNTAINS

TEXAS MEXICO

BASIN JUNCTION

Basin Road

PANTHER JUNCTION

Terlingua (Ghost Town)

Study Butte

Villa de la Mina

Entrance

170

To Lajitas

The Window (4,600 ft.)

CHISOS BASIN

PANTHER PASS

Lost Mine Peak (7,550 ft.)

Lost Mine Trail

Visitor Center
(park headquarters)

MEXICO

Maverick

Terlingua Creek

RATTLESNAKE MOUNTAINS

BURRO MESA

Ross Maxwell Scenic Dr.

BURRO MESA POUROFF

Chisos Mountain Lodge

High Chisos Complex

PINE CANYON

JUNIPER CANYON

Casa Grande (7,325 ft.)

Nugent Mountain

SOUTH RIM

ERNST BASIN

RIO GRANDE OVERLOOK

Rio Grande Village

BOQUILLAS CANYON OVERLOOK

MESA DE ANGUILA

Rio Grande

SANTA ELENA CANYON

SOTOL VISTA OVERLOOK

BLUE CREEK RANCH

CHISOS MOUNTAINS

Visitor Center

HOT SPRINGS

Boquillas del Carmen

SANTA ELENA CANYON OVERLOOK

DORGAN HOUSE

Elephant Tusk (5,249 ft.) ▲

Rio Grande

San Vicente

COTTONWOOD

Castolon

Santa Elena

▲ Mule Ears Peaks (3,881 ft.)

▲ Dominguez Mountain (5,156 ft.)

▲ Talley Mountain (3,765 ft.)

SIERRA QUEMADA

BIG BEND NATIONAL PARK

HOT SPRINGS
An easy raft trip through Hot Springs Canyon begins at the site of an old spa that billed itself in the 1920's as the fountain of youth Ponce de Leon never found. The bathhouse foundation still fills with 105-degree water from the thermal spring.

MEXICO

Mariscal Mountain (3,932 ft.) ▲

MARISCAL CANYON

TEXAS MEXICO

0   5   10   15 miles

INFORMATION FOR VISITORS

Big Bend's southern border is the Rio Grande River, an unbroken section of the international boundary between Mexico and the United States. There is no southern entrance to the park. The north entrance is 42 miles south of Marathon on Hwy. 385. To reach the park's west entrance, take Hwy. 118 from Alpine (80 miles), or Texas Ranch Road 170 from Presidio to Hwy. 118 (70 miles). There is no public transportation to or within the park. The closest commercial airports are Midland International, 230 miles to the northeast, and El Paso, 325 miles to the northwest. Panther Junction serves as the park headquarters. There are four campgrounds within the park and many primitive backcountry campsites (free permits required). The park is open year-round although fall and winter are the best times to visit (summer temperatures can reach 110°F). For more information: Superintendent, Big Bend National Park, Big Bend N.P., TX 79834. (915) 477-2251.

HOT-FOOTING IT

Lizard dinner in tow, a greater roadrunner races across the desert. The wily, aggressive bird can reach speeds of 20 miles an hour.

HOLED UP

A fledgling New World elf owl (right) nests snugly inside an abandoned woodpecker hole as protection from the extremes of desert cold and heat. Below, a swath of blue desert sky is reflected in the quiescent waters of Santa Elena Canyon. During the slow course of geologic time, the water-borne abrasives of the Rio Grande have carved out Big Bend's steep-cliffed river chasms.

Midland, Texas, and park headquarters is a full day's drive from Dallas or Houston. The Chisos Mountain Lodge has only 72 rooms and they are usually booked far in advance. There are three campgrounds, but only limited provisions and medical services. Although the park is open year-round, clothing should be considered carefully. In winter, temperatures can range from sub-freezing in the mountains to 90°F on the desert floor. In summer, the daytime temperatures can reach 110°F and fall by half at dusk.

Yet, this remoteness and diversity are what give the Big Bend its special mystique. It is three distinct ecological worlds—river, desert, mountain—but they mesh with remarkable congruity. Along the river, prickly-pear cacti grow beside a virtual wetland in the shadow of a desert mountain. Despite the aridity (8 to 20 inches of rainfall a year) the desert blazes in spring with Texas bluebonnets,

Clusters of agave present a prickly obstacle for passersby. The spiny-margined leaves terminate in needle-sharp points that store a mildly poisonous chemical. After about 15 years of growth, the agave sends out a thick stalk and a cluster of nectar-rich flowers. After this spectacular display, the plant has exhausted its supply of energy and dies.

the huge yellow blossoms of giant daggers, vivid strawberry cactus and spiny ocotillo stems topped by crimson cones. Prairie verbena, rock-nettle, cholla and a dozen other cacti and wildflowers give life and texture to the somber tones of the ridges and volcanic outcroppings.

LIFE IN THE DESERT FLOURISHES The Big Bend is home to 75 species of mammals, 55 species of reptiles and 1,000 plant varieties, and more than 430 species of birds have been sighted in the park. At the park's lower, drier elevations, mule deer, their oversized ears deployed like radar dishes, may come almost close enough to touch. On the paved roads, during early evening, you may be able to park and watch a family of javelinas, ugly and ill-mannered wild pigs, feeding on the flesh of lechuguilla plants.

Much of the park can be explored by automobile, though to explore more than the paved roads, a four-wheel drive, high-clearance vehicle is recommended. From the park headquarters, a paved road goes southeast 20 miles to Rio Grande Village, where you can park and hike along the river, through a dense stand of river reed and mesquite, across a butte with a sweeping view of the Dead Horse Mountains. A side trip, on an unpaved but improved dirt road, leads to the river and the gray stone remains of what was once Hot Springs, Texas. The hulls of an old post office and a motel are still standing. A 200-yard trail follows the river to a one-time bathhouse over a warm spring that emerges from the earth. The 105° spring is still impounded in a shallow rock pool and is often used by weary hikers to melt away the day's fatigue.

Another paved road, known as the Ross Maxwell Scenic Drive, meanders west of the Chisos, past

DESERTED DESERT

*Crumbling under the desert sun,
the remains of an adobe farm,
Dorgan House, are silhouetted
against a dramatic Big Bend sunset.
Farmers and ranchers worked this
floodplain area near the village
of Castolon until the 1930's.*

LOCAL RESIDENTS

*Below, two javelinas, also called col-
lared peccaries, forage in the brush.
The nearsighted, piglike herbivores
have the reputation of being foul-
smelling and fierce, but actually
pose no danger to park visitors.*

fields of wildflowers and volcanic debris, and ends
at Santa Elena Canyon. You can hike nearly a mile
into the canyon to a place where boulders as big
as houses block further progress.

The third paved route goes from the park headquarters into the Chisos Mountain Basin seven
miles away. There, you can take a room at the lodge,
camp, ride horseback or take in one of the Big
Bend's most spectacular dances of nature—sunset through The Window, a V-shaped notch in the
mountain range that provides a perfect frame for
the haunting blue moonscape.

Despite its rugged immensity, the Big Bend is
best experienced on foot. There are more than 150
miles of hiking trails in the park, but be prepared:
the altitudes exact a toll and on longer trails,
water—even food—will have to be backpacked
along. Some trails begin where "primitive roads"

An ocotillo, also called a coachwhip, displays its spring show of brilliant red flowers on what appear to be dead branches. In drought, the ocotillo looks like a lifeless collection of sticks jutting out of the desert sand. But soon after a rainstorm, the plant sprouts hundreds of tiny leaves that quickly drop off again when arid conditions return.

end, where access by ordinary passenger car is risky or impossible.

Grapevine Hills Trail is to the north, away from the mountains, and is an easy 2.2-mile walk through a sandy wash strewn with granite boulders. It ends where balanced rocks frame a view of Nugent Mountain. Like the rest of the park, the Grapevine Hills are so silent that the scurry of lizards and the wingbeats of ravens are audible.

TRAILS TO STORIED VISTAS

Lost Mine Trail (4.8 miles round trip) provides the best introduction to the flora and fauna of the High Chisos. The trail begins at 5,600-foot-high Panther Pass on the Basin Road and ascends, in zigzag fashion, to a lookout point about a mile away from the peak of Casa Grande. From there,

you can see down into Pine and Juniper Canyons and more than 100 miles beyond.

For serious hikers only is the strenuous 14-mile round trip to the South Rim of the Chisos, 2,500 feet above the desert floor, and its storied vistas: the rusty-red Sierra Quemada—the burned mountains—Santa Elena Canyon and the Rio Grande, 20 miles away. In clear weather, the view extends 100 miles into Mexico. The trail begins in the Chisos Basin and can be completed in a day, but it is done best as an overnighter. There are campsites on the South Rim, but some are closed when the endangered peregrine falcon elects to nest there.

The Big Bend is a place not for quick consumption, but for gradual absorption. Many come here time after time for the replenishment of the soul—to visit the river in its stone box, and to sit by the rainbows waiting for rain.

Its formidable adobe walls hint at a military past, but Fort Leaton actually served as a 19th-century trading post. Built on the San Antonio-Chihuahua Trail, the outpost was an important supply center for the nearby towns of Presidio and Chihuahua.

NEARBY SITES & ATTRACTIONS

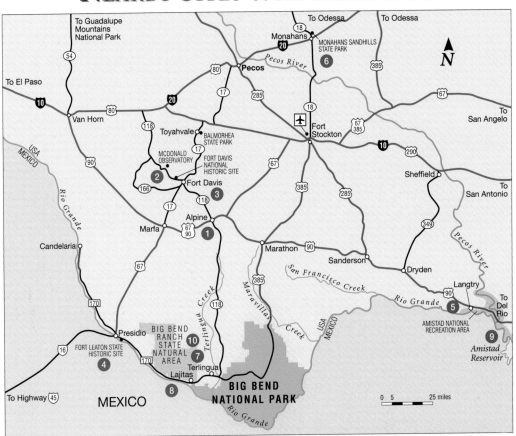

1 ALPINE

Nestled in the valley of the Davis Mountains almost a mile above sea level, Alpine is the closest town and jumping-off point to Big Bend National Park. Founded in the 1880's as a ranching depot, the picturesque town now serves as the gateway to the park and a center of activity for nearby cattle ranches. The Museum of Big Bend, on the campus of Sul Ross State University, traces the history of Indian, Spanish and American settlement in the Big Bend area. At the junction of Hwys. 118 and 90, 103 miles north of Big Bend National Park.

2 MCDONALD OBSERVATORY

Atop the 6,800-foot summit of Mount Locke in the Davis Mountains, the University of Texas McDonald Observatory scans the clear desert sky. The observatory houses five telescopes, which range in size from 30 inches in diameter to 107 inches. Visitors can take guided tours of the observatory; a self-guided tour explains how a telescope works. The Visitors' Center has exhibits of the solar system and the universe. On Hwy. 118, 15 miles north of Fort Davis.

3 FORT DAVIS NATIONAL HISTORIC SITE

Fort Davis, located near one of the few sources of water in the Pecos Mountains, was built in 1854.

Relics from a vanished epoch, these eroding adobe tombstones still stand in the cemetery of Terlingua, a deserted mining town.

Soldiers garrisoned at the fort protected westward-bound mail and freight trains, and travelers on the San Antonio-El Paso Road. Soldiers garrisoned at the fort in 1857 were given an unusual assignment when Secretary of War Jefferson Davis imported camels to be tested for use by the army in American deserts. The fort was taken by the Confederates during the Civil War and later destroyed by the Apache Indians. In 1867, a post-Civil War fort was constructed here of stone and adobe; the fort saw active service until 1891. Today, some of these buildings have been restored including the officers' quarters, enlisted men's barracks and the hospital. Located just outside the town of Fort Davis off Hwy. 17.

4 FORT LEATON STATE HISTORIC SITE

This massive adobe fortress was built as a civilian settlement in 1848 by the "noble desperado" Ben Leaton. Leaton was a scalp hunter turned entrepreneur whose trading practices with the Comanche and Apache brought charges from the Mexicans and Americans that he was encouraging the Indians to raid Mexican settlements for goods to swap. The fort's restored rooms and interpretative exhibits allow visitors a glimpse at Texas frontier days. The fort is a gateway to the Big Bend Ranch State Natural Area. Located 4 miles southeast of Presidio on Hwy. 170.

5 LANGTRY

Founded in the late 1800's, Langtry was once home to the notorious Judge Roy Bean, the self-appointed "law west of the Pecos." Bean meted out Texas-style frontier justice from the porch of his saloon-courtroom—the Jersey Lily—now adjacent to the Visitor Center. Bean placed Langtry on the map by his strange actions, such as fining a dead man $40 for wearing a pistol. According to Bean's version of history, both the town and the saloon were named for the British actress Lily Langtry, rumored to have been a mistress of the Prince of Wales (later Edward VII), and certainly the object of Bean's not-so-secret passion. A cactus garden identifies all the species of cacti native to west Texas. On Hwy. 90, 138 miles east of Big Bend.

6 MONAHANS SANDHILLS STATE PARK

One of the most unusual state parks in the Southwest preserves 3,840 acres of white sand and sparse desert vegetation for as far as the eye can see. The wind-carved sand dunes create a landscape reminiscent of the Sahara. Remarkably, the largest oak forest in the nation grows here. But these are no ordinary oak trees: they are Havard oaks, which seldom grow taller than 3 feet and send down massive root systems as far as 90 feet. "Sand surfing" is permitted on the dunes. Located off Hwy. 20, 6 miles northwest of Monahans.

7 TERLINGUA GHOST TOWN

Gold, silver or quicksilver? Early Texas pioneers mined for these valuable minerals and Terlingua quickly sprang up to house the would-be millionaires. Once the quicksilver (also known as mercury) mines were exhausted, the town folded its tents and died. Restored stores, hotels and mining offices recall Terlingua's more prosperous days. The most impressive abandoned adobe structure is that of the mine owner's winter home. Terlingua is also the site of the annual World Championship Chili Cookoff every November. Off Hwy. 170, 10 miles west of Big Bend.

8 LAJITAS

This recreated Old West town was originally a major border-crossing point and trading post where fur trappers sold their skins for goods. General John "Blackjack" Pershing housed his troops here in 1913 when he was on the trail of Mexican revolutionary Pancho Villa. The Barton Warnock Environmental Center includes a restored miner's home and a blooming cactus garden. Near the junction of Hwys. 170 and 118, 18 miles northwest of Big Bend National Park.

9 AMISTAD NATIONAL RECREATION AREA

The immense reservoir formed by the confluence of the Devil's River, Rio Grande, and Pecos River creates a perfect locale for boating, water skiing, swimming and fishing. At Panther Cave, accessible only by boat, visitors can see Indian pictographs on the cave walls. Facilities include 10 major boat ramps, marinas, primitive campgrounds and picnic areas. Located on Hwy. 90, 250 miles east of Big Bend National Park.

10 BIG BEND RANCH STATE NATURAL AREA

This 264,000-acre untamed region of desert, canyons and the Rio Grande lies adjacent to the western border of Big Bend National Park. There are no visitors' facilities at this new state-run reserve, but the area is popular with experienced wilderness buffs for its hiking trails and river rafting. Bus excursions stop at a prehistoric Indian Camp and at Sauceda, the old ranch headquarters where herds of longhorn cattle graze. East of Lajitas on Highway 170.

The angled afternoon sun casts ribbons of shadows across the Monahans Sandhills. The vast dune fields, sculpted by the wind, stretch hundreds of miles into Mexico.

Twilight illuminates the University of Texas' McDonald Observatory, one of the pre-eminent observatories in the world. Once a month, at the approach of the full moon, the observatory opens its 107-inch telescope to the public.

GRAND CANYON

*One of nature's spectacular creations,
its rugged, stepped landscape breaks
the bank of superlatives.*

No matter how much you've heard about the Grand Canyon, nothing can really prepare you for it. From the south, the road climbs gradually upward, across grassy scrubland through a thin forest of pinyon, juniper and ponderosa pine. Occasionally a view opens to the north, but there is nothing notable on the horizon, nothing to hint at what lies ahead. You could wonder what all the fuss is about until suddenly, there it is, a vast open space bounded by layer upon layer of colored rock, stair-stepping downward past interior valleys, buttes and promontories, ending finally in the black-walled Inner Gorge where the Colorado River, largely unseen from above, grinds its way to the sea.

More than a mile deep in places, 277 miles long, and as much as 18 miles across, the Canyon appears monolithic, beyond human proportions—large almost to the point of vulgarity. Glowing red under the Arizona sun it offers itself in a stunning but immodest panorama, as if it has nothing to hide.

SWIRLING WATERS
Water running off the North Rim eroded Deer Creek Narrows, which feeds into the Colorado River. Deer Creek Falls, near the river, is a popular spot for rafting and boating.

MULTIHUED MAJESTY
Overleaf: A storm sky broods over the Grand Canyon at Cape Royal, creating a play of shadow and light on the canyon walls. Cape Royal is one of three main lookouts on the North Rim, which is 1,000 feet higher than the South Rim.

But like all great things, the Grand Canyon reveals its enormous complexity in stages—never all at once, and never without some coaxing. From above, from below, in good weather and in storms, in winter and summer, and in its ten thousand different nooks and corners, the Canyon is always changing. You can see it hundreds of times and still find something new with each visit, whether hiking the superb trails, running the Colorado River in a rubber raft, cross-country skiing on the Kaibab Plateau, or just sitting quietly at a viewpoint. To those who listen, the Canyon speaks eloquently in terms that, once heard, can never be forgotten.

Among the sun-baked rock ledges, surrounded by desert-hardened creatures such as chuckwallas, rattlers and horned toads, the Canyon holds delicate secrets. Moist hollows are scattered like hidden treasures. They drip with springwater and fill with the gentle fragrance of wildflowers. In April and May, after winter rains have soaked the soil, the scene explodes in blossoms, some of the most exquisite of which emerge from unlikely plants— the prickly-pear cactus or the gnarly shrub called cliffrose. Of more than 1,500 species of plants found here, only about two dozen are cacti. And while lizards scurry in great numbers, there are also songbirds and butterflies and tree frogs, along with maidenhair ferns, columbines and cattails—all part of the Grand Canyon's surprising diversity.

The variety is due in part to differences in elevation and exposure. Just as its rock layers form distinct levels, so do the Canyon's climatic zones. Generally, the deeper you go into the Canyon, the warmer and drier it gets. At the highest point in the park, on the North Rim, conditions resemble those of Canada's boreal forest, while at river level plants and animals are similar to those found in Arizona's Sonoran Desert. Traveling from the North Rim to the river is, in a sense, equivalent to going from British Columbia to southern Arizona.

The journey begins at more than 9,000 feet in a cool forest of aspen, spruce and fir, where winter snows lie deep and linger into late May or June. This forest is home to mule deer, coyotes, mountain lions, great horned owls, wild turkeys, and the rare white-tailed Kaibab squirrels. As the plateau slopes down toward the rim, conditions become warmer. The forest grades into pinyon, juniper, Gambel oak and mountain mahogany—plants capable of withstanding the formidable combination of cold winters and hot, dry summers.

There is a mixture of plants spilling off the North Rim into the inner Canyon. Moisture-loving species live on protected north-facing slopes, while desert plants thrive on the drier exposures facing south. Going deeper, trees vanish altogether, until at about

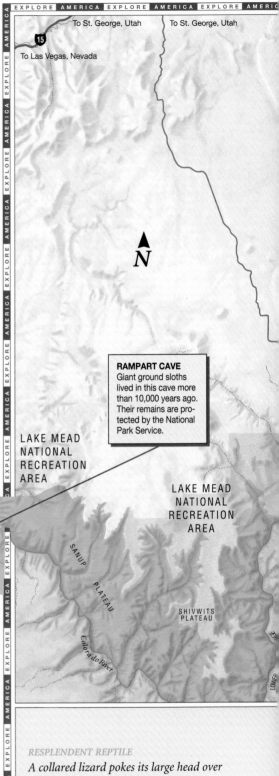

To St. George, Utah   To St. George, Utah

To Las Vegas, Nevada

N

RAMPART CAVE
Giant ground sloths lived in this cave more than 10,000 years ago. Their remains are protected by the National Park Service.

LAKE MEAD NATIONAL RECREATION AREA

LAKE MEAD NATIONAL RECREATION AREA

RAMPART CAVE

SANUP PLATEAU

SHIVWITS PLATEAU

Colorado River

RESPLENDENT REPTILE
A collared lizard pokes its large head over a rock waiting for prey. Named for the black and white bands that wrap around the back of its neck, the lizard feeds on insects and other lizards. There are 48 species of amphibians and reptiles in the park.

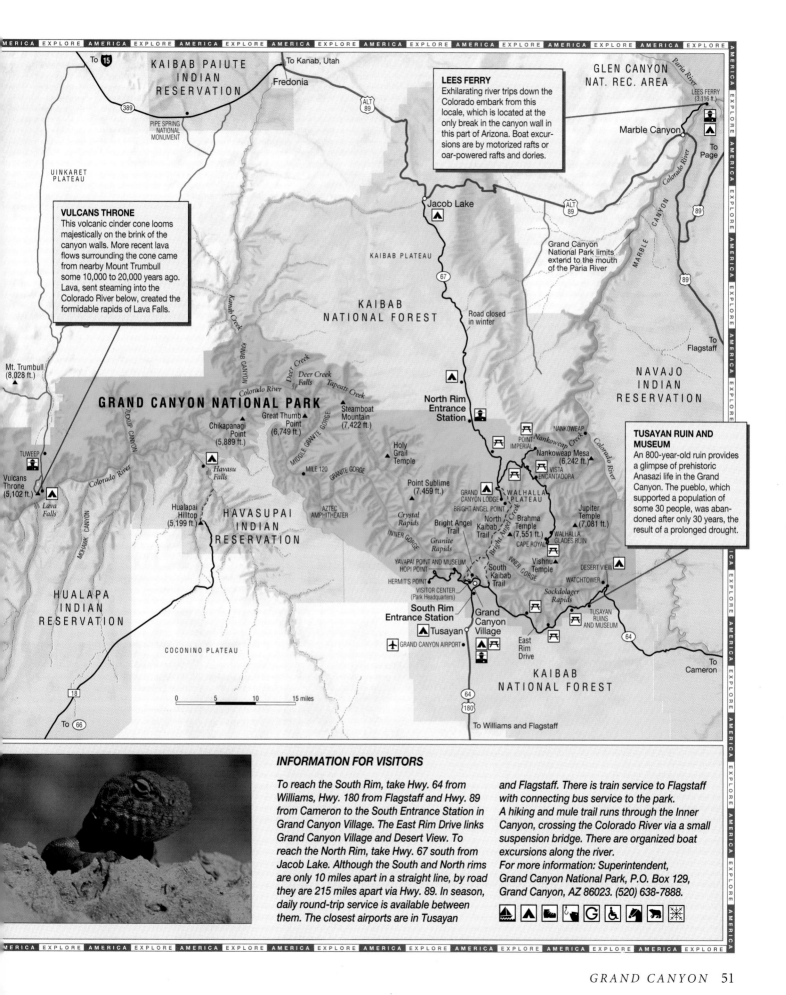

KAIBAB PAIUTE INDIAN RESERVATION

To Kanab, Utah

Fredonia

To 15

389

PIPE SPRING NATIONAL MONUMENT

UINKARET PLATEAU

ALT 89

GLEN CANYON NAT. REC. AREA

Paria River

LEES FERRY (3,116 ft.)

LEES FERRY
Exhilarating river trips down the Colorado embark from this locale, which is located at the only break in the canyon wall in this part of Arizona. Boat excursions are by motorized rafts or oar-powered rafts and dories.

Marble Canyon

To Page

89

VULCANS THRONE
This volcanic cinder cone looms majestically on the brink of the canyon walls. More recent lava flows surrounding the cone came from nearby Mount Trumbull some 10,000 to 20,000 years ago. Lava, sent steaming into the Colorado River below, created the formidable rapids of Lava Falls.

Jacob Lake

ALT 89

KAIBAB PLATEAU

KAIBAB NATIONAL FOREST

67

Road closed in winter

Grand Canyon National Park limits extend to the mouth of the Paria River

MARBLE CANYON

Colorado River

89

To Flagstaff

Mt. Trumbull (8,028 ft.)

KANAB CANYON

Kanab Creek

Colorado River

Deer Creek

Deer Creek Falls

Tapeats Creek

GRAND CANYON NATIONAL PARK

Chikapanagi Point (5,889 ft.)

Great Thumb Point

Steamboat Mountain (7,422 ft.)

MIDDLE GRANITE GORGE

MILE 120

Holy Grail Temple

GRANITE GORGE

North Rim Entrance Station

NANKOWEAP

POINT IMPERIAL

Nankoweap Creek

Nankoweap Mesa (6,242 ft.)

VISTA ENCANTADORA

NAVAJO INDIAN RESERVATION

Colorado River

TUSAYAN RUIN AND MUSEUM
An 800-year-old ruin provides a glimpse of prehistoric Anasazi life in the Grand Canyon. The pueblo, which supported a population of some 30 people, was abandoned after only 30 years, the result of a prolonged drought.

TUWEEP

Vulcans Throne (5,102 ft.)

Lava Falls

Colorado River

TUCKUP CANYON

Havasu Falls

Hualapai Hilltop (5,199 ft.)

HAVASUPAI INDIAN RESERVATION

AZTEC AMPHITHEATER

Point Sublime (7,459 ft.)

Crystal Rapids

INNER GORGE

Granite Rapids

GRAND CANYON LODGE

WALHALLA PLATEAU

BRIGHT ANGEL POINT

Bright Angel Trail

North Kaibab Trail

Bright Angel Creek

Brahma Temple (7,551 ft.)

CAPE ROYAL

Jupiter Temple (7,081 ft.)

WALHALLA GLADES RUIN

Vishnu Temple

DESERT VIEW

MOHAWK CANYON

HUALAPA INDIAN RESERVATION

COCONINO PLATEAU

YAVAPAI POINT AND MUSEUM

HOPI POINT

HERMIT'S POINT

VISITOR CENTER (Park Headquarters)

South Rim Entrance Station

Tusayan

GRAND CANYON AIRPORT

Grand Canyon Village

South Kaibab Trail

INNER GORGE

East Rim Drive

WATCHTOWER

Sockdolager Rapids

TUSAYAN RUINS AND MUSEUM

64

To Cameron

KAIBAB NATIONAL FOREST

64

180

To Williams and Flagstaff

18

To 66

0   5   10   15 miles

INFORMATION FOR VISITORS

To reach the South Rim, take Hwy. 64 from Williams, Hwy. 180 from Flagstaff and Hwy. 89 from Cameron to the South Entrance Station in Grand Canyon Village. The East Rim Drive links Grand Canyon Village and Desert View. To reach the North Rim, take Hwy. 67 south from Jacob Lake. Although the South and North rims are only 10 miles apart in a straight line, by road they are 215 miles apart via Hwy. 89. In season, daily round-trip service is available between them. The closest airports are in Tusayan and Flagstaff. There is train service to Flagstaff with connecting bus service to the park. A hiking and mule trail runs through the Inner Canyon, crossing the Colorado River via a small suspension bridge. There are organized boat excursions along the river.

For more information: Superintendent, Grand Canyon National Park, P.O. Box 129, Grand Canyon, AZ 86023. (520) 638-7888.

MERICA EXPLORE AMERICA EXPLORE AMERICA EXPLORE AMERICA EXPLORE AMERICA EXPLORE AMERICA EXPLORE AMERICA EXPLORE AMERICA EXPLORE AMERICA EXPLORE

GRAND CANYON 51

5,000 feet, a scrubland of blackbrush, yucca, Mormon tea, various cacti and agave appears. This is a habitat favored by lizards, jack rabbits, desert bighorn sheep, coyotes and a host of small rodents—notably the remarkable kangaroo rat. A mouse-sized creature, it hops like its Australian namesake and can survive without ever taking a drink of water. It relies on the moisture contained in the dry seeds it eats.

FROM THE TOP DOWN And still the Canyon goes deeper, between 2,000 and 3,000 feet, where Lower Sonoran conditions prevail. Here the barrel cacti, the ocotillo and mesquite trees of southern Arizona make their home. Temperatures rise above 120°F at times and while thunderstorms drench the forested rim, this zone can remain parched for months on end. From a human point of view it would be a cruel landscape were it not for the Colorado River and its many tributary streams. To a hiker descending a long dusty trail there is no greater earthly miracle than the sudden, almost magical appearance of desert water, flowing cool and clear over smooth rock. Water bursts from springs, seeps out of gravel in canyon bottoms and supports lush oases of vegetation, including willows and big shady cottonwood trees. The streams are home to beavers, dippers, herons, rainbow trout, frogs and other undesert-like creatures.

There isn't much mystery about how the Grand Canyon was made—it was eroded. Virtually all of what once filled this great space has been carried off by water, primarily the Colorado River. The bulk

WATCHFUL EYE

The domed ceiling and interior walls of a 70-foot-tall tower are painted with murals depicting Hopi Indian legends. Inspired by the architecture of Indian towers in the region, designer-architect Mary E.J. Colter built the Watchtower in 1932. It is the highest point on the South Rim and a popular lookout spot.

of the work was accomplished in no more than five or six million years, and perhaps less than that. This means that although the oldest rock at the bottom of the inner gorge is 1.7 billion years old, in geological terms the Canyon itself is a relatively new creation.

Moving water has amazing strength. Its ability to transport material grows exponentially as its speed increases. A stream moving two miles per hour, for instance, will carry 64 times as much material as the same stream moving at one mile per hour. And at 10 miles per hour, as in a flood, the stream's carrying capacity is a million times greater. Experts have been able to calculate the Colorado River's carrying capacity at various water levels and compare those numbers to the quantity of material eroded from the Canyon. Astonishing as it might seem, a river of this size can indeed transport a Grand Canyon's volume of sediment.

If that were the end of the story, it would be simple to tell, and geologists would not still be trying to unravel it all. What challenges them even today is that in carving the Canyon, the river performed what seems like an impossible trick—it cut through the Kaibab Plateau, a gigantic 9,000-foot-high fold in the earth's surface. Rivers normally flow around

A row of small alcoves (left), used as granaries by the Anasazi, were carved into the canyon walls 1,000 feet above the Colorado River at Nankoweap. Strategically located near the fields, the granaries protected the harvest from both looters and the weather. Split-twig figurines (below), dating back 4,000 years, are the oldest record of human occupation in the Grand Canyon. Each tiny figure resembled a game animal and was made from a single young willow twig. They were hidden deep inside caves as hunting talismans.

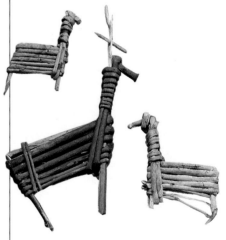

such highlands, not through them. What could have happened here?

It was once thought that the plateau rose beneath the ancient, pre-existing Colorado; in other words, that the river had cut downward as the land was being pushed up. The same sort of thing has happened in other parts of the world and it seemed to be a logical explanation. But then geological evidence was found on the western end of the Canyon showing that six million years ago, the Colorado River as we know it today did not exist, and therefore neither did the Grand Canyon. So much for a simple explanation.

A TALE OF TWO RIVERS

Currently, the most widely accepted theory is a tale of not one but two rivers. This theory describes a complex series of events going back over 50 million years, to a time when the land had a substantially different shape and was overlain by thick rock layers that have long since been eroded away. At that time, the ancestral Colorado River was relatively small, wandering across an open landscape, flowing eventually toward the northwest into what is now the state of Nevada. At some point, the Gulf of California began opening along a rift in the crust of the earth and a new river was created, flowing into that rift. Gradually, this new river eroded into the highlands at its source, extending its reach toward the northeast until it finally broke into the drainage system of the ancestral Colorado, and captured that river's water.

Thus, around 5.5 million years ago, one river was born from two—a new river with a steep gradient and plentiful water—and the carving of Grand Canyon began in earnest.

The river, however, could not have done it alone. Without help it would only have dug a deep, narrow slit with no side canyons. Instead, numerous tributary streams acted like conveyor belts, hauling material to the Colorado, which in turn carried it downstream. Of course, this constant widening of the Canyon has happened at an incremental rate not readily visible to visitors. The geological clock ticks at what seems to us a very slow rate.

But not always. From time to time, a large section of some cliff face breaks away in a thunder of falling stone and rock dust. One recent fall occurred in 1991, just across the side canyon from Bright Angel Point on the North Rim. The scar will be clearly visible for years. Had it not occurred in the win-

Marble Canyon is named for its red-streaked walls, stained by iron oxides and other minerals that seep out of the rock and disguise the natural gray. The Colorado River veers sharply as it flows through Marble Canyon. Its water either appears blue-green or muddy brown depending on the amount of sediment it carries.

ter, when no one was around, hundreds of people would have witnessed the event.

Equally impressive—and stranger than science fiction—are the erosion events called debris flows. These occur in side canyons when small amounts of water (less than 40 percent) mix with clay, sand and boulders, providing just enough lubrication for the whole mass to begin moving. Usually started by landslides, the big ones go for miles at speeds of up to 46 feet per second, finally ending at the Colorado River where they deposit boulders, some of them as big as a house. These boulders alter the flow of the river, either creating new rapids or increasing the speed of existing ones. The noise from these debris flows is deafening.

For geologists, the exposed rock itself is perhaps the most revealing feature of the Canyon. Lying in largely undisturbed layers, the rocks describe nearly two billion years of North American history. Starting from the top, the most recent layer is the Kaibab limestone, loaded with fossil seashells that are easy even for the untrained eye to find. At the bottom, the so-called basement rock of the Inner Gorge, is the 1.7-billion-year-old Vishnu complex—a fine-grained, metamorphosed, black rock with red marbling. It is the bedrock of an ancient mountain range.

GEOLOGY ON A GRAND SCALE

Between the Vishnu and the Kaibab lies the rest of the story, as told by layers of mostly sedimentary rocks, including limestone, sandstone and mudstone. By analyzing these layers, geologists read them like the neatly stacked pages of a vast history book. The record is surprisingly complete except for one major gap, where whole chapters have been torn out. This gap occurred in the distant past when a series of rock layers, twisted and tilted, were eroded flat, as if sliced off by a carpenter's plane. Eventually, deposition resumed, but the eroded materials were forever lost. Today, the point of contact between the new layers and the old planed surface is called the Great Unconformity. It is visible, just below the Tonto Platform, from most points in the central Canyon.

Although the park itself was established in 1919, and enlarged to its present size in 1975, human habitation goes back much further. We know—from the animal figurines made of split twigs found deep inside Canyon caves, perhaps placed there as part of a hunting ritual—that people lived here as early as 4,000 years ago.

About 2,000 years later, the Anasazi (called Hisat Sinom, meaning the ancient ones, by their Hopi descendants) appeared on the scene. They were farmers who lived in permanent communities—characterized in later years by their famous stone dwellings, often perched beneath overhanging sandstone cliffs. For reasons that still puzzle archeologists, the Anasazi had left the area by around A.D. 1200. But their legacy survives in practically every nook and cranny, in the form of buildings and other artifacts. Two ruins are easily accessible to visitors: on the South Rim, Tusayan was a community of about 30 people. On the North Rim, near the tip of the Walhalla Plateau, Walhalla Glades Ruin was used by farmers who migrated seasonally between the rim and the river.

In places like Greece, or Egypt, these little ruins would be of passing interest, lost in the shadow of temples and pyramids. But in the relatively young United States, 1,000-year-old villages and relics take on a large significance. They housed the ghosts

of our land, and pondering them gives us a chance to bridge the centuries that lie between us.

That connection can be made through the simplest of relics—a hand print in the dried mortar of a masonry wall, a flat stone in the sun where someone once sat, a straw figurine or a fragment of a pottery bowl appealing to us across the years with the quality of its craftsmanship. Through these things there comes a flash of recognition. These people were real and cut from the same cloth as we. And then the flash goes the other way, back in time. From our knowledge of ourselves and how we

would react to such conditions, we can imagine things for which we have no physical evidence. In an ancient ruin, for example, we can hear the sounds of voices: children laughing, mothers calling, adults talking quietly. We do not know the language those ancient people spoke, but the music of human voices is everywhere the same and the imagining comes easily.

The first non-Indians to see Grand Canyon were Spanish treasure-seekers, members of Francisco Vasquez de Coronado's expedition in search of the fabulous Seven Cities of Cibola. Instead of golden capitals, however, the Spanish found Pueblo Indian communities along the Rio Grande River whose people were farmers living in stone buildings, and owning no riches worth plundering. Disappointed, Coronado sent parties into the surrounding region hoping to find something better. It was one of those parties, under the command of Garcia Lopez de Cardenas, and guided by Hopis, that rode to the South Rim in 1540. Surviving accounts of that first visit are very sketchy. Although the Spanish were impressed by the size of the place, they saw the Canyon chiefly as a barrier to further exploration. Whether they felt inspiration in the presence of

TROPICAL PARADISE

Havasu Falls (above) is one of three prominent waterfalls in Havasu Canyon. Its blue-green waters cascade from a notch in the rock walls, tumbling into a jewel-like pool below. The waterfall, located outside the park on the Havasupai Indian Reservation, is accessible by helicopter tours, hiking and riding trails.

CANYON OASIS

Clumps of pink phlox (left) brighten the North Rim each spring. The North Rim receives about 28 inches of rainfall a year. Coniferous forests, meadowlands and a great variety of wildflowers flourish in this environment.

such grandeur, or only disappointment and thirst, will never be known.

After Cardenas, it was more than two centuries before Europeans again entered the Grand Canyon region. Explorers and adventurers, dreamers and scoundrels were drawn to this epic landscape. Some built reputations here. Others lost everything. The most famous explorer was John Wesley Powell, leader of the first descent of the Colorado River through the Canyon in 1869. There were also miners and developers and artists and scientists. The Canyon nurtured the new science of geology and had much to do with the great appreciation for the Western landscape.

RUNNING THROUGH RED ROCK

Today, as ever, at the heart of the Canyon runs the river—creator and prime mover of this remarkable landscape. It is said that if you know the river, you know the Canyon. From Lees Ferry to Lake Mead, it falls 2,215 feet, dropping through a series of powerful rapids that no one who has run them can ever forget: Crystal, Lava Falls, Sockdolager, Granite, Hermit and others.

The river begins far upstream in the snowy mountains of Colorado, drawing strength from tributaries such as Wyoming's Green River, pouring cold and clear into Utah's red rock country. Here the river becomes warm in the summer sun, and picks up the sediment for which it was named: Colorado, Spanish for red.

The river once flowed red all the way to the Gulf of California. It built a great delta there, until a series of dams created settling ponds and diverted the water to booming cities. Hoover Dam, built in the mid-1930's, created what is now Lake Mead. The most recent dam, Glen Canyon Dam, stands just above the Grand Canyon and contains Lake Powell. Emerging from the depths of the lake, the old red river now flows cold and green. Like a string of jade among the red sandstones, it is beautiful to look at, but the dam-controlled river environment is far different from what it once was. In permanently cold water, a new assortment of fish and insects has replaced native species. With no new sand being brought down from upstream, the beaches are disappearing. And with the disappearance of spring floods, vegetation along the riverbank has grown more dense, with different species dominating the scene.

These impacts fuel a heated controversy between demands that the natural river environment be maintained and the need for electrical power from the dam. By adjusting flow rates, some of the effects can be mitigated, but others will remain as long as the dam remains.

How long will that be? For a larger perspective, consider the biggest dam of all, caused by lava that flowed across the lower end of the Canyon 1.2 million years ago. It was more than 2,000 feet high. It stopped the river completely for an estimated 22 years, creating a lake that reached what is now upper Lake Powell. Even so, the river had its way eventually, destroying the dam just as it had dug the Canyon—through time and slow persistence.

In the end, if the Grand Canyon teaches us one thing, it is the impermanence of all things.

NEARBY SITES & ATTRACTIONS

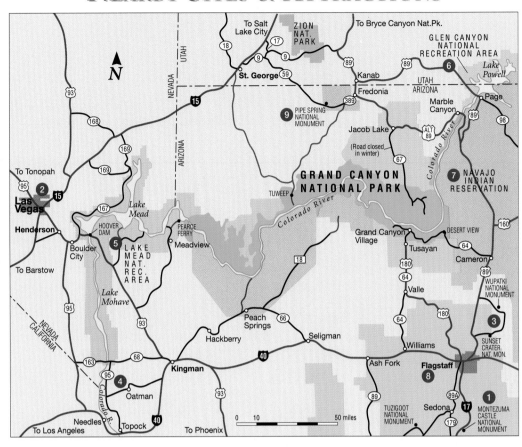

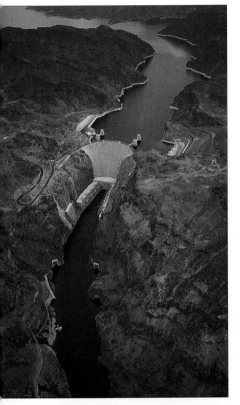

Hoover Dam, completed in 1935, is a remarkable feat of engineering. About 5,000 men toiled for five years to complete the structure, pouring enough concrete to build a two-lane highway from New York to San Francisco.

❶ MONTEZUMA CASTLE NATIONAL MONUMENT

Sinagua Indians began constructing this five-story, 20-room complex in the 12th century. The ancient dwelling, tucked into a recess in a yellow limestone cliff about 100 feet above the Verde Valley, was well protected. It is considered to be one of the best pre-served prehistoric structures in the Southwest. The monument was named by early settlers who thought it was built by the Aztecs. The Sinagua were excellent artisans, and examples of their stone tools—axes, knives and hammers—woven cotton clothing as well as ornaments of shells, turquoise and red stone are on display in the Visitor Center. The interior of the "castle" is not open to visitors. Located in Camp Verde off Hwy. 17.

❷ LAS VEGAS, NEVADA

In pioneer days, Las Vegas was just a stopping spot along the the Old Spanish Trail, but the town's future was secured when the state of Nevada legalized gambling in 1931. Today, the city is one of the entertainment capitals of the world. Visitors can also take in the Nevada State Museum and Historical Society and the Las Vegas Museum of Natural History, both of which exhibit the culture and history of southern Nevada from 1200 to the present. Located west of the park on Hwys. 93 and 15.

❸ WUPATKI AND SUNSET CRATER NATIONAL MONUMENTS, ARIZONA

Sinagua and Anasazi Indians living in this region in 1064-65 were forced to flee when a nearby volcano erupted and spewed ash over an 800-square-mile area. They returned a few decades later to cultivate the rich volcanic soil. Wupatki (Hopi for tall house) grew to be a prominent pueblo, consisting of a three-story residential complex of more than 100 rooms as well as an adjacent amphitheater and ballcourt. The buildings were made of slabs of red Moenkopi sandstone, limestone and basalt. By 1225 the Indians left Wupatki, probably because of droughts. Today, visitors can tour the ruins, including several typical rooms in the housing unit. Sunset Crater is 18 miles away. The volcanic eruption of 1065 deposited minerals around the crater's rim and coated the upper slopes of the 1,000-foot cone with the vivid colors of a sunset. A one-mile, self-guiding nature trail allows visitors to explore several interest-ing volcanic features. Sunset Crater is located 15 miles north of Flagstaff off Hwy. 89; a loop road connects the two sites.

❹ OATMAN

Oatman was an important gold-mining town and business center in the early part of the 19th century. By 1931, the town had a population of 15,000, boasted 20 saloons and had produced almost 2 million ounces of gold. The mines closed in 1942 and the buildings were boarded up or transformed into shops. Wild burros, descendants of those brought to the town by the early prospectors, roam the length of Main Street and throughout the surrounding hills. The Oatman Museum, housed in the Oatman Hotel—the only two-story adobe structure in Mohave County—contains a collection of photographs and artifacts depicting the town's rowdy history. Located on Hwy. 66, 31 miles west of Kingman.

5 HOOVER DAM-LAKE MEAD NATIONAL RECREATION AREA

Locally dubbed the eighth wonder of the world, Hoover Dam is the centerpiece for the nation's first national recreation area. Built in 1935, the 1,244-foot-long dam, located in a bend in the Colorado River, towers 726 feet high and is more than 660 feet thick at the base. The dam helped tame the river and created Lake Mead, a 110-mile-long body of water set in a desert-like landscape. The lake supplies water to major cities including Los Angeles and San Diego and hydroelectric power to Nevada, Arizona and southern California. The recreation area, which borders the northwestern area of the Grand Canyon, is popular with fishermen, waterskiers, sailors, scuba-divers and swimmers. Located on Hwy. 93, 8 miles east of Boulder City.

6 GLEN CANYON NATIONAL RECREATION AREA

Glen Canyon, located downstream of Cataract Canyon and upstream from Grand Canyon, slices through southern Utah and northern Arizona. The canyon's towering red- and buff-colored cliffs contrast dramatically with the bright desert sky overhead. Glen Canyon Dam, built as a water reservoir and power generator, also created a recreational lake. The 186-mile-long Lake Powell is renowned as a water-sports vacationland, offering swimming, waterskiing, fishing and sailing in a desert-and-canyon setting. The lake has also made Rainbow Bridge accessible to boaters. This perfectly arched natural bridge of stone is 290 feet high and spans 275 feet. Wildlife enthusiasts may spot bald eagles, peregrine falcons, desert bighorn sheep and mountain lions. Located on Hwy. 89 just northeast of Grand Canyon National Park.

7 NAVAJOLAND

Navajoland, the largest reservation in North America, comprises more than 25,000 square miles of territory in the states of Utah, Arizona and New Mexico. Set in a landscape of mountain ranges, sage-covered valleys, wind-carved canyons, and lakes and ponds, the reservation preserves an array of historic sites, tribal parks and national monuments. It also offers camping, hiking and horseback riding. Self-guiding walking trails lead past important Anasazi ruins. Highlights include the Navajo Tribal Museum, which reflects the rich Navajo history and culture, and the Navajo Arts and Crafts Enterprise, which showcases Navajo turquoise and silver

jewelry, baskets, rugs and other crafts. Navajoland borders the eastern side of Grand Canyon National Park and extends into New Mexico. From the North Rim, take Hwy. 89 east; from the South Rim, take Hwy. 64 east.

8 FLAGSTAFF

Named for a pine tree that was used by early settlers as a flagpole, Flagstaff was founded by a sheep herder in 1876. There are a number of historic sites in the town. Kinlichi, Navajo for red house, is a massive 13,000-square-foot, 40-room log mansion. The house, located in the Riordan State Historic Park, was built by lumber magnates Michael and Timothy Riordan and contains most of its original furnishings. The Museum of Northern Arizona traces the history of native settlement of the Colorado Plateau from 15,000 B.C. to the present. The Lowell Observatory displays an exhibit on the work of Dr. Percival Lowell, who claimed that the canals on Mars were constructed by intelligent beings. Southeast of Grand Canyon on Hwys. 180, 89, 40 and 17.

9 PIPE SPRING NATIONAL MONUMENT

This spring-fed oasis is located in the arid northern Arizona desert. The monument was named when a cowboy shot the bottom out of his friend's pipe. Pueblo Indians were the first to settle here more than 1,000 years ago, followed by the nomadic Paiute Indians and Spanish missionaries. Mormon pioneers established a cattle ranch here in the 1860's. They built a fortified ranch house, fancifully called Windsor Castle, as well as houses, a church, workshops and corrals. At its peak in 1879, the ranch had 2,269 head of cattle and produced about 80 pounds of cheese daily. The first telegraph office in the state operated from the Castle. Today, costumed guides interpret pioneer life in the restored ranch houses and outbuildings. Located north of the park on Hwy. 389, 15 miles west of Fredonia.

Las Vegas is a phantasmagoria of lavish casinos and glitzy hotels illuminated by two million light bulbs and more than 43 miles of neon tubing.

Montezuma Castle was named by early European settlers who thought the 12th-century Sinagua Indian structure had been built by the Aztecs.

YELLOWSTONE

*Oldest of all the parks, Yellowstone
is not manicured, nor orchestrated,
nor a zoo. It is wild.*

Yellowstone National Park fools the eye. To a visitor driving through its 2.2 million acres of rolling plateaus, great expanses of forest and high country meadows in flower, it looks, at first glance, like a disarmingly gentle world. Bison herds browse by the side of the road, seemingly unperturbed by motorists stopping to take photographs. Trout dimple the surface of deep pools as the lines of wading fly fishermen arc over the crystalline water. Swans paddle toward a visitor. A fumarole vents steamy wisps into thin mountain air.

All seems to be in order here. But nature in Yellowstone National Park is not always tame or gentle. Beneath the park, so close to the surface you will swear you can feel your feet warming, boils molten rock. Underlain by massive reservoirs of this semi-liquefied substance, called magma, Yellowstone has been ripped by dozens of volcanic eruptions over the last two million years. It could—it will—happen again.

Some 200 geysers erupt occasionally, blowing fountains of hot water and steam toward the heavens. Huge pools of mud bubble thickly like soup set on simmer. Yellowstone broods while it vents its hydrothermal frustration. To walk its geyser basins over vent-fractured surfaces, which tenuously separate a vast underground furnace from blue sky overhead, is to expe-

NIMBLE CLIFF CLIMBER

In a habitat too rugged for most grazing animals, a young bighorn sheep nibbles on sparse grass and sedges. Protected from hunters, Yellowstone's bighorns enjoy relative safety—few animals have the skill to follow these adept climbers. Males can weigh up to 275 pounds, while the smaller females weigh 75 to 150 pounds. Both males and females display magnificent curved horns. During the mating season, males take leaping charges at each other, butting heads to establish dominance. The crack of their colliding horns sometimes echoes through the mountains.

HOME ON THE RANGE

Overleaf: Yellowstone's free-ranging bison, also known as buffalo, appear tame as they graze across the snow-draped Upper Geyser Basin, but visitors are cautioned against getting too close. North America's largest land animals can weigh 2,000 pounds and sprint at an impressive 30 miles an hour.

rience a geologic house of wonders. This is a living museum of tension and upheaval where the primal forces of volcanic power push closer to the surface than anywhere on earth.

Yellowstone's untamed voice speaks just as loudly through the grunts of sow grizzlies as it does through a hot plume of steam. From their cars, if they are lucky, park visitors can gaze out across Hayden Valley near Canyon Village and spot a grizzly mother with cubs in a distant meadow. Watching from afar is safe, but to approach is to court disaster. Farther north, a pair of massive bull elk clash on a hillside not 200 yards from the Mammoth Hot Springs Hotel. Their antlers locked, they joust to determine which one will control breeding rights in a harem of a dozen females. Watch from behind a window or from the hotel porch and the elk will ignore you as harmless. Infringe on their wildness by getting too close and you may be perceived as a threat. Even Yellowstone's bison—seemingly docile, and as slow on their feet as they appear of mind—will charge anyone who ventures too close, on the mistaken assumption that these beasts are tame.

They are not, nor is the land they roam. It is an unpredictable, sometimes dangerous 3,472 square miles of spectacular landscape: a combination of geysers—the world's largest concentration—hot springs and mud volcanoes inhabited by some of North America's greatest populations of large mammals. Geologically, biologically and meteorologically, Yellowstone is wild.

Tucked into the northwest corner of Wyoming, spilling over into Montana and Idaho, Yellowstone attracts nearly three million visitors a year, making it one of America's favorite parks. Yet many visitors never stray from its 370 miles of roads. Five entrances, spaced evenly around the park's perimeter, funnel motorists onto a figure eight of highways offering access to the major attractions, as well as the best views of wildlife.

The highway life does have its drawbacks, however. Summer traffic can turn park roads into wilderness gridlock. Protected from hunting, animals inside the park—especially bison—show little fear and sometimes saunter onto roadways and plunk themselves down. If a bear, moose or bison is spotted near the road, motorists stop for a look. Before long a traffic jam has developed. With so much to see, and so many who enter to see it, the best way to avoid crowded conditions in Yellowstone is either to visit during non-summer months—September and May are gorgeous, winter is spectacular—or to park the car and explore on foot or on horseback.

Yellowstone boasts more than 1,200 miles of hiking and riding trails. In winter, though most of the

INFORMATION FOR VISITORS

Five entrances lead to the park. In Montana: Hwy. 20 from West Yellowstone leads to the West entrance; Hwy. 89 from Gardiner takes visitors to the North entrance; Hwy. 212 from Silver Gate and Cooke City serves the Northeast entrance. From Wyoming: Hwy. 89 connects the South entrance with Grand Teton National Park; Hwy. 16 from Cody leads to the East entrance. The airport at West Yellowstone is open only during the summer months; airports at Bozeman and Billings, Montana, and at Cody and Jackson, Wyoming, operate year-round.

Spur roads connect the five entrances to the 142-mile Grand Loop Road, which forms a figure eight through the heart of the park. Grand Loop crisscrosses the Continental Divide; to the east, waters flow to the Atlantic Ocean; to the west, they go to the Pacific. The Grand Loop Road brings visitors to five geyser basins: Upper, West Thumb, Midway, Lower and Norris. Visitors are not permitted to swim or bathe in thermal pools or streams within the park.

For more information: Superintendent, P.O. Box 168, Yellowstone National Park, WY 82190. (307) 344-7381.

RELIABLE RHYTHM

Old Faithful spews a 1,000-gallon plume of water and steam 150 feet into the air every 75 minutes. This geyser has not missed a performance in more than 120 years of observation.

62

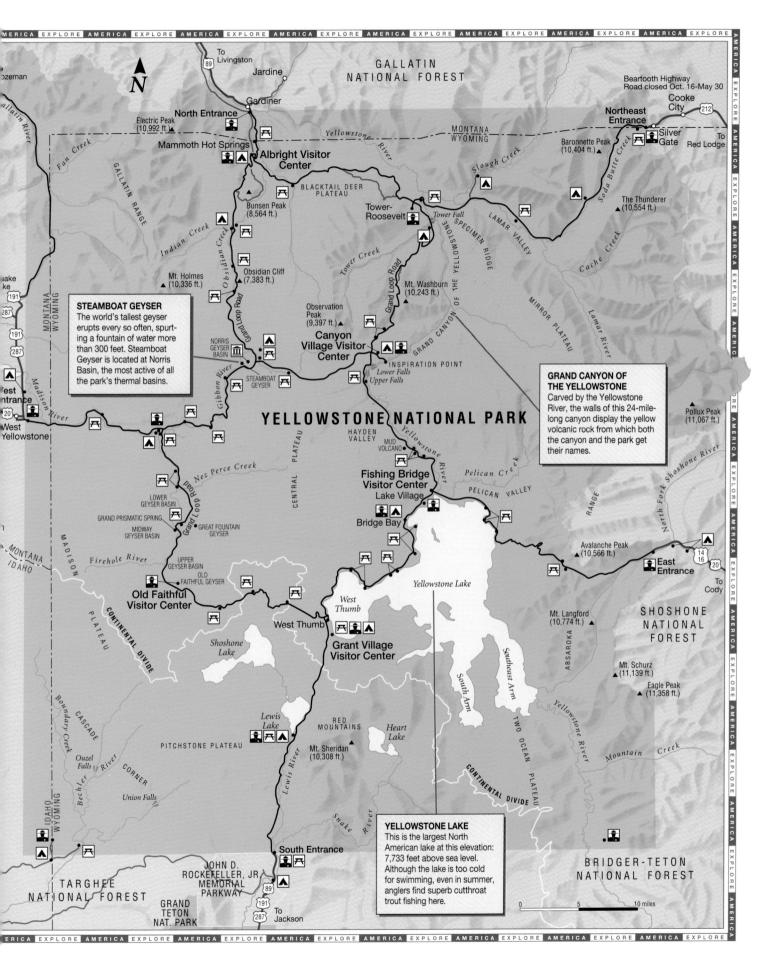

To Livingston

Jardine

GALLATIN
NATIONAL FOREST

Gardiner

Beartooth Highway
Road closed Oct. 16-May 30

Cooke
City

North Entrance

Electric Peak
(10,992 ft.)

**Northeast
Entrance**

Silver
Gate

To
Red Lodge

Mammoth Hot Springs

**Albright Visitor
Center**

MONTANA
WYOMING

Baronnette Peak
(10,404 ft.)

BLACKTAIL DEER
PLATEAU

Bunsen Peak
(8,564 ft.)

**Tower-
Roosevelt**

Tower Fall

Slough Creek

Soda Butte Creek

The Thunderer
(10,554 ft.)

Obsidian Cliff
(7,383 ft.)

SPECIMEN RIDGE

LAMAR VALLEY

Cache Creek

Lamar River

Mt. Holmes
(10,336 ft.)

Tower Creek

Mt. Washburn
(10,243 ft.)

GRAND CANYON OF THE YELLOWSTONE

MIRROR PLATEAU

STEAMBOAT GEYSER
The world's tallest geyser
erupts every so often, spurt-
ing a fountain of water more
than 300 feet. Steamboat
Geyser is located at Norris
Basin, the most active of all
the park's thermal basins.

Observation
Peak
(9,397 ft.)

**Canyon
Village Visitor
Center**

NORRIS
GEYSER
BASIN

INSPIRATION POINT

Lower Falls

Upper Falls

**GRAND CANYON OF
THE YELLOWSTONE**
Carved by the Yellowstone
River, the walls of this 24-mile-
long canyon display the yellow
volcanic rock from which both
the canyon and the park get
their names.

STEAMBOAT
GEYSER

Pollux Peak
(11,067 ft.)

YELLOWSTONE NATIONAL PARK

HAYDEN
VALLEY

MUD
VOLCANO

Yellowstone River

PELICAN VALLEY

Pelican Creek

North Fork Shoshone River

West
Entrance

West
Yellowstone

Nez Perce Creek

CENTRAL PLATEAU

**Fishing Bridge
Visitor Center**

Lake Village

RANGE

Avalanche Peak
(10,566 ft.)

**East
Entrance**

To
Cody

LOWER
GEYSER BASIN

GRAND PRISMATIC SPRING

MIDWAY
GEYSER BASIN

GREAT FOUNTAIN
GEYSER

Bridge Bay

MONTANA
IDAHO

Firehole River

UPPER
GEYSER BASIN

OLD
FAITHFUL GEYSER

**Old Faithful
Visitor Center**

Yellowstone Lake

West
Thumb

West Thumb

**Grant Village
Visitor Center**

Mt. Langford
(10,774 ft.)

SHOSHONE
NATIONAL
FOREST

Mt. Schurz
(11,139 ft.)

Eagle Peak
(11,358 ft.)

ABSAROKA

Southeast Arm

CONTINENTAL DIVIDE

PLATEAU

Shoshone
Lake

Lewis
Lake

RED
MOUNTAINS

Heart
Lake

South
Arm

TWO OCEAN PLATEAU

Yellowstone River

CASCADE

Bechler River

Mt. Sheridan
(10,308 ft.)

CONTINENTAL DIVIDE

Mountain
Creek

Ouzel
Falls

PITCHSTONE PLATEAU

Boundary Creek

Union Falls

CORNER

IDAHO
WYOMING

Snake River

YELLOWSTONE LAKE
This is the largest North
American lake at this elevation:
7,733 feet above sea level.
Although the lake is too cold
for swimming, even in summer,
anglers find superb cutthroat
trout fishing here.

BRIDGER-TETON
NATIONAL FOREST

South Entrance

JOHN D.
ROCKEFELLER, JR.
MEMORIAL
PARKWAY

To
Jackson

GRAND
TETON
NAT. PARK

TARGHEE
NATIONAL FOREST

0   5   10 miles

EXPLORE AMERICA EXPLORE AMERICA EXPLORE AMERICA EXPLORE AMERICA EXPLORE AMERICA EXPLORE AMERICA EXPLORE AMERICA EXPLORE AMERICA EXPLORE AMERICA EXPLORE

YELLOWSTONE 63

roads are only open to snowmobiles and snow coaches, these trails are open to cross-country skiing. Just 100 yards from a paved road the park becomes a less humanized place. Yellowstone's aura of sage-dotted meadows, cool rivers and pine scent starts to emerge.

TALL TALES, BUT TRUE

Two hundred yards from the road, you'll start to imagine what explorer and trapper John Colter felt, by himself, in the winter, when fate led him through Yellowstone. But it wasn't Yellowstone when Colter first saw it in 1807. Then it was uncharted wilderness, filled with silvery streams, beavers, clouds of white steam—and potential. Hired by St. Louis fur traders to scout beaver-rich trapping grounds west of the Missouri River, Colter set out on his trek in late autumn. Thought to be the first white man ever to see Yellowstone, he journeyed alone through its forests and valleys on snowshoes, then returned with wondrous stories to tell.

The earth seethed with steam, he claimed. Geysers gushed skyward. Rivers thundered through canyons. Waterfalls added a roar that could be heard miles away. Although no one really believed him, similar stories kept filtering back to St. Louis. By the 1840's numerous other trappers and hunters had followed Colter's footsteps. They came back with their own tales—of mud bubbling up in great sulfurous cauldrons and of men having to follow elk tracks through hissing geyser basins so as not to fall through the hot crust.

By 1872, the area's marvels were well documented. That was the year Congress passed a bill establishing Yellowstone as the nation's—indeed

SIMMERING COLOR

An eagle's-eye view reveals the giant florid spirals of Grand Prismatic Spring. Algae, bacteria and an assortment of minerals create the vivid colors and sulfur gives it its distinctive rotten-egg smell. A boardwalk, skirting the 370-foot-diameter pool, allows visitors to peer safely into the near-boiling spring. It also helps preserve this delicate hydrothermal area.

64

the world's—first national park. Geologically speaking, what John Colter viewed many years ago has changed very little. Today's park visitors view the same super-heated variety show that he did, marveling at all the ways rain and melted snow can seep underground, then be boiled into steam and forced back through large cracks in the earth.

Once returned to the surface, that water may bubble in a pool of exquisite beauty, its temperature approaching 200°F. Smelling of sulfur, it may push through pink mud with an ominous "plop" as it does in the park's Mud Volcano near Fishing Bridge. Or, it may build up as pressure, then explode with a roar, flashing skyward in the form of steam in a geyser. How high it will go depends on the geyser. Great Fountain Geyser, in the park's Lower Geyser Basin, sometimes reaches 200 feet. The highest flier, Steamboat Geyser, set the record

with an eruption of 400 feet. No geyser on earth has ever shot higher. Then there is Old Faithful: staunch, reliable, but not aiming to beat records. On a good day it may rocket 150 feet, thrusting 7,000 gallons of boiling water skyward in an eruption that lasts from 2 to 5 minutes. A number of Yellowstone geysers climb higher, to be sure. Some throw plumes that elicit more "oohs" from a crowd. But none blasts away with more rock-solid surety than Old Faithful. Since its discovery well over a century ago, it has performed on schedule—currently every 75 minutes, give or take a few—some 850,000 times.

The scenario always unfolds the same way: First, like a warm-up comedian building the crowd for the headliner, Old Faithful hiccups a few 5- to 10-foot-high columns of pale greenish water from its rocky, coral-like mouth. Then comes the big blast, shooting straight up before trailing off in feathery wisps as the wind catches hold of the steam.

Every day through the summer, observers sit and chat on benches that surround the geyser in a safely distant semicircle. This show plays during colder months, too, but with fewer spectators. Old Faithful is especially beautiful in winter, when its steam coats the trees with a ghostly white shroud of frost. Heat in the ground melts the snow around

LIVING SCULPTURE
The sculpted tiers and cascading terraces of travertine around Mammoth Hot Springs began to take shape 8,000 years ago when thousands of gallons of water per day bubbled up through soluble limestone and left behind telltale deposits. Mammoth Hot Springs continues to lay down up to two tons of limestone per day.

Teddy Roosevelt watched birds in Yellowstone, in 1903. He came with John Burroughs, the poet and naturalist. They saw pygmy owls, dippers and mountain bluebirds. White pelicans nested on Yellowstone Lake. Sandhill cranes danced and uttered their guttural calls from high meadows. Such birding delights still await Yellowstone visitors. Bald eagles still fish in the park's lakes and rivers. Ospreys still haunt the 1,200-foot-deep Grand Canyon of the Yellowstone River, their nests atop pillars of colored rock that rise like minarets from the canyon floor. Golden eagles still swoop through the sagebrush in search of jack rabbits. Bald eagles are occasionally sighted too. These are the constants that rule Yellowstone, where the workings of nature are given free rein and where wildlife adapts to the changes.

THE FIERY WAYS OF NATURE

Great changes came when devastating fires burned through the park in 1988. Thirty-six percent of Yellowstone's 2.2 million acres of parched forest felt flames that hot summer. Fanned by high winds, the flames leaped from treetop to treetop, devouring ancient forests with shocking speed. Pine resin boiled. Boulders exploded. Much of the fire-touched land—mostly dense lodgepole pine stands that went up like tinder—burned so fiercely that mere matchsticks remained.

Yet Yellowstone and its creatures adapted. Visitors to the park just two years after the fires found thousands of lodgepole pine seedlings crowding the same forest floors that had been blackened by furnace-hot blazes. In some burned areas, wildlife watchers found bison, elk and other large mammals actually thriving. The food types they require had increased when burned forest tracts were opened to sunshine, allowing grasses and other browse plants to take root.

Even park visitors have benefited from the fires. Many mountainside trails that once cut through dense forest now offer spectacular views. The burned trees that once blocked these views lie rotting, their nutrients feeding young pines that have taken their place.

Visitors who walk the woodland trails of Yellowstone 50 years from now will be shaded by the trees that have risen from the ashes of 1988's blackened forest. That is the way Yellowstone works. Centuries pass and the natural world runs through cycles of time-honored change. Old Faithful gushes, bull elk bugle in autumn, seasons paint meadows with flowers, then drape them with snow. Left on its own in this beautiful place, nature seems to have found a true balance.

WORK OF NATURE

Like the ruins of a fortress, weathered spires of volcanic rock stand guard behind Tower Fall. Tumbling 132 feet on a precipitous path to join the Yellowstone River, the waterfall is the centerpiece of a landscape of craggy slopes, rolling hills and virgin forest.

geysers and hot springs. Elk and bison convene there to browse, chewing grass while the steam turns to ice on their shaggy pelts.

Outside the park, and no matter the season, human encroachment continues to shrink wildlife habitat. Species such as the grizzly bear and trumpeter swan have declined dramatically in the region since the days of John Colter's foray. Others, such as bison, already have vanished from lands they once roamed by the millions.

Inside the park, however, spared the pressure of hunting, some of these animals (the bison, for example) are thriving. Others, such as bears, just manage to hold their own. But though they sometimes seem to have developed a degree of tolerance for the human presence, these animals are not tame, nor should they be approached. When their "space" is violated, they will react—either by charging or running away. You may be lucky enough to photograph trumpeter swans feeding in the Madison River shallows or an elk browsing on the next hill. However, approaching on foot within 100 yards of bears or within 25 yards of any other wildlife, even birds, is prohibited.

During the summer of 1988, Yellowstone suffered the largest-scale devastation in the history of America's national parks: close to 800,000 acres of forest were scorched by fierce fires that blazed their way through the park. This kind of natural holocaust is an important stage in the life cycle of a great forest. Nutrients are recycled back to the earth, and seedlings are afforded the light they need to survive.

UNPREDICTABLE PREDATOR

Before European settlement, the grizzly roamed much of the North American continent. Today, one of the last sizable grizzly populations in the U.S. is found in Yellowstone Park. The bear's name stems from the silver-tipped fur it develops with age. Mature adults weigh from 300 to 600 pounds.

NEARBY SITES & ATTRACTIONS

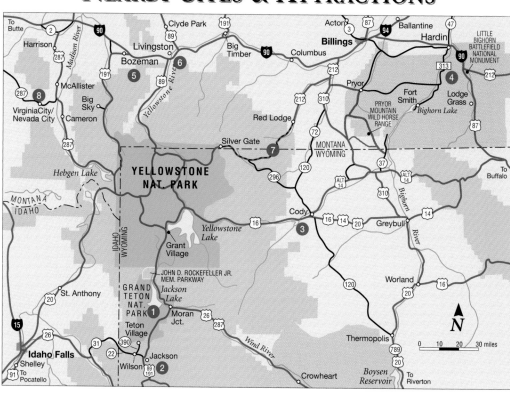

Aspiring cowboys, young and old, can admire their Wild West heroes at the Buffalo Bill Museum in Cody, Wyoming.

1 GRAND TETON NATIONAL PARK

The Teton Range soars more than a mile to preside over shimmering lakes, glaciers, brilliantly colored wildflower meadows and the meandering Snake River. Open year-round, the park is home to one of the largest elk herds in the world; visitors may also spot bison, moose and, more infrequently, black bears and grizzlies. Bald eagles and ospreys nest along the Snake River. More than 200 miles of hiking trails—from easy to challenging—crisscross the valley and mountains. In winter, the park is frequented by cross-country skiers and snowmobilers. Entrances to the park are on the John D. Rockefeller Jr. Memorial Parkway.

2 JACKSON

Nestled against the foothills of the Gros Ventre Range, the town has a world-class collection of North American wildlife art housed in the Wildlife of the American West Art Museum. A second popular museum, the Jackson Hole Museum, displays fur trappers' tools of the trade and Plains Indian artifacts. During the summer, visitors can ride around town in an authentic stagecoach and experience the flavor of the Wild West during the daily shoot-out on main street. A chairlift climbs to the top of Snow King Mountain and provides a spectacular overview of the Jackson Hole Valley. More than 8,000 elk winter in the National Elk Refuge, just north of Jackson; visitors tour the refuge by sleigh during the winter months. Located on Highway 89, 12 miles south of Grand Teton National Park.

3 BUFFALO BILL HISTORICAL CENTER, CODY

The Center is a complex of four museums, all of which specialize in western Americana; one whole museum is devoted to William F. "Buffalo Bill" Cody. Visitors can tour Cody's childhood home, moved from LeClaire, Iowa, in 1933. Cody's Congressional Medal of Honor, presented to him in 1872 for Indian fighting, is on display at the Buffalo Bill Museum, along with a stagecoach and billboards from his Wild West Show. The Plains Indian Museum highlights the history, culture and art of the nomadic Plains Indian tribes. The Cody Firearms Museum's diverse collection has everything from crossbows

Founded during the heyday of the 1860's, Nevada City, Montana—just half a mile from Virginia City—has more than 50 restored buildings from its gold-rush days.

to contemporary military and sporting guns. Old Trail Town, near Cody, evokes the frontier era with its collection of original buildings, including the cabin used by Butch Cassidy and the Sundance Kid. The center is in Wyoming, 50 miles east of Yellowstone National Park on Highway 16.

4 LITTLE BIGHORN BATTLEFIELD NATIONAL MONUMENT

One of the last stands of the Northern Plains Indians against U.S. Army soldiers took place here during the Battle of the Little Bighorn. Stone markers indicate where Lt. Col. Custer and his men died (the site was formerly called Custer Battlefield). A visitor center, museum and guided battlefield tours give visitors the historical significance of the battle. Interpretative programs are offered on the Plains Indians' traditional way of life. Open year-round, the battlefield is located 15 miles southeast of Hardin on the Crow Indian Reservation.

5 BOZEMAN

Along with historic houses that date back to 1883, Bozeman has many museums to tour. Learn about Montana's past at the State University's Museum of the Rockies. Full-size reconstructions depict dinosaur colonies that were excavated in Montana, and visitors can see fossilized dinosaur eggs as well as the remains of flying reptiles that lived more than 80 million years ago. There are exhibits of Plains Indians' clothing, tools and weapons, as well as displays on the life styles of the pioneer settlers. Montana's "Big Sky" is revealed at The Taylor Planetarium. The American Computer Museum traces the history of computers with displays of mechanical adding machines to state-of-the-art electronic computers. Approximately 60 miles north of Yellowstone National Park on Interstate 90.

6 LIVINGSTON

Located on the Yellowstone River, the town grew because of its geographical importance to the Northern Pacific Railroad. Today, the downtown area boasts more than 400 designated historic buildings, most of which are open to the public. One of them, Depot Center, was designed in 1902 by the same company that designed Grand Central Terminal in New York City. The railway station in Livingston was used by passengers when most trips to Yellowstone National Park were made by train. On Interstate 90, 23 miles east of Bozeman.

7 BEARTOOTH HIGHWAY

Designated a National Forest Scenic Byway in 1989, the Beartooth Highway runs between Red Lodge and the Northeast Entrance to Yellowstone National Park. This 69-mile drive offers a diversity of landscapes: snow-capped mountain peaks, glacial cirques, pink snow in summer (created by the decay of a tiny plant that gives the snow a pink glow), and

The clustered markers on Custer Hill indicate where some of the soldiers of the 7th Cavalry gathered for their last stand during the Battle of the Little Bighorn.

alpine meadows carpeted with delicate wildflowers. The route, part of Highway 212, takes approximately 3 hours to drive and is closed during the winter.

8 VIRGINIA CITY/NEVADA CITY

When news of a gold strike in 1863 spread across the nation, thousands of prospectors rushed to the Alder Gulch area. Virginia City and Nevada City were two of the towns that grew up along the gulch as rough, makeshift mining camps. Virginia City quickly grew into a city of 10,000 people and also served as the territorial capital from 1865 to 1875. Every summer, the Virginia City Players present 19th-century entertainment. A restoration effort in Nevada City enables visitors to step back in time to the heyday of the gold rush. The city has preserved many of its houses and public buildings. The general store sells merchandise from the era. The two cities are located on Hwy. 287, one-and-a-half miles from each other; visitors can travel between them on a narrow gauge railroad.

The Teton Range rises dramatically from the flat valley floor of Jackson Hole (19th-century fur trappers named these protected valleys "holes"). Horseback riding is one of many visitor activities.

YOSEMITE

"No temple made with hands can compare with Yosemite. Every rock in its walls seems to glow with life."

n the journal he kept during an 1869 ramble through what is now Yosemite National Park, the renowned naturalist John Muir seemed to use the word "sublime" on every page. It would be easy to dismiss the effusive prose as exaggeration, a product of Muir's passion for the High Sierra, but that is a judgment call that should be made only after journeying to Yosemite. A simple way to test his choice of words is to rise before dawn, drive up to the 7,214-foot-high lookout at Glacier Point, and there, as if in a darkened movie theater, wait for the show to begin.

At the first glimmer of daybreak the 12,000- and 13,000-foot peaks strewn along Yosemite's eastern boundary appear, first in silhouette, then as dim gray eminences, and finally as snow-topped mountains whose edges burn orange as the rising sun ignites them from behind. As the sky brightens further, closer peaks such as Clouds Rest and Starr King emerge from the night. Soon it becomes apparent that Glacier Point is aloft in the very heart of the Sierra. At last, the sun crests the divide and paints colors into the landscape: the blues of the creeks and the Merced River, the dark

FAMOUS FACE
Yosemite's most celebrated landmark, Half Dome, soars 4,733 feet above the flat floor of Yosemite Valley, its 2,000-foot vertical cliff facing the valley. Naturalist John Muir called Half Dome "the most beautiful and most sublime of all the wonderful Yosemite Rocks."

MIRRORED GRANDEUR
Overleaf: The boldly sculpted form of North Dome, located at the opposite end of the Yosemite Valley from El Capitan, is reflected in the Merced River. This five-mile-long river snakes its way along the valley floor and is popular with rafters. North Dome was created by a geological process that caused its huge outer slab of rock to split and fall away.

green of the conifer forest, and, above all, the vibrant hues of the muscular granite formations that are Yosemite's signature. As it awakens to the sunlight, the rock seems almost to take on life, changing from charcoal to chocolate to luminous bronze, copper and gold before finally dressing in the silver-gray it wears in broad daylight.

As the sun climbs still higher, its fingers of light reach into the shadows 3,000 feet below Glacier Point and unveil the valley: Yosemite Valley, the hallowed place. The valley is anchored by Half Dome on the east and El Capitan on the west, each rising thousands of feet above the upturned faces that gather below to pay homage. Scattered around the valley are other granite landmarks so striking that they too bear names: Royal Arches, Washington Column, Cathedral Spires, and the Three Brothers, to name but a few. From the lofty rims of the encircling cliffs, creeks make their dying leaps, tumbling hundreds, even thousands of feet to give themselves to the Merced. Glacier Point affords a dramatic view of the patriarch of this park's cascades, Yosemite Falls, which drops a dizzying 2,425 feet. Finally, there is the valley floor, its flower-filled meadows, oak woodlands and meandering river a sharp contrast to the rugged tumult of the high country.

But the view from Glacier Point is more than a show, more than an opportunity for a scenic snapshot. It is also a window on Yosemite's processes, especially the fundamental workings of the earth itself. The point is surrounded by the handiwork of glaciers, rivers, wind, rain, snow, volcanic action and clashing continental plates. Perhaps such manifestations of nature's workings are precisely what makes the park's enthralling views so enthralling; they remind us of the harmonious complexity of the planet, of the eons that have been devoted to its design. The word for the view from Glacier Point is, without a doubt, "sublime."

Becoming sublime takes time, however, and Yosemite got a head start about 200 million years ago when two great land masses slowly collided, causing rock to liquefy into magma. Some of the magma squeezed to the surface and punched out a string of volcanoes; some cooled and hardened before reaching the surface, forming Yosemite's granite. This mountain-building process continued for nearly 150 million years until the ancestral Sierra had been created. Then wind and water scoured away the crust overlying the granite, freeing it from the ground so it could soar.

But the Sierra didn't really move up in the world until about 25 million years ago, when the eastern edge of the range lifted as much as 11,000 feet. This dramatic tilt runs from 2,000 feet in the west to more than 13,000 feet in the east, which accounts

INFORMATION FOR VISITORS

Four main highways lead into the park. The year-round access roads are Hwy. 140 and Hwy. 120 eastbound from Merced and Manteca respectively, and Hwy. 41 north from Fresno. Hwy. 120 westbound from Lee Vining, near Mono Lake, is closed in winter. For road and weather information, call (209) 372-0200. Bus, air and rail service is available to Merced and Fresno, with connecting bus services to Yosemite. Once in the park, visitors can board a free shuttle bus to tour Yosemite Valley. The shuttle bus operates 12 months of the year. A section of the nationally acclaimed Pacific Crest Trail crosses the less-visited northern section of the park. There are 15 park campgrounds; four are open year-round. Reserve eight weeks in advance. There are several hotels and inns within the park, ranging from the luxurious Ahwahnee to the more modest Yosemite Lodge. Pioneer Yosemite History Center, with costumed interpreters, reenacts the park's history.

For more information: Superintendent, Yosemite National Park, P.O. Box 577, Yosemite, CA 95389. (209) 372-0200.

STOP AND SMELL THE FLOWERS
Experienced ranger-naturalists conduct free guided walks throughout the park. These tours provide visitors with an invaluable insight into Yosemite's flora and fauna.

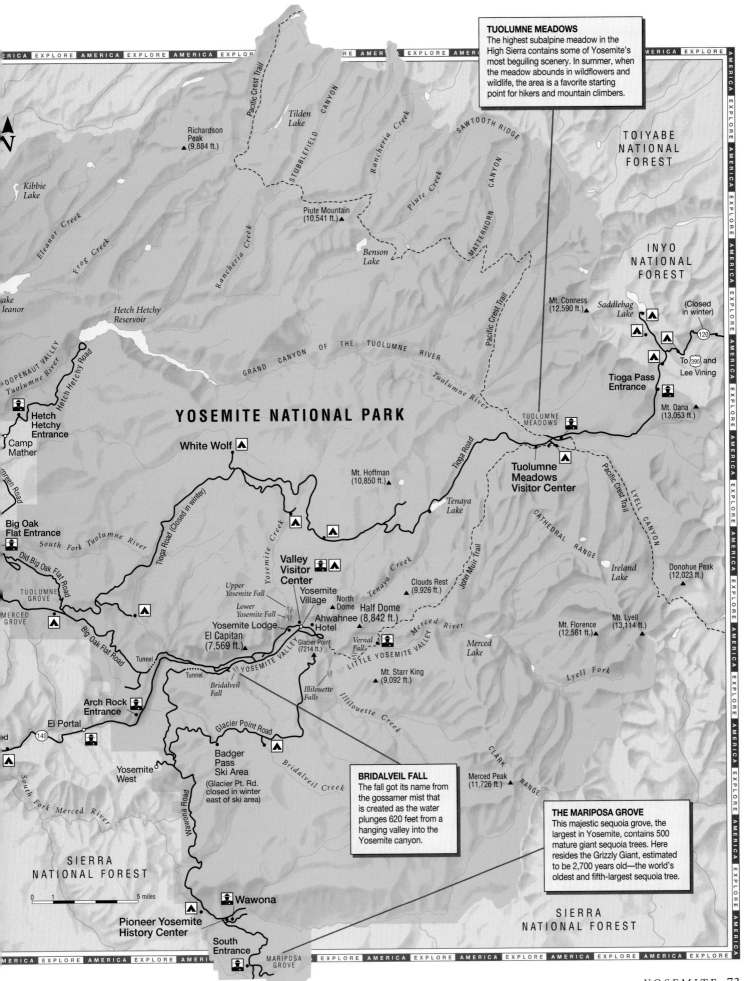

TUOLUMNE MEADOWS
The highest subalpine meadow in the High Sierra contains some of Yosemite's most beguiling scenery. In summer, when the meadow abounds in wildflowers and wildlife, the area is a favorite starting point for hikers and mountain climbers.

TOIYABE NATIONAL FOREST

INYO NATIONAL FOREST

Richardson Peak (9,884 ft.)

Kibbie Lake

Tilden Lake

Pacific Crest Trail

STUBBLEFIELD CANYON

Rancheria Creek

SAWTOOTH RIDGE

Piute Mountain (10,541 ft.)

Piute Creek

MATTERHORN CANYON

Benson Lake

Eleanor Creek

Frog Creek

Rancheria Creek

Pacific Crest Trail

Mt. Conness (12,590 ft.)

Saddlebag Lake

(Closed in winter)

120

ake leanor

Hetch Hetchy Reservoir

GRAND CANYON OF THE TUOLUMNE RIVER

Tuolumne River

To 395 and Lee Vining

Tioga Pass Entrance

Mt. Dana (13,053 ft.)

DOOPENAUT VALLEY Tuolumne River

Hetch Hetchy Road

YOSEMITE NATIONAL PARK

TUOLUMNE MEADOWS

Hetch Hetchy Entrance

Camp Mather

White Wolf

Mt. Hoffman (10,850 ft.)

Tioga Road

Tuolumne Meadows Visitor Center

rreen Road

Big Oak Flat Entrance

South Fork Tuolumne River

Tioga Road (Closed in winter)

Yosemite Creek

Tenaya Lake

Tenaya Creek

CATHEDRAL RANGE

LYELL CANYON

Pacific Crest Trail

Old Big Oak Flat Road

TUOLUMNE GROVE

Valley Visitor Center

Clouds Rest (9,926 ft.)

John Muir Trail

Ireland Lake

Donohue Peak (12,023 ft.)

MERCED GROVE

Big Oak Flat Road

Upper Yosemite Fall

Yosemite Village

North Dome

Half Dome (8,842 ft.)

Merced River

Lower Yosemite Fall

Ahwahnee Hotel

Yosemite Lodge

El Capitan (7,569 ft.)

Glacier Point (7214 ft.)

Vernal Fall

LITTLE YOSEMITE VALLEY

Merced Lake

Mt. Florence (12,561 ft.)

Mt. Lyell (13,114 ft.)

Lyell Fork

Tunnel

YOSEMITE VALLEY

Mt. Starr King (9,092 ft.)

Arch Rock Entrance

Tunnel

Bridalveil Fall

Illilouette Falls

Illilouette Creek

El Portal

140

Glacier Point Road

CLARK RANGE

Yosemite West

Badger Pass Ski Area

Bridalveil Creek

BRIDALVEIL FALL
The fall got its name from the gossamer mist that is created as the water plunges 620 feet from a hanging valley into the Yosemite canyon.

Merced Peak (11,726 ft.)

South Fork Merced River

(Glacier Pt. Rd. closed in winter east of ski area)

THE MARIPOSA GROVE
This majestic sequoia grove, the largest in Yosemite, contains 500 mature giant sequoia trees. Here resides the Grizzly Giant, estimated to be 2,700 years old—the world's oldest and fifth-largest sequoia tree.

Wawona Road

SIERRA NATIONAL FOREST

SIERRA NATIONAL FOREST

0 1   5 miles

Wawona

Pioneer Yosemite History Center

South Entrance

MARIPOSA GROVE

EXPLORE AMERICA EXPLORE AMERICA EXPLORE

Upper and Lower Yosemite Falls (below) surge with life during late spring and early summer. The falls drop nearly half a mile in three giant steps that direct melting winter run-off from the high meadows to the valley floor. The combined height of Upper and Lower Yosemite Falls is 2,425 feet, making it the highest waterfall in North America and the second-highest in the world. Only Angel Falls in Venezuela, at 3,281 feet, is higher.

for the great diversity of life zones that makes Yosemite a place of infinite surprise. The tilt also made Yosemite's watercourses much steeper, and the rush of water down the slopes started carving the Sierra into the rough range it is today.

What the tilted rivers started, glaciers finished—not that geologic change is ever finished. For two to three million years, up until a mere 15,000 years ago, a cooler climate produced as many as 10 glacial periods, sometimes burying half of Yosemite beneath thick sheets of ice. Massive glaciers also shoved along many of the park's waterways, scouring them into textbook examples of U-shaped glacial canyons and valleys. Some of Yosemite's granite gleams with a metallic gloss called "glacial polish," which resulted when glaciers loaded with abrasive rock and sand rasped across exceptionally hard stone, giving it a truly long-lasting shine. Glacial polish also shimmers at the bottom of Tenaya Creek, which Indians named "Py-we-ack," the "river of the glistening rocks." Often glaciers

did a lot more than polish. Where rock was weak, glaciers ground away the more vulnerable stone or tore off huge blocks, sculpting many of the park's spires and domes.

LINCOLN SAVED THE VALLEY

It was the magnificent geology of Yosemite that led to its formal recognition. Though the 1872 designation of Yellowstone as a park generally is cited as the start of America's national park system, an argument can be made that the honor belongs to Yosemite. Most of its acreage was not set aside until 1890, but in 1864 President Lincoln signed legislation protecting Yosemite Valley and the Mariposa Grove. Perhaps he longed to do something for beauty in the midst of the ugliness of the Civil War.

Since the park's founding, annual visitation has increased from a few people to a few million, which inevitably has caused some problems. Yosemite

Valley in particular is in danger of being loved to death as more than 18,000 visitors jam it on an average summer day, leading to snarled traffic, smog and damage to the land. Visitors can help relieve the pressure by using the free shuttle buses and by arriving in a season other than summer. Perhaps most importantly, park-goers should move beyond Yosemite Valley, especially if they hope to fully appreciate this multifaceted land.

Each so-called off-season offers distinct opportunities to experience the rhythms of Yosemite. Spring brings the renewal of life. Wildflowers bloom and trees bud. Black bears emerge from their winter dens, trailing frisky cubs behind them. Mule deer, including a full complement of gangly fawns, mow the meadows along the Merced. Waterfalls gorged on snow-melt surge over the valley rim and explode against the rocks below.

In many ways, autumn is summer without the crowds, because most of the people have gone but the snow hasn't yet come. However, the bold col-

ors of the dogwood, oak and maple at lower elevations and the resplendent gold of the aspens in the high country proclaim the shift to fall. Autumn also is the rutting season for deer; bucks can be spotted snorting in the meadows as they try to shove other males around with their antlers.

Winter is the most peaceful season. Not only are the crowds at low ebb, but this is a time of rest for nature, as well. Visitors can venture out on their own or in some cases with ranger-naturalists to explore the transformed winter park via snowshoes, snowmobiles or cross-country skis. The tracks of a bobcat; an improbable bouquet of winter wildflowers flaring from a protected nook on the warmer north side of the valley; the fantastic shapes fashioned out of frozen spray below the waterfalls—many particulars reward winter visitors, but the whole of Yosemite in winter is greater than the sum of its parts. Hiking along the valley floor, hearing only the crunch of their snowshoes, travelers are swathed in the hushed tranquility of the sleeping wilds.

BEAUTY BEYOND THE VALLEY

Most visitors to Yosemite never leave this valley, though fully 99 percent of Yosemite's 750,000 acres lies outside Yosemite Valley and 94 percent of the park is designated wilderness. Perhaps they're afraid that if they leave the valley they'll leave behind the grandeur, but they're mistaken.

Burly granite domes, rivers, graceful waterfalls, and even other deep valleys and canyons exist elsewhere in the park, too. And grandeur of sorts not found in Yosemite Valley also awaits.

Take the giant sequoias. It is doubtful that anyone could look upon these living counterparts of Yosemite's granite pinnacles and not think them grand. Certainly they impressed one A.T. Dowd, a professional hunter who was one of the first people to report their existence. One day in 1852, Dowd was out hunting for meat to feed the men at a mining camp near Yosemite when he happened upon a grove of giant sequoias. Astonished, he rushed back and blurted out that he had seen huge trees four times bigger than any trees he'd ever encountered, but his skeptical companions hooted him out of camp. A crafty fellow, Dowd stayed away long enough to be convincing and then came back and said that he'd killed a grizzly and needed five men to help haul the meat.

He led the five unsuspecting witnesses to the sequoia grove, and the word went out about the presence of the largest living things on earth.

How big are giant sequoias? Well, the General Grant Tree in Mariposa Grove, the most extensive of Yosemite's three sequoia groves, measures 29

feet in diameter, tops out at 290 feet, and weighs at least 2 million pounds—and it may not even be the grove's biggest tree. Giant sequoias also can live more than 3,000 years. But statistics don't adequately convey their immensity. Back in the 1800's when sequoias were first logged, their bulk often was demonstrated by what people could put up on them. Taking photos of throngs of loggers, teams of horses, cavalry troops and the like on top of downed sequoias became a cottage industry. One entrepreneur built a two-lane bowling alley on one of the fallen giants. The massive, roofed-over stump of another at various times housed the staff and printing press of a newspaper, served as a stage for theatrical performances, and was used as a ballroom for up to 48 dancers at a time.

Strangely, few young sequoias are growing in Mariposa Grove. That is because park managers repressed all fires for 100 years, not realizing that their effort to protect the sequoias was keeping the trees from reproducing. Sequoias need fire to prompt the seeds to fall from the cones tucked high in the crowns of the mature trees. They also need fire to clear competing, shade-tolerant trees from the forest understory. In the 1960's scientists began to understand the ways of the giant sequoias and the park service initiated a program of prescribed burns to get the grove back on track.

Giant sequoias, waterfalls, glacial valleys, towering granite domes—the park's plethora of majestic features tends to monopolize the attention of visitors. That's understandable, but to deepen their insight into Yosemite, park-goers should narrow their focus at times and observe the small things or look closely at the big things. Visitors to the giant sequoia groves, for example, ought to take time to scrutinize the cinnamon-brown bark of one of those pillars of the forest community.

As its deep furrows reveal, sequoia bark is extraordinarily thick—as thick as two feet. It is also

A HELPING HAND

Yosemite is home to the peregrine falcon, an endangered species that had been brought to the verge of extinction by exposure to pesticides. The Park Service helps boost the resident falcon population by removing and hatching the fragile, thin-shelled eggs in a laboratory incubator and then returning the chicks to the nest for adoption by the adult birds of prey.

THE BIG CHIEF

The 3,000-foot vertical walls of El Capitan (opposite page) shimmer softly through a winter mist. These colossal cliffs, located at the opposite end of Yosemite Valley from Half Dome, challenge experienced rock climbers from around the world.

fibrous and lacks resin. These qualities protect the trees from the fires they need to reproduce. The bark of ponderosa pines also warrants a close-up, especially the rich yellow-tan color (they are commonly called yellow pines) and the scales, which look like parts of a jigsaw puzzle. A cousin of the ponderosa pine, the Jeffrey pine is the most fragrant bark in the park. Visitors who flake off a small piece and smell the underside report aromas from butterscotch to peanut butter, but the majority of noses smell vanilla.

Other travelers are lured away from the park's grand features by the wildflowers of Tuolumne Meadows. High astride the Tioga Road at 8,600 feet, Tuolumne Meadows cannot muster the warmth for spring until June, but when it happens, this two-and-a-half-mile-long basin erupts with technicolor blooms as plants hustle to reproduce in the brief subalpine growing season. Crimson, rocket-shaped shooting stars; tiny, bright blue Sierra forget-me-nots; clusters of purple-red Sierra primroses; the pink, perfect pachyderm likenesses of little elephant heads—the bounty of blossoms compels visitors to stop and smell the flowers.

The same patient approach to observing plants also is advisable for watching Yosemite's animals, for the park is no Serengeti teeming with big beasts. Mule deer and coyotes are common; black bears often are seen—or at least heard—at night as they prowl around campsites searching for poorly stored food. Visitors would have to be extremely lucky to glimpse a mountain lion or a bighorn sheep. But that is no reason to give up on the wildlife.

Take a good look at the squirrels rummaging around in the meadows to see if they are California ground squirrels—it's easy to tell because they have white polka dots all over their backs. A high-pitched squeak alerts onlookers to scan for pikas—cute, guinea-pig-like relatives of rabbits that bustle about collecting grasses for their winter haystacks, which can be two feet high. Picnickers should beware the gray jay, also known as the "camp robber," as these aggressive scroungers have been known to snatch food from people's hands. Especially vigilant visitors may spot some of the members of the weasel family. Anyone nursing stereotypes of weasels as scraggly critters will be surprised by the beauty and grace of most of Yosemite's species, such as minks, ermines, martens, wolverines and river otters.

Among the park's small creatures the yellow-bellied marmot arguably is the biggest crowd-pleaser. Marmots inhabit many high-country rock piles, living in colonies that consist of a territorial male, several females and some of their offspring. On sunny days the colony's dominant male often can be seen melted over a prominent rock, a bag of bones loosely bundled in yellow-brown fur. The females move about the rocks doing all the work.

PLAYING FOR THE CROWDS

Juvenile marmots spend much of their day chasing each other and wrestling. Sometimes they sit up and box wildly with their front paws while averting their faces, other times they clutch each other and roll down a hillside while locked together, like two adversaries in some old-fashioned Western. When members of a colony meet, they usually greet each other by sniffing cheeks and arching their tails, and sometimes one grooms the other. If a yellow-bellied interloper from another colony is spotted by the territorial male, he'll scurry from his throne and drive the intruder away, whistling at it in a way that can aptly be described as a shriek. The antics of the marmots impart an important lesson about wildlife-watching; looks may attract our attention, but behavior holds it. No creature underscores this better than the American dipper.

The dipper is a stocky, gray, drab bird that is a little smaller than a robin. People who aren't familiar with it probably would give a dipper about a two-second glance if they saw it standing on a rock beside a rushing creek. However, the dipper would surely get their attention if it chose that moment to leap into the white water. Dippers forage for aquatic insects by diving into streams and striding along the bottom. They can blithely amble through rapids too swift and powerful for people to stand in.

At some point travelers should eschew roads, visitor centers, campgrounds and anything else that distracts from the park's wildness to visit the backcountry. People who don't have the means to spend a week trekking the John Muir Trail or making the circuit of the High Sierra Camps should at least take a few hours and go to the side of a ridge far from civilization. Yosemite's whispered messages can be heard much more clearly away from the whine of car engines. By tarrying in the park's wilderness and tuning in to its ways, a traveler can sense his place in the natural world, his relation to the animals, plants, rivers and rocks.

John Muir put it well in his 1869 Yosemite journal: "An eagle soaring above a sheer cliff, where I suppose its nest is, makes another striking show of life, and helps to bring to mind the other people of the so-called solitude—deer in the forest caring for their young; the strong, well-clad, well-fed bears; the lively throng of squirrels; the blessed birds, great and small, stirring and sweetening the groves....All these come to mind....But most impressive of all is the vast glowing countenance of the wilderness in awful, infinite repose."

NEARBY SITES & ATTRACTIONS

A wooden church's spire is the tallest structure still standing in the once wealthy town of Bodie. The ghost town's authentic, unrestored buildings give visitors an eerie glimpse of life during the heyday of the gold rush.

Mineral King Canyon in Sequoia National Park was named optimistically by miners who hoped the canyon would yield a fortune in silver. The silver rush of the 1870's soon petered out, however, and the mines closed. The canyon was annexed to the park in 1978.

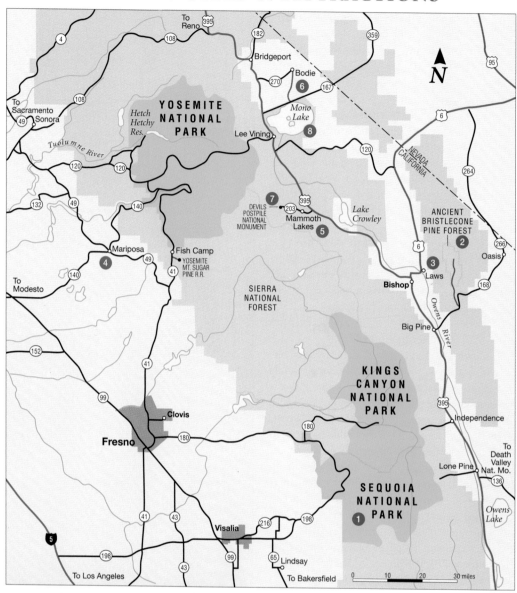

① SEQUOIA-KINGS CANYON NATIONAL PARKS

Sequoia-Kings Canyon National Parks cover nearly a million acres of preserved wilderness. Hiking trails connect cathedral-like forests, lake-dotted meadows, sheer-walled canyons and some of the tallest mountain peaks on the continent. Mount Whitney, at 14,495 feet, is the highest point in the contiguous U.S. Groves of sequoia trees, the largest living things on earth, grow along the moist, unglaciated ridges of the Sierra's west slope. Sequoia's Giant Forest is home to the 2,500-year-old General Sherman tree, a gargantuan specimen with a girth almost 103 feet in circumference. Located 70 miles south of Yosemite on Hwy. 395.

② ANCIENT BRISTLECONE PINE FOREST

The world's oldest trees—gnarled and wind-carved bristlecone pines—grow on the arid slopes of the

White Mountains at elevations of 10,000 to 12,000 feet. The timeworn trees, some of them 4,000 years old, grow very slowly, as little as one inch in girth every hundred years. Over the centuries, wind-driven sand, hail, ice and snow have sculpted the bristlecones into astonishing shapes with coiled, spiraling roots. Located 3 miles north of Hwy. 168.

3 RAILROAD MUSEUM, LAWS

The Laws-to-Keeler branch of the Southern Pacific was the last narrow gauge railway line to operate west of the Rocky Mountains. The service made its first trip to Laws in 1883 and ran until 1959, serving as a lifeline for the mines and communities of Eastern California and Western Nevada. Today railroad hobbyists can see the small engine, nicknamed the "Slim Princess" because of the line's 36-inch tracks. The museum also has a fine collection of railroad memorabilia and 19th-century artifacts such as musical instruments and books from bygone railroad days. Located 5 miles north of Bishop on Hwy. 6.

4 MARIPOSA

Memories of the gold-rush days survive in this historic gold-mining town located in the foothills of the towering Sierra Nevada. The Mariposa Museum and History Center, considered to be one of America's best small museums, presents an authentic picture of gold-rush life, including a full-size working stamp mill, a vintage newspaper office and period interiors. The town's most celebrated building is the Grecian-styled County Courthouse, built in 1854 from local white pine. The California State Mining and Mineral Museum, located on the outskirts of town, features its own permanent world-class exhibits of minerals as well as touring exhibits. Located at the junction of Hwy. 140 and Hwy. 49.

5 MAMMOTH LAKES RECREATION AREA

This year-round resort is the gateway to more than 200,000 acres of stunning backpacking, mountain climbing, and fishing country. The area boasts one of the largest ski areas in the country: Mammoth Mountain Ski Resort sometimes stays open until the Fourth of July. Other winter activities include cross-country skiing and wind skiing on the meadows. A local National Forest Visitor Information Center organizes guided nature walks and ski tours. Located 3 miles off Hwy. 395 along a mountain road.

6 BODIE

After gold was discovered in the Mono Lake region in 1852, thousands of would-be prospectors rushed to the scene. From 1876 to 1880 Bodie's population mushroomed to 10,000 and the town quickly gained the dubious reputation as the toughest and most lawless gold-mining camp in California. Today, Bodie is a ghost town with more than 150 authentic buildings. Visitors can stroll down streets that look

much the way they did when the last resident left 50 years ago. Located 20 miles southeast of Bridgeport off Hwy. 395.

7 DEVILS POSTPILE NATIONAL MONUMENT

Columns of basaltic rock, resembling 60-foot teetering logs, stand along the Middle Fork of the San Joaquin River. The columns, known as the Devils Postpile, were formed almost 100,000 years ago when hot lava cracked as it cooled. Walkers can hike two miles south of the monument to Rainbow Falls, a cascade of 101 feet over a sheer rock face. The John Muir Trail also intersects the monument. Located 17 miles off Hwy. 395 along a mountain road.

8 MONO LAKE

This crusty moonlike landscape of spires and knobs, some of them as much as 13,000 years old, was exposed when Mono Lake's level dropped about 40 feet; the tufa towers were formed underwater by buildups of calcium carbonate. Today, a boardwalk and pathways allow visitors to explore the tufa towers along the lake's shoreline and its bordering marshes. Visitors can also watch grebes and phalaropes feed on brine shrimp and, by special permission, observe one of the largest nesting colonies of California gulls. The lake's water is denser and saltier than ocean water; a swim here is an unforgettably buoyant experience. Located just off Hwy. 395, 5 miles north of Lee Vining.

Oddly shaped limestone columns, called tufa towers, break the cobalt-blue surface of Mono Lake.

A vintage Shay steam locomotive takes passengers on a four-mile excursion through the magnificent mountains of the Sierra National Forest. The trip begins just outside the south entrance to the park near Fish Camp. The original Sugar Pine narrow gauge railroad operated from 1899 to 1931 and transported almost a billion and a half feet of lumber from the forests of the Sierra Nevada.

OLYMPIC

*With its coastal climate and
rain-washed mountain slopes,
Olympic is a gift from the sea.*

In the far northwestern corner of Washington
state, the Olympic Mountains rise abruptly into
a spectacular jumble of steep, glacier-clad ridges
and peaks, and deep, forested river canyons. The
tallest of the peaks, dubbed Mount Olympus by
British captain John Meares in 1788, has given
the range and the isolated peninsula it occupies
its name. Meares was one of many British,
American and Spanish explorers in the area in
the late 1700's, and in bequeathing the fanciful
epithet to the mountain, he initiated an enduring
enchantment with the remote range that is half-
hidden in the clouds.

More than 1,400 square miles of the untram-
meled heart of the Olympic Peninsula have been
preserved within the boundaries of Olympic
National Park. It encompasses rugged mountains,
wild, free-flowing rivers, a pristine wilderness
coast and the largest preserve of old-growth forest in the temperate world.

It was this abundance of resources and wildlife
that led Theodore Roosevelt to establish the
Olympic National Monument in 1909. In 1938
Franklin D. Roosevelt signed the bill that created

SERRATED PEAKS

Morning light illuminates the eastern side of the Olympic Mountains. About 55 million years ago, the Olympic Peninsula lay under the sea. Rock now found on the tops of the mountains contains fossils of long-extinct marine life.

RAIN MAKER

Overleaf: A soft cloud of mist lies trapped in the valley between the meadows of High Divide and Mt. Olympus. Weather is unpredictable here—within minutes brilliant sunshine can give way to torrential rain.

Olympic National Park, and 50 years later Congress included more than 95 percent of the park in the National Wilderness System. Today, visitors to Olympic find a magnificent landscape little changed from the snowy range that first inspired Captain Meares more than two centuries ago—a corner of wilderness North America with all its power, riches and beauty intact.

From the high ridges and peaks of the western Olympics, valleys drop into mist-laden evergreen forests and rivers ribbon westward toward the blue plane of the Pacific. But the ocean's influence here goes far deeper than climate and setting. The Olympic Peninsula owes its origins to the sea and the primal forces that lie hidden beneath it.

Over a period of 25 million years, an undersea mountain range that would become the Olympic Mountains was grafted onto the continent, bending and buckling up out of the coastal waters and forming a new coastline.

For the next 10 to 12 million years, the Olympics continued to rise, only to be ceaselessly worn, carved, and quarried by the equally relentless powers of wind, water and glacial ice. As moist air from

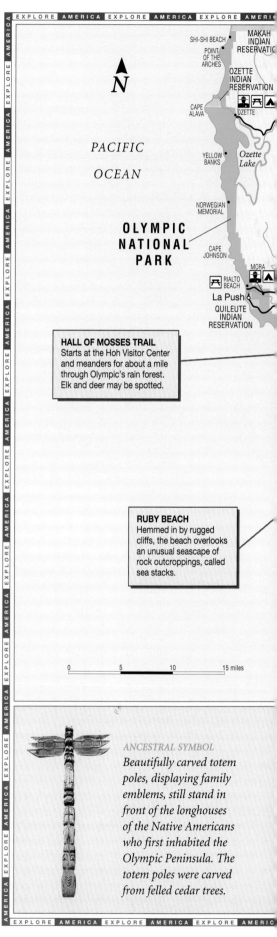

PACIFIC OCEAN

SHI-SHI BEACH

MAKAH INDIAN RESERVATIO

POINT OF THE ARCHES

OZETTE INDIAN RESERVATION

CAPE ALAVA

OZETTE

YELLOW BANKS

Ozette Lake

NORWEGIAN MEMORIAL

OLYMPIC NATIONAL PARK

CAPE JOHNSON

MORA

RIALTO BEACH

La Push

QUILEUTE INDIAN RESERVATION

HALL OF MOSSES TRAIL
Starts at the Hoh Visitor Center and meanders for about a mile through Olympic's rain forest. Elk and deer may be spotted.

RUBY BEACH
Hemmed in by rugged cliffs, the beach overlooks an unusual seascape of rock outcroppings, called sea stacks.

0   5   10   15 miles

ANCESTRAL SYMBOL

Beautifully carved totem poles, displaying family emblems, still stand in front of the longhouses of the Native Americans who first inhabited the Olympic Peninsula. The totem poles were carved from felled cedar trees.

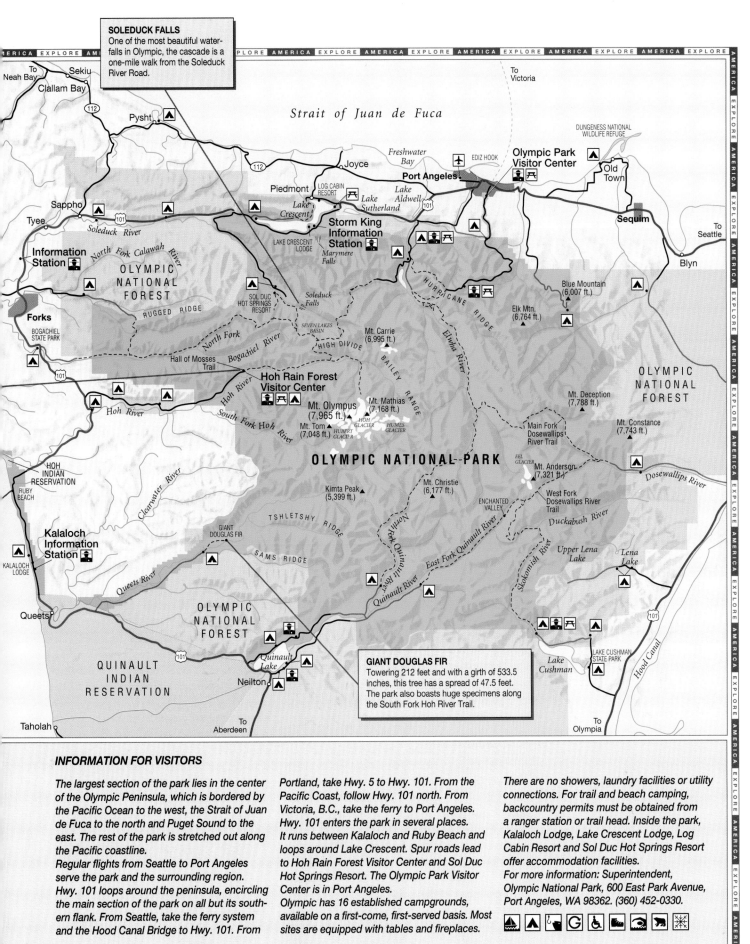

SOLEDUCK FALLS
One of the most beautiful waterfalls in Olympic, the cascade is a one-mile walk from the Soleduck River Road.

Strait of Juan de Fuca

To Neah Bay
Sekiu
Clallam Bay
Pysht
112

To Victoria

DUNGENESS NATIONAL WILDLIFE REFUGE

Freshwater Bay
EDIZ HOOK
Olympic Park Visitor Center

Joyce
Piedmont
LOG CABIN RESORT
Lake Sutherland
Lake Aldwell
Port Angeles

Old Town

Sequim

To Seattle

Sappho
Tyee
101
Soleduck River
Lake Crescent
LAKE CRESCENT LODGE
Storm King Information Station
Marymere Falls
101

Blyn

Information Station
North Fork Calawah River
OLYMPIC NATIONAL FOREST
RUGGED RIDGE
SOL DUC HOT SPRINGS RESORT
Soleduck Falls
SEVEN LAKES BASIN

Blue Mountain (6,007 ft.)
Elk Mtn. (6,764 ft.)

HURRICANE RIDGE

Forks
BOGACHIEL STATE PARK
North Fork
Bogachiel River
HIGH DIVIDE
Mt. Carrie (6,995 ft.)

Elwha River
BAILEY RANGE

Hall of Mosses Trail
Hoh River
Hoh Rain Forest Visitor Center
Mt. Mathias (7,168 ft.)
Mt. Olympus (7,965 ft.)
Mt. Tom (7,048 ft.)
HOH GLACIER
HUMES GLACIER
HUBERT GLACIER

Mt. Deception (7,788 ft.)

OLYMPIC NATIONAL FOREST

Mt. Constance (7,743 ft.)

South Fork Hoh River

HOH INDIAN RESERVATION
RUBY BEACH

OLYMPIC NATIONAL PARK

Clearwater River
Kimta Peak (5,399 ft.)
Mt. Christie (6,177 ft.)
EEL GLACIER
Mt. Anderson (7,321 ft.)

Dosewallips River
Main Fork Dosewallips River Trail
West Fork Dosewallips River Trail
ENCHANTED VALLEY
Duckabush River

Kalaloch Information Station
KALALOCH LODGE

TSHLETSHY RIDGE
GIANT DOUGLAS FIR
SAMS RIDGE
North Fork Quinault River
East Fork Quinault River
Quinault River

Skokomish River
Upper Lena Lake
Lena Lake

Queets River

Queets
101

OLYMPIC NATIONAL FOREST

LAKE CUSHMAN STATE PARK
Lake Cushman
Hood Canal

QUINAULT INDIAN RESERVATION
101
Quinault Lake
Neilton

GIANT DOUGLAS FIR
Towering 212 feet and with a girth of 533.5 inches, this tree has a spread of 47.5 feet. The park also boasts huge specimens along the South Fork Hoh River Trail.

Taholah
To Aberdeen

To Olympia

INFORMATION FOR VISITORS

The largest section of the park lies in the center of the Olympic Peninsula, which is bordered by the Pacific Ocean to the west, the Strait of Juan de Fuca to the north and Puget Sound to the east. The rest of the park is stretched out along the Pacific coastline.

Regular flights from Seattle to Port Angeles serve the park and the surrounding region. Hwy. 101 loops around the peninsula, encircling the main section of the park on all but its southern flank. From Seattle, take the ferry system and the Hood Canal Bridge to Hwy. 101. From

Portland, take Hwy. 5 to Hwy. 101. From the Pacific Coast, follow Hwy. 101 north. From Victoria, B.C., take the ferry to Port Angeles. Hwy. 101 enters the park in several places. It runs between Kalaloch and Ruby Beach and loops around Lake Crescent. Spur roads lead to Hoh Rain Forest Visitor Center and Sol Duc Hot Springs Resort. The Olympic Park Visitor Center is in Port Angeles.

Olympic has 16 established campgrounds, available on a first-come, first-served basis. Most sites are equipped with tables and fireplaces.

There are no showers, laundry facilities or utility connections. For trail and beach camping, backcountry permits must be obtained from a ranger station or trail head. Inside the park, Kalaloch Lodge, Lake Crescent Lodge, Log Cabin Resort and Sol Duc Hot Springs Resort offer accommodation facilities.

For more information: Superintendent, Olympic National Park, 600 East Park Avenue, Port Angeles, WA 98362. (360) 452-0330.

MERICA EXPLORE AMERICA EXPLORE AMERICA EXPLORE AMERICA EXPLORE AMERICA EXPLORE AMERICA EXPLORE AMERICA EXPLORE AMERICA EXPLORE

OLYMPIC 85

the Pacific rose against the mountains, it cooled, dumping prodigious amounts of rain and snow. Rivers and glaciers worked to erode the uplifted mass into peaks and valleys. Over time, at least six ice-age advances have chiseled the mountains into the breathtaking shapes visible now.

THREE WORLDS IN ONE Even in today's relatively warm climate, the Olympics are mantled with snow for more than half the year. Snowfall on Mount Olympus can reach 150 feet, and rainfall in one of the park's western valleys commonly exceeds 140 inches a year. This pall of wetness that cloaks the Olympics from November to June is the key that makes Olympic National Park what it is.

From coastline to mountaintop, the park is blessed with myriad plant types. As the snowpack recedes from the high mountains in late spring and summer, rivulets and waterfalls frame a daz-

zling world of mossy cliffs, brilliant wildflower meadows and still mountain lakes. As summer progresses, black-tailed deer, Roosevelt elk and the ubiquitous black bear migrate to the high country, drawn by lush meadow growth and ripening seeds and berries. Visitors, too, flock to the high mountains in summer, but they must be willing to travel by foot or horseback, for Olympic is above all else a wilderness park. It reveals its secrets best to those willing to take in the country slowly, page by page, like a good book.

By the last weeks of September, days become short. The snowpack has all but vanished from the ridges. Glaciers glint blue-white on the higher peaks and meadows redden with the autumn blush of huckleberry leaves. Soon the herds of elk, the scattered bands of deer, the fat, shaggy black bears and other wildlife will retrace their routes down to the forests that fill the valleys.

There are few places on earth that support an old-growth forest ecosystem as complete, as rich-

A mountain goat kid takes its first steps in the snow. Since the careless introduction of the goats to the peninsula in the 1920's, they have eroded the thin soil and altered plantlife patterns. Park officials are removing the goats from the park.

Spring in the High Divide is a hurried growing season when plants such as this false hellebore quickly bud. Soon these subalpine meadows will be blanketed with wildflowers.

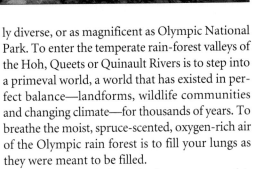

ly diverse, or as magnificent as Olympic National Park. To enter the temperate rain-forest valleys of the Hoh, Queets or Quinault Rivers is to step into a primeval world, a world that has existed in perfect balance—landforms, wildlife communities and changing climate—for thousands of years. To breathe the moist, spruce-scented, oxygen-rich air of the Olympic rain forest is to fill your lungs as they were meant to be filled.

The Olympic rain forest harbors a great multiplicity of giant-sized trees. A combination of soils, climates and topography has created a magnificent population of Douglas fir, western hemlock, Sitka spruce and western red cedar. But rather than dwarfing visitors who walk among them, the great trees of the rain forest have a way of lifting spirits, of reminding us once more of the miracle of life we share with them. Many of these giants are more than 500 years old and stand more than 300 feet high. Their high canopy of interwoven branches is dense, and a soft green light filters

OLYMPIC 87

A cluster of ochre sea stars clings to a rock during low tide. Sea stars live in the middle intertidal zone, feeding largely on mollusks. The creatures feed only underwater, and during low tide they manage to move between tidal pools using their five radial arms to gain forward momentum.

side vegetation, so important for wintering elk and deer. For when the mountains are locked in snow and storm fronts move in tandem from the Pacific Ocean, the lowland forest nurtures and protects much of Olympic's wildlife as it has for millennia.

When Captain Meares sighted the Olympic Peninsula in 1788, he encountered a wild coastline incised with swift rivers and broken by steep cliffs and rugged headlands. The forests stretched unbroken from tidewater to the snowpeaks of the interior. Visitors to Olympic National Park's wilderness coast today find the view that met Captain Meares essentially unchanged.

SEACOAST RICHNESS

From the smooth sandy beaches of Kalaloch at the southern end of Olympic's ocean strip to the headlands and sea stacks of Point of the Arches on the rocky northern coast, more than 57 miles of undeveloped coastline have been preserved. (A sea stack is an island-like pinnacle of land that was gnawed by the sea from the headland.) It is the longest stretch of wilderness coast remaining in the lower 48 states and it beckons beach walkers, campers and backpackers throughout the year.

Winter is the season when the unbridled power of the coast is most vivid. Storms batter the windswept coastal spruces and pound the headlands with tremendous force. Huge logs are cast seaward as the mouths of rivers become torrents. Viewed from a snug cabin at Kalaloch or La Push, there are few sights more dramatic than a winter storm on the coast. And few things are more satisfying than a driftwood fire when the storm clears and winter stars shine through the broken clouds like beacons.

By early spring the storms abate and the coast is taken once more with a calmer mood. Morning light slants through misty trees and the beach is washed smooth and fresh. Eagles and ospreys perch among the tallest trees and shorebirds begin to return from their southerly ranges. This is also the time when one of the most profoundly moving sights graces the Olympic coast—the northward migration of whales. For thousands of years the gray whales have followed their migratory routes from southern calving grounds to the Arctic feeding grounds.

Few things are more inspiring to behold than their distant plumes as they breach and sound offshore. The return of the whales is a signal that the natural systems are still intact, a reassurance and a sign of hope. But for the human societies that preceded ours, they were much more than that.

For the coast people, the Makah, Quileute and Quinault, the returning whales were a gift that

through tiers of limbs and hanging clubmoss draperies.

The song of a winter wren weaves its way through the low shrubs and ferns, and always in the distance is the sound of water. A thick carpet of moss dotted with pale flowers cushions the forest floor. Continuous browsing by elk has lent an open, parklike elegance to these valleys, and the ancient trees rise in great fluted columns toward the diffused light of the heavens.

In the fall the rain forest teems with life. Roosevelt elk are down from the high summer meadows and the valleys ring with the mating calls of the bulls. (Created primarily to protect these magnificent animals, Olympic was almost named Elk National Park.) The deer, too, are in the midst of their rutting season, and a host of wildlife from Douglas squirrels and long-tailed voles to dark-eyed juncos are kept busy harvesting summer's bounty. Higher up in the subalpine zone of the mountains the Olympic marmots are preparing to hibernate in their burrows under the snow.

Less conspicuous amid the autumn fervor but just as important to the overall life of the forest community are the salmon that return up the rivers to spawn and die beneath the great trees. Spawned salmon provide an important source of rich, ocean-derived nutrients for many of the park's wildlife at a critical time in their seasonal cycles. Bald eagles, black bears, ravens, raccoons, river otters and crows are among some of the animals who feed on the returning salmon.

These animals in turn serve a valuable function in the forest ecology. By dragging salmon carcasses from river banks and leaving them scattered through the brush, they aid the growth of stream-

meant the survival of their people. For traditional whaling people there was no greater achievement and no greater devotion than the ritualized practice of hunting whales. The native lifestyles that developed on the Northwest Coast were rich in ritual, artistry and skill. Over thousands of years they built a culture out of cedar and mussel shell, spruce root and bone. Amid the natural bounty of the Northwest Coast, theirs became one of the most sophisticated hunting and gathering societies in North America. That the descendants of those early people live on in their ancestral sites at Neah Bay, La Push, Hoh and Tahola, speaks well for the strength, dignity and endurance of their way of life.

After the long leisurely days of summer—days of digging clams, exploring tide pools, or savoring long walks in the evening light—the fall rains come as a shock. But rain brings the first salmon runs back to the rivers of the Olympic Peninsula and with the return of the salmon the cycle is complete.

Far inland, bears are cleaning the last of mountain blueberry bushes and the elk are retracing their ancient routes to the valley forests. Soon the mountain passes will be blocked with snow and the wilderness of the Olympic Mountains will be total and inviolate.

For many people, there will be an occasional ski or snowshoe trip to see them through the winter months. But for many more there will remain the simple joy of knowing that a corner of this busy land endures unchanged, remains for now and always a wilderness.

LOW TIDE ON SHI SHI
The sea-worn cliffs and driftwood-strewn beach at Shi Shi during low tide are a paradise for beach explorers. But incoming tides are hazardous and hikers are warned to stick to overland trails. In the space of approximately one day, the Pacific Coast has two high tides and two low tides.

NEARBY SITES & ATTRACTIONS

A snowy owl, an infrequent visitor to the lower 48 states, surveys the scene for prey at Dungeness National Wildlife Refuge. Only when its usually abundant food source, the lemming, becomes scarce does the snowy owl migrate out of its traditional northern tundra range. The refuge is located on Dungeness Spit, which projects 5 1/2 miles into the Strait of Juan de Fuca. The Spit forms a quiet bay (bottom) where wildlife lives, feeds and finds protection from the pounding surf. The best time to visit is during the spring and fall migration when thousands of scoters, widgeon, bufflehead, grebes and plovers may be sighted.

① PORT ANGELES

Framed by snowcapped mountains, this small but bustling port is the gateway to Olympic National Park. The Park Headquarters and Visitors' Center houses exhibits on the park and provides information on campgrounds, trails, naturalist programs and weather conditions. The town's busy waterfront is a hub of activity: huge ships load slings of logs for transport, ferries transport visitors to and from the Canadian city of Victoria, British Columbia, and scores of recreational vessels jostle for moorage. The lively city pier features an observation tower, promenade decks and a picnic area. The Arthur D. Feiro Marine Lab, a marine zoo with more than 80 species of sealife, octopi, wolf eels, sea cucumbers and sea slugs, is also on the pier. Located north of the park on Hwy. 101.

② PORT TOWNSEND

Port Townsend was founded in 1851 and soon teemed with the activity of lumber mills, gold-rush fever and pioneers. Today, it is considered one of the best examples of a Victorian seacoast town north of San Francisco. Much of the city has been designated a national historic district; guided side-walk tours in Old Port Townsend capture the spirit of the town's salty past with walks by former opium dens and "parlor houses." Two of the town's gen-teel addresses—handsomely gabled 19th-century homes—are open to summer visitors. The Jefferson County Historic Museum contains a collection of artifacts and photographs of the town's early days. Located northeast of the park; Hwy. 101 to Hwy. 20.

③ FORT WORDEN STATE PARK

A small outpost was erected here in 1855 to protect the settlement of Port Townsend from Indian attack. Abandoned in 1856, the outpost was rebuilt in 1897-

Log rafts in Port Angeles Harbor wait to be loaded onto timber ships bound for the Orient. Since the 1860's, tugboats have piloted logs harvested from the Olympic Peninsula to the pole yard and lumber mill at Port Angeles. Logging and fishing are still mainstay industries for the port—the deepest natural harbor in the northwest.

1910 as part of a defense strategy to guard Puget Sound cities and the important shipyard at Bremerton. The 498-acre estate contains a collection of restored Victorian officers' houses, barracks, parade grounds and elaborate artillery bunkers. The fort was used in the filming of the popular movie, *An Officer and a Gentleman.* One mile north of Port Townsend on Hwy. 20.

4 MAKAH MUSEUM, NEAH BAY

In 1970, a storm eroded some beachfront on the Ozette Reservation, exposing a perfectly preserved 300- to 500-year-old Makah Indian village. The site is now recognized as one of the most significant archeological finds in North America. The Makah Museum in Neah Bay displays the best preserved and most dramatic artifacts excavated from the site, along with changing exhibits. Other attractions include full-scale replicas of a 15th-century long-house and a whaling canoe, prehistoric baskets, clothing, weavings of bird feathers and animal hair, whale and sealing harpoons and intricately carved totem poles. On Hwy. 112.

5 CAPE FLATTERY

From the quiet village of Neah Bay, a half-mile hike along a wooded trail leads to the most northwesterly point on the contiguous United States. Here, at certain times of the year, dozens of bald eagles can be seen gliding and diving for fish. The cape's deserted beaches offer sensational sunsets and magnificent views of the lighthouse on Tatoosh Island, Hole-In-The-Wall, Vancouver Island and the Pacific coastline. Whales may be spotted feeding in the kelp beds from March through May. Off Hwy. 112.

6 DUNGENESS NATIONAL WILDLIFE REFUGE

Each spring and fall, thousands of migratory birds touch down at this wildlife sanctuary, the longest sand spit in the U.S. Dungeness Spit runs 5½ miles

into the Strait of Juan de Fuca, forming a quiet bay and refuge for a large variety of resident shorebirds and waterfowl. Harbor seals and sea lions bask on the tip of the Spit, deer venture into the sanctuary to feed, and the tideflats are home to crabs, clams, oysters and other shellfish. An easy half-mile hiking trail wends its way through upland forest to a bluff overlooking the Spit. The Dungeness Lighthouse, at the tip, is the oldest lighthouse north of the Columbia River. Clam digging is permitted within the refuge, but oysters cannot be harvested by the public. East of Port Angeles on Hwy. 101.

7 CLALLAM BAY/SEKIU

During the summer months, commercial and recreational fishing boats crowd the harbor between these neighboring towns on the Strait of Juan de Fuca. That's because the Strait is a prime fishing ground for salmon and halibut. Boats can be rented in the town or from fishing resorts located along the coast. Many visitors prefer just to soak up the restful beauty of these snug harbor towns, or wander down to the strait-side park with its easy access to the shoreline. On Hwy. 112.

8 FORKS

This century-old town lies at the fork of the Calawah and Bogachiel rivers. Centrally located, the town is a hub for fishing, hunting and camping activities in the Olympic Peninsula's northwest. Professional fishing guides direct visiting fishermen to the area's six top rivers for the winter and summer runs of the steelhead trout and salmon. The city is a frequent starting point for visitors traveling to nearby beaches and the famous Hoh Rain Forest. The region receives more than 100 inches of rain a year and is well known as an excellent mushroom-gathering area. Forks' past as a booming timber center is not forgotten: the town's long history of lumbering is immortalized in the Timber Museum, filled with photographs and logging memorabilia. On Hwy. 101.

Bathed in the glow of sunset, the lighthouse at Fort Worden seems transplanted from a New England coastline. The beacon was built in 1919 to replace the original lighthouse erected on this site in 1879. In the background, across Puget Sound, rises the snowy crest of Mount Baker, at 10,778 feet the third highest peak in Washington's Cascade Range.

DENALI

It is everything Alaskan: majestic with mountains, glaciers and rivers, and incomprehensibly immense.

This is indeed a landscape to inspire the human spirit: mountain after mountain, glacier beyond glacier, tundra rolling into tundra as far as the eye can see, and farther. At six million acres, Denali National Park and Preserve is approximately the size of Massachusetts—nearly three times larger than the largest and most venerated national park in the lower 48 states, Yellowstone.

The park straddles the Alaska Range and includes as its centerpiece the highest mountain in North America, Mount McKinley—more properly called Denali, the native name meaning The High One—crowning the continent at 20,320 feet above sea level. Thousands of mountaineers have tested their mettle on this mountain, and more than 50 have lost their lives to it.

There are other mountains as well, most of them nameless and all of them rugged, cascading from snowy summits to serrated ridges and thence into distant lowlands that have seldom, if ever, felt the tread of human feet.

One can only imagine what such keen observers of nature as the author Henry David

NAME DROPPING

Local legend has it that a turn-of-the-century miner inadvertently named Denali's four-mile-long lake (above) when he exclaimed to his partner, "I wonder how we missed this before!" Originally nicknamed I Wonder Lake, the name has been shortened to Wonder Lake. Moose are sometimes seen here feeding on aquatic plants.

COLORS OF SUMMER

With Healy Ridge as a dramatic backdrop, a hiker soaks up the grandeur of the vast landscape and the vibrant colors of the tundra. Plant growth takes place at a rapid pace under the bounty of the midnight sun.

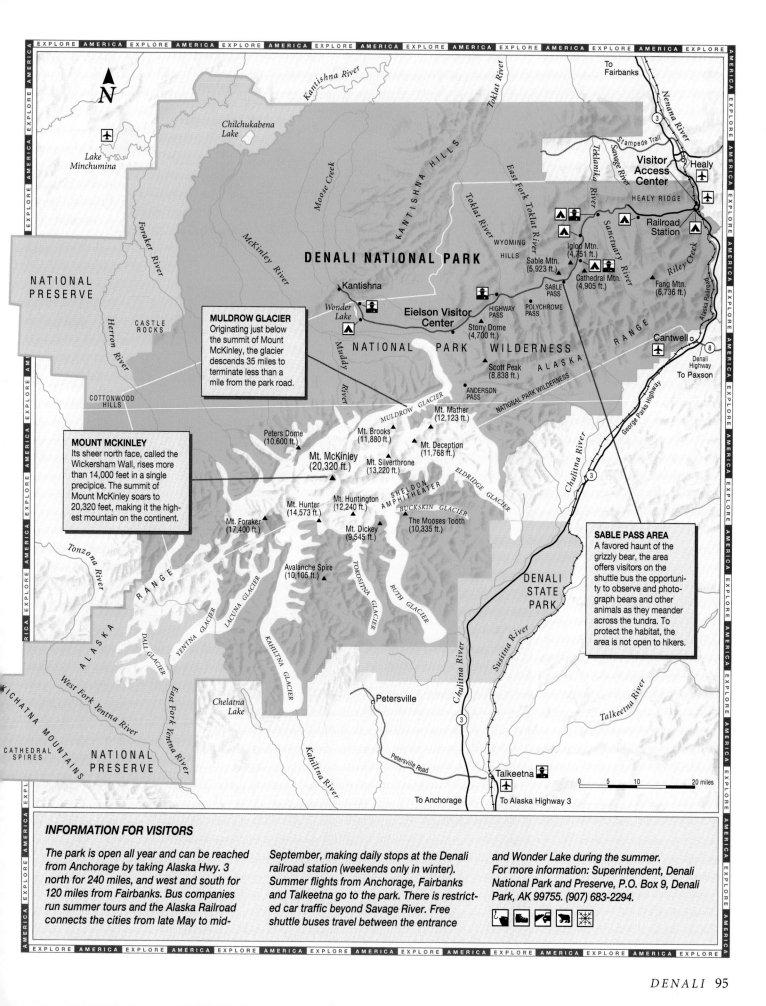

To Fairbanks

Kantishna River

Toklat River

Chilchukabena
Lake

Lake
Minchumina

Moose Creek

KANTISHNA HILLS

East Fork Toklat River

Teklanika River

Savage River

Stampede Trail

**Visitor
Access
Center**

Healy

HEALY RIDGE

McKinley River

Toklat River

WYOMING
HILLS

Igloo Mtn.
(4,751 ft.)

Sanctuary River

**Railroad
Station**

NATIONAL
PRESERVE

Foraker River

CASTLE
ROCKS

DENALI NATIONAL PARK

Sable Mtn.
(5,923 ft.)

Cathedral Mtn.
(4,905 ft.)

Fang Mtn.
(6,736 ft.)

Riley Creek

Kantishna

Wonder
Lake

**Eielson Visitor
Center**

SABLE
PASS

HIGHWAY
PASS

POLYCHROME
PASS

Alaska Railroad

Herron River

MULDROW GLACIER
Originating just below
the summit of Mount
McKinley, the glacier
descends 35 miles to
terminate less than a
mile from the park road.

Stony Dome
(4,700 ft.)

Cantwell

Denali
Highway
To Paxson

COTTONWOOD
HILLS

Muddy River

NATIONAL   PARK   WILDERNESS

ALASKA

RANGE

Scott Peak
(8,838 ft.)

ANDERSON
PASS

NATIONAL PARK WILDERNESS

MULDROW GLACIER

Mt. Mather
(12,123 ft.)

Chulitna River

George Parks Highway

MOUNT McKINLEY
Its sheer north face, called the
Wickersham Wall, rises more
than 14,000 feet in a single
precipice. The summit of
Mount McKinley soars to
20,320 feet, making it the highest mountain on the continent.

Peters Dome
(10,600 ft.)

Mt. Brooks
(11,880 ft.)

Mt. Deception
(11,768 ft.)

Mt. McKinley
(20,320 ft.)

Mt. Silverthrone
(13,220 ft.)

ELDRIDGE GLACIER

SHELDON
AMPHITHEATER

Mt. Hunter
(14,573 ft.)

Mt. Huntington
(12,240 ft.)

BUCKSKIN GLACIER

Mt. Foraker
(17,400 ft.)

Mt. Dickey
(9,545 ft.)

The Mooses Tooth
(10,335 ft.)

SABLE PASS AREA
A favored haunt of the
grizzly bear, the area
offers visitors on the
shuttle bus the opportunity to observe and photo-
graph bears and other
animals as they meander
across the tundra. To
protect the habitat, the
area is not open to hikers.

**DENALI
STATE
PARK**

Tonzona River

RANGE

Avalanche Spire
(10,105 ft.)

TOKOSITNA GLACIER

RUTH GLACIER

ALASKA

YENTNA GLACIER

LACUNA GLACIER

KAHILTNA GLACIER

DALL GLACIER

West Fork Yentna River

East Fork Yentna River

Chelatna
Lake

Susitna River

KICHATNA MOUNTAINS

CATHEDRAL
SPIRES

**NATIONAL
PRESERVE**

Kahiltna River

Petersville

Petersville Road

Talkeetna River

0   5   10   20 miles

To Anchorage

Talkeetna

To Alaska Highway 3

INFORMATION FOR VISITORS

The park is open all year and can be reached
from Anchorage by taking Alaska Hwy. 3
north for 240 miles, and west and south for
120 miles from Fairbanks. Bus companies
run summer tours and the Alaska Railroad
connects the cities from late May to mid-

September, making daily stops at the Denali
railroad station (weekends only in winter).
Summer flights from Anchorage, Fairbanks
and Talkeetna go to the park. There is restrict-
ed car traffic beyond Savage River. Free
shuttle buses travel between the entrance

and Wonder Lake during the summer.
For more information: Superintendent, Denali
National Park and Preserve, P.O. Box 9, Denali
Park, AK 99755. (907) 683-2294.

Denali, far away from big-city lights, is among the best places on earth to view the aurora borealis, or northern lights. The lights appear most frequently near the Arctic Circle, though they have been seen as far south as Florida.

A LANDSCAPE OF SURPRISE

Overleaf: The multihued ridges and valleys in Polychrome Pass create a panoramic view for shuttle-bus passengers. Iron oxide in the rocks is responsible for the striking color. To the south, the 600-mile-long Alaska Range arcs across the state and divides south-central Alaska from the interior.

Thoreau or conservationist John Muir would have written had they experienced this place. Yet another such observer, Charles Sheldon, did experience Denali's wilderness. He roamed the area by foot, snowshoe and with a sled-dog team, summer through winter, from 1906 to 1908. Upon his return to the East he embarked on a campaign to create a national park in the heart of Alaska. Alaska was still a territory then, not a state, and the National Park Service was some 10 years shy of being born. Yet Charles Sheldon had a mission. It was not the landscape in general or the mountains in particular that Sheldon wanted to protect; mountains can take care of themselves. It was the other great hallmark of the area: the wildlife.

There was good reason to be concerned. A 1905 gold rush in Alaska had attracted hordes of miners, and in order to feed them, hunters had begun to kill Dall sheep, moose, caribou and other big game.

Sheldon's efforts bore fruit after nearly 10 years of work, in 1917, when President Woodrow Wilson signed a bill creating the 1.9-million-acre Mount McKinley National Park. With passage of the Alaska National Interest Lands Conservation Act in 1980 (which created seven new national parks in Alaska), Mount McKinley National Park was enlarged and renamed Denali National Park and Preserve.

At first, few visitors came to the park. A small staff of rangers patrolled in winter by snowshoe and sled-dog team, and in summer by foot and pack horse. In 1923 the Alaska Railroad was completed from Anchorage to Fairbanks, joining the park with what would become Alaska's two largest cities, and visitors slowly began to trickle in. Then a single dirt road was built through the park, traversing its mountains, rivers, tundra and spruce forest. Completed in 1937, the road linked the railroad with Wonder Lake and the mining settlement of Kantishna, 90 miles to the west, and the trickle of visitors grew.

They came to experience the "Subarctic Serengeti," as Denali has been called, for nowhere else in North America is there so easily seen such a spectacle of wild, magnificent mammals—Dall sheep, caribou, moose, wolves, grizzlies—moving to the rhythms of spring and autumn, migration and adaptation, predator and prey. Add to them foxes, marmots, pikas, porcupines, snowshoe hares, wolverines and lynx, 37 species of mammals in all—and overhead are more than 150 species of birds. Some of them arrive each summer from shores as distant as Hawaii, Central America and Siberia to raise their young. Others stay the year round, surviving temperatures of -40°F.

Located between 62° and 64° north latitude, Denali is less than 200 miles from the Arctic Circle, twice as close to the North Pole as it is to the Equator. Winters are long, cold and dark; summers short, cool and blessed with light. At summer solstice, the sun rises at four o'clock in the morning and sets at midnight, swinging across the sky and washing the land with pale morning pastels and rich evening ambers.

WILDFLOWERS BRIGHTEN THE TUNDRA It can rain for days on end—weeks, in fact—yet even these times are special. They nourish the constellations of wildflowers that hug the earth in relatively wind-free pockets, brightening the tundra with myriad colors in rosette, mat and button shapes: a splash of yellow arctic poppies here, of red Lapland rosebay there. White mountain avens, blue harebells, pink woolly louseworts, purple mountain saxifrages, all compete for attention at the peak of the blooming period, usually in late June or early July. A good field botanist can take a one-day hike from habitat to habitat—river bar to spruce forest, wet tundra to alpine ridge—and find more than 100 species of flowering plants.

Perhaps a golden eagle will sail by; more than 50 pairs have been counted nesting in and around the park. Or perhaps a gyrfalcon will slice the sky and plummet earthbound after a ptarmigan or arctic ground squirrel. From almost any ridgetop in the park, a large, braided river may be seen sparkling in the sunlight more than 1,000 feet below. The Savage, Sanctuary, Teklanika and Toklat Rivers all flow from the Alaska Range northward, where they eventually join the mighty Yukon River and turn west for the Bering Sea.

Lying down to absorb the sun's warmth on an alpine ridge, a hiker could very well drift asleep, and awake later to the sound of hooves clicking on the rocky terrain nearby. A band of rams might be only 20 feet away, their golden eyes framed by handsome, curling horns, studying everything

around them, always watchful for their chief predator, the wolf. A human visitor, especially one who remains quiet and keeps a respectful distance, does not concern them, and as unexpectedly as the rams arrive, they leave, grazing across the ridge.

Every day of the summer offers new possibilities in Denali. Someone might encounter a band of Dall sheep, someone else a small herd of caribou or—to really get the heart pumping—a grizzly bear. Even from afar, a grizzly cannot fail to make an impact on a visitor's sensibilities. It's not only the bear itself, but what it implies—wilderness in all directions—that makes Denali a great park.

Many of the 200 to 300 grizzlies that live here belong to a blond race called Toklat, unique to the park. So rich and light are their coats that they appear at times to glow. Their flaxen fur seems to change from one golden tone to another as they patrol the tundra, feeding on roots and berries, digging for ground squirrels, sniffing the air with noses held high. Though the grizzlies are primarily vegetarians, they sometimes give chase to caribou, moose and Dall sheep. Each May and June the bears prey upon a significant number of newborn caribou and moose.

KEEPING
TRACK OF THE
WILD

Wildlife research is a hallmark of Denali, which was designated in 1982 an International Biosphere Reserve by the United Nations. Studies originally began in 1939 when biologist Adolph Murie spent three years observing wolves in the park, and concluded—in an era of predator control when wolves were being systematically shot in U.S. parks—that by culling out the weak, old and infirm members of the species on which they prey, wolves actually strengthen those species and the ecosystems in which they live.

It is a lucky visitor in Denali who sees a wolf, though in some years sightings are quite commonplace along the road that threads through the

WEATHERING THE STORM
The hardy willow ptarmigan, perched nonchalantly atop a spruce tree during a snowstorm, is one of the few birds that live in the park year-round.

A CARIBOU CARAVAN
A herd of caribou rambles across the autumn landscape to its winter home in the northwestern area of the park and preserve. Unlike other members of the deer family, both sexes of these northern reindeer grow antlers. Delicate-looking but hardy alpine flowers such as the harebells, crowberries and cranberries seen at right flourish in this seemingly harsh environment.

THE HIGH ONE
Dwarfed by the great bulk of Mount McKinley (opposite page), one of the park's yellow shuttle buses wends its way to Wonder Lake. The park road begins in stunted spruce forest called taiga, a Russian word meaning land of little sticks, and gradually climbs to treeless tundra. The buses stop just about anywhere along the 85-mile route to allow passengers to view wildlife and to get off or on.

park. Eleven packs of wolves live mostly within the park, and another half dozen packs move regularly back and forth across the park's boundaries. Each wolf pack has an average territory of approximately 385 square miles.

Depending on the abundance of prey—caribou, moose, Dall sheep, and to a lesser degree squirrels, beavers, snowshoe hares, marmots and salmon—the numbers and pack size of the wolves change, rising to as many as 30 wolves per pack, and falling to fewer than 10. Fluctuations of this kind are the rule, not the exception, for many species of large mammals in the far north. The Denali caribou herd, for example, which numbered an estimated 20,000 in the mid-1900's, dropped to 1,000 in the 1970's before beginning to climb again in the late 1980's to 3,000. Experts may wonder why and propose their theories, but none of the evidence is conclusive. Alaska's native people seem to accept that the mysteries of nature may always remain hidden. "No one knows the ways of the wind or the caribou," they say.

With completion of the George Parks Highway in 1972, paralleling the railroad between Anchorage and Fairbanks, park visits doubled from 44,000 to 88,000 in one year. Park managers soon faced the pivotal question: At what point does increased tourism threaten the integrity of a park? People, roads, lodges, restaurants and curio shops already were making an impact on other national parks.

Alaska offered a chance to do things differently. Thus, in 1972 a shuttle bus system was inaugurated in Denali, and private vehicles were banned from the 85-mile-long park road (except under very limited circumstances).

The shuttle buses serve a twofold purpose: by reducing traffic on the road they minimize the risk of accidents and maximize the opportunities for visitors to view wildlife that might otherwise be displaced by heavier traffic. Visitors sit alertly in their seats, scanning the landscape for animals. "Bear!" someone might shout to the driver. The bus stops and, from the safety of the vehicle, a whole group of excited passengers can admire the grizzly (the park's reclusive black bears are virtually never seen) as the great beast moves over the tundra, crosses the road, and walks by only 10 feet away.

In 1992, the 75th anniversary of Mount McKinley National Park, Denali's shuttle and tour buses ran full almost every day from late May to mid-September. It is to be hoped that those who shape the future will heed the words of pioneering biologist Adolph Murie, who spent 25 summers in Denali. "The national park idea represents a far-reaching cultural achievement," he wrote, "for here we raise our thoughts above the average, and enter a sphere in which the intangible values of the human heart and spirit take precedence....Our task is to perpetuate this freedom and purity of nature, this ebb and flow of life."

NEARBY SITES & ATTRACTIONS

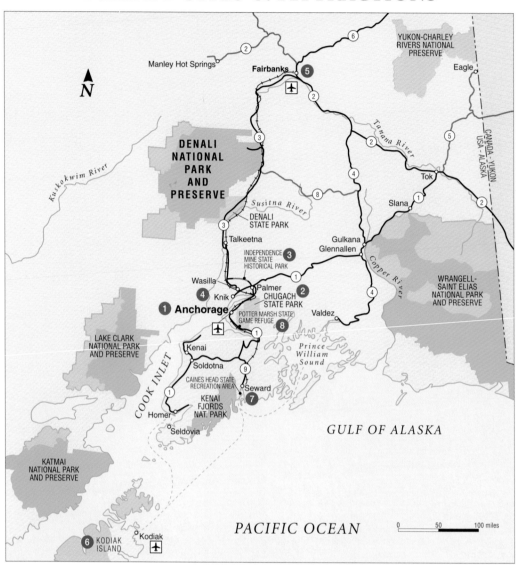

Glass-domed cars, hooked onto the Alaska Railroad's Fairbanks-Denali-Anchorage train, convert it into The Midnight Sun Express or The McKinley Explorer. During the summer months, passengers are entertained with a 20-hour view of the Alaskan landscape.

❶ ANCHORAGE

Home to more than half the state's population, Anchorage is Alaska's largest cultural and recreational center. Exhibits on local history and native tradition are presented at the National Bank of Alaska Heritage Library and Museum and the Museum of History and Art. Nature lovers can visit the Alaska Zoo and the city's two wildlife museums. In March, city streets become trails for the start of the world's premier sled-dog event, the grueling Iditarod Race from Anchorage to Nome.

❷ CHUGACH STATE PARK

This rugged 495,000-acre state park is just 10 minutes by car from Anchorage. Open all year, the park's vast network of trails is a haven for hikers, climbers and cross-country skiers, and the spring run of fish in the park's southern section draws scores of anglers. Pink, king, chum and silver salmon are found in the park. Sport fishing licenses are required. Alpine ranges provide a dramatic backdrop for viewing the park's mammals, songbirds and wildflowers. Five access roads from Anchorage lead to the park.

❸ INDEPENDENCE MINE STATE HISTORICAL PARK

During the 1930's, Independence Mine was one of Alaska's richest gold mines. Today, its few restored buildings provide visitors with a look at a gold mining operation. The visitor's center is located in the mine manager's house. Mining buffs can view a mineral display and peer down a mine tunnel. The park is also a year-round recreation center. Walking trails wind between the buildings; in winter, they convert to cross-country trails. Nearby Hatcher Pass Lodge, at 5,000 feet, offers excellent views of the Talkeetna Mountains and the Chugach Range. The park is on Fishhook Road, 22 miles northeast of Wasilla.

Cameras and binoculars at the ready, a group of bird watchers enjoy the wildlife at Potter Marsh State Game Refuge. Spring is the best time to visit, when migrating birds make the refuge their temporary home.

4 MUSHERS' HALL OF FAME, KNIK

Legends of yesteryear were born when intrepid dog mushers and their faithful huskies braved the northern wilderness to transport mail and supplies. The Knik Museum honors these men and dogs. Nearby, on Knik Road, is the Iditarod Race Headquarters and Museum with memorabilia and videos of the world's most demanding sled-dog race, the annual 1,049-mile Iditarod Race from Anchorage to Nome. The Knik Museum is located on the Knik-Goose Bay Road; the Iditarod Museum is located just south of Wasilla on the Knik Road.

5 FAIRBANKS

Gold! The frontier spirit is still alive here in Alaska's second-largest city. Visitors can step back into the wild and woolly past at Alaskaland, the high-kicking replica of a turn-of-the-century gold-rush town. An authentic sternwheeler cruises down the Chena and Tanana Rivers, past deserted cabins and the intriguing Indian fish wheels, which scoop salmon from the rivers as they turn. Fairbanks is also home to the University of Alaska Museum and the Dog Mushing Museum and serves as the gateway to Alaska's wilderness. Air taxis shuttle visitors into the "bush" to visit outlying native communities, or into wilder and more remote areas for fishing, river trips, or back-country camping. Each July, native people from Alaska, Canada, and the Commonwealth of Independent States (the former U.S.S.R.) gather for the World Eskimo-Indian Olympics, which features traditional games of strength and endurance such as the knuckle hop and the blanket toss.

6 KODIAK ISLAND

With traces of the 8,000-year-old Koniag and Aleut cultures still present, this island qualifies as one of the oldest and most historic regions in Alaska. In 1784, the first Russian settlement was established at Three Saints Bay, spelling disaster for the native Koniag population, many of whom were killed or taken hostage. The settlement soon relocated to Kodiak. The town's Baranov Museum, housed in an original Russian American Company fur warehouse,

has displays on the Koniag and Aleut cultures, as well as on Russian and later settlers. Even though the island is only 600 miles from the Arctic Circle, a moist, mild marine environment encourages lush summer greenery. Jagged peaks and a convoluted coastline of fjords and bays were sculpted during the last ice age. The island's rugged interior has not yet been explored. Kodiak is served by daily flights from Anchorage and by ferry from Seward and Homer.

7 CAINES HEAD STATE RECREATION AREA

Whether arriving on foot or by boat, visitors must time their trips around the tides to visit this 6,000-acre site, which includes an abandoned World War II fort. The construction of the South Beach Garrison was one of the most expensive and hazardous defense projects of the war. Soon after completion, in April 1944, the fort was ordered abandoned. A coastal hiking trail follows the shale beaches to Resurrection Bay, strategic spot for defending the Port of Seward from possible Japanese attack. Visitors can prowl underground passages and rooms of the former command center at Fort McGilvray, perched on a 650-foot cliff. The site is within walking distance of Seward.

8 POTTER MARSH STATE GAME REFUGE

Pintail ducks, teal, whistling swans, bald eagles, Canada geese and terns are among the 130 species of birds that touch down in the Potter Marsh State Game Refuge. A 1,550-foot-long boardwalk skirts the marsh and allows visitors to get a close-up view of the four distinct habitats located within the 2,300-acre reserve. Interpretive displays along the boardwalk provide information about the refuge's wildlife and plants. Located 10 miles southeast of downtown Anchorage.

The skyline of Anchorage is outlined against the Chugach Mountain Range. This city is as far north as Helsinki, Finland, and as far west as Honolulu, Hawaii.

During the winter, cross-country ski trails zigzag between the abandoned buildings of Independence Mine. The state historical park is popular with both summer and winter visitors.

HAWAII VOLCANOES

---

*This is a haunting landscape
where life manages to endure in the
face of destruction.*

Visiting Kilauea, the fiery heart of Hawaii
Volcanoes National Park, is like having a
grandstand seat at Creation. It is the world's
largest active volcano and the world's only drive-
up volcano. Motorists can pull right up to the
edge of the immense crater and peer into what
looks like the gaping, smoldering pit of hell. Or
they may watch an eruption spew spectacular
fountains of fire while buttering their breakfast
toast at Volcano House, the lodge on the very lip
of Kilauea's huge crater.

Kilauea is on the island of Hawaii, called the
Big Island because it is twice as large as all the
other Hawaiian islands combined. And the Big
Island grows bigger still, thanks to the action of
Kilauea and the tons of fresh lava that continue to
add flesh to this amazing chunk of real estate in
the middle of the Pacific.

The park encompasses the summit crater of
Kilauea, sections of the Kalapana coast downslope of the volcano, as well as the summit and
upper part of another active volcano, Mauna Loa.

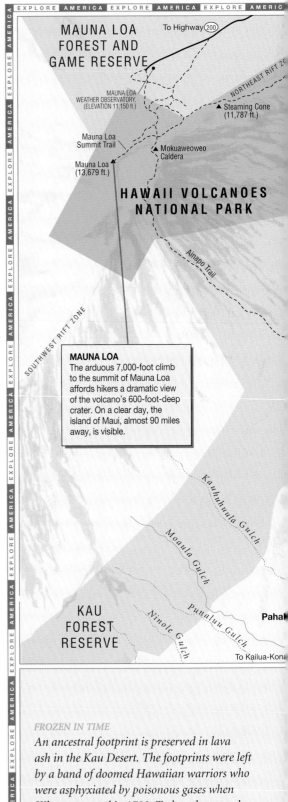

MAUNA LOA
FOREST AND
GAME RESERVE

To Highway (200)

MAUNA LOA
WEATHER OBSERVATORY,
(ELEVATION 11,150 ft.)

NORTHEAST RIFT ZO

▲ Steaming Cone
(11,787 ft.)

Mauna Loa
Summit Trail

Mokuaweoweo
Caldera

Mauna Loa
(13,679 ft.)

HAWAII VOLCANOES
NATIONAL PARK

SOUTHWEST RIFT ZONE

Ainapo Trail

MAUNA LOA
The arduous 7,000-foot climb
to the summit of Mauna Loa
affords hikers a dramatic view
of the volcano's 600-foot-deep
crater. On a clear day, the
island of Maui, almost 90 miles
away, is visible.

Kauhuhula Gulch

Moaula Gulch

Punaluu Gulch

KAU
FOREST
RESERVE

Ninole Gulch

Paha

To Kailua-Kona

CAPRICIOUS LAVA FLOW

A steaming blanket of dark lava from Kilauea creeps across devastated Chain of Craters Road. The lava covered an eight-mile stretch of road between the national park and Kalapana on Hawaii's east coast. There are no plans to reestablish a new road until the eruptions stop. Kilauea is one of the most active volcanoes in the world.

RIVERS OF FIRE

Overleaf: Against the night sky, fiery lava fountains illuminate the shoulder of Kilauea Volcano. The escaping lava forms black rivers of semi-liquefied rock that flow downslope to the ocean. At the shore, great plumes of steam burst forth where the lava stream is quenched by the sea. Hawaii's famous coal black beaches, acres of pulverized volcanic lava, are formed when lava explodes into pieces as it enters the sea.

The Hawaiian Islands are actually the tops of a vast range of undersea volcanic mountains that stretch across 1,500 miles of the Pacific Ocean. According to the geological "hot spot" theory, the islands were formed at a single spot, then drifted away to the northwest by the slow movement of the Pacific plate. Molten rock bubbling up from the center of the earth at a hot spot in the submarine crust formed a colossal volcano that spewed forth lava in great pillows and mounds, patiently building the foundation of island after island over thousands of years.

Finally—hissing and steaming—a mountain would rear its fierce head above the waves and continue its long climb skyward. These mid-ocean mounts are so high that two of them, Mauna Loa and Mauna Kea, measured from their bases on the floor of the ocean, rise more than 30,000 feet. That makes them the tallest mountains on the planet.

The process of creation is never finished. Off the coast of the Big Island, in a fire so intense that an ocean cannot quench it, a new island—Loihi—is being born. Scientists estimate it will be tall enough to break the ocean's surface in about 10,000 years.

The drama that occurs when fire meets water was center stage for visitors to the park from 1986 until 1991. Flows of lava, pouring down Kilauea in rivers of fire, surged over the cliffs and seethed into the surf in towering clouds of steam. The awesome, primitive spectacle was just a five-minute walk from the road.

The new land that comes from a volcano starts out sterile and lifeless. Algae and lichen are the first forms of life to take root, followed by ferns. Eons ago, seeds and spores of plants were carried by

FROZEN IN TIME

An ancestral footprint is preserved in lava ash in the Kau Desert. The footprints were left by a band of doomed Hawaiian warriors who were asphyxiated by poisonous gases when Kilauea erupted in 1790. Today, they may be safely viewed along Footprints Trail, a 1.6-mile trek that leads visitors through an eerie but intriguing landscape.

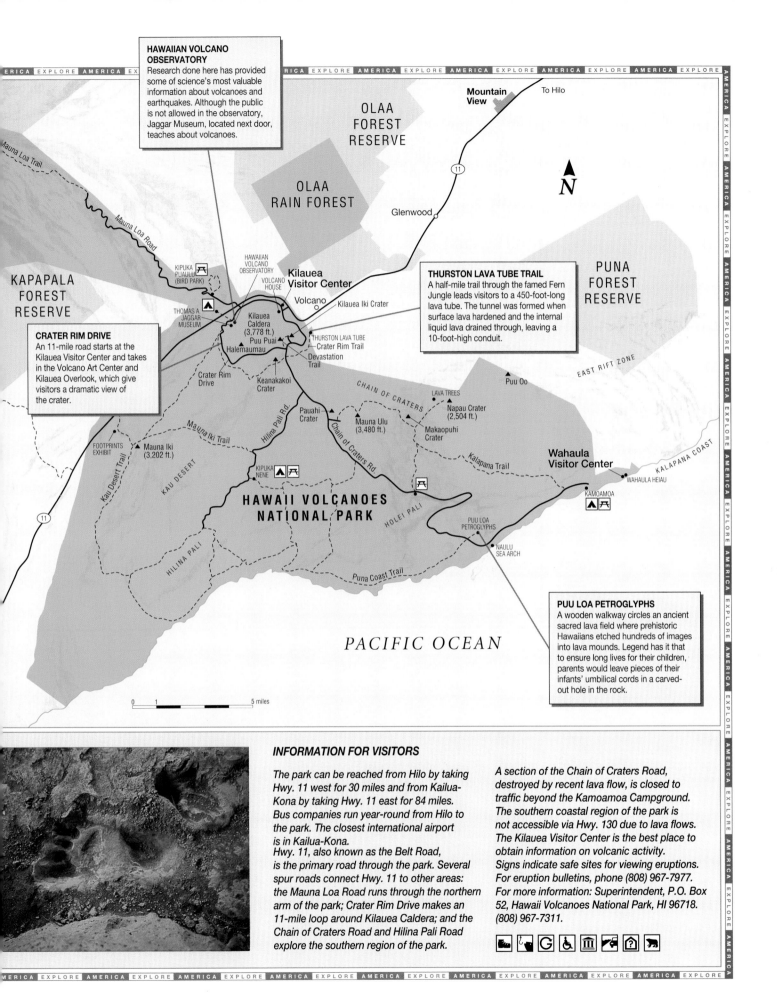

HAWAIIAN VOLCANO OBSERVATORY
Research done here has provided some of science's most valuable information about volcanoes and earthquakes. Although the public is not allowed in the observatory, Jaggar Museum, located next door, teaches about volcanoes.

OLAA FOREST RESERVE

OLAA RAIN FOREST

Mountain View

To Hilo

11

Glenwood

Mauna Loa Trail

Mauna Loa Road

KAPAPALA FOREST RESERVE

HAWAIIAN VOLCANO OBSERVATORY

VOLCANO HOUSE

KIPUKA PUAULU (BIRD PARK)

Kilauea Visitor Center

Volcano

Kilauea Iki Crater

PUNA FOREST RESERVE

THOMAS A. JAGGAR MUSEUM

Kilauea Caldera (3,778 ft.)

Puu Puai

Halemaumau

THURSTON LAVA TUBE

Crater Rim Trail

Devastation Trail

THURSTON LAVA TUBE TRAIL
A half-mile trail through the famed Fern Jungle leads visitors to a 450-foot-long lava tube. The tunnel was formed when surface lava hardened and the internal liquid lava drained through, leaving a 10-foot-high conduit.

CRATER RIM DRIVE
An 11-mile road starts at the Kilauea Visitor Center and takes in the Volcano Art Center and Kilauea Overlook, which give visitors a dramatic view of the crater.

Crater Rim Drive

Keanakakoi Crater

CHAIN OF CRATERS

LAVA TREES

Puu Oo

EAST RIFT ZONE

Pauahi Crater

Mauna Ulu (3,480 ft.)

Napau Crater (2,504 ft.)

Makaopuhi Crater

Hilina Pali Rd.

Chain of Craters Rd.

Mauna Iki Trail

FOOTPRINTS EXHIBIT

Mauna Iki (3,202 ft.)

Kalapana Trail

Wahaula Visitor Center

KALAPANA COAST

WAHAULA HEIAU

Kau Desert Trail

KIPUKA NENE

KAU DESERT

HAWAII VOLCANOES NATIONAL PARK

KAMOAMOA

HILINA PALI

HOLEI PALI

PUU LOA PETROGLYPHS

NAULU SEA ARCH

Puna Coast Trail

11

PUU LOA PETROGLYPHS
A wooden walkway circles an ancient sacred lava field where prehistoric Hawaiians etched hundreds of images into lava mounds. Legend has it that to ensure long lives for their children, parents would leave pieces of their infants' umbilical cords in a carved-out hole in the rock.

PACIFIC OCEAN

0   1   5 miles

INFORMATION FOR VISITORS

The park can be reached from Hilo by taking Hwy. 11 west for 30 miles and from Kailua-Kona by taking Hwy. 11 east for 84 miles. Bus companies run year-round from Hilo to the park. The closest international airport is in Kailua-Kona.
Hwy. 11, also known as the Belt Road, is the primary road through the park. Several spur roads connect Hwy. 11 to other areas: the Mauna Loa Road runs through the northern arm of the park; Crater Rim Drive makes an 11-mile loop around Kilauea Caldera; and the Chain of Craters Road and Hilina Pali Road explore the southern region of the park.

A section of the Chain of Craters Road, destroyed by recent lava flow, is closed to traffic beyond the Kamoamoa Campground. The southern coastal region of the park is not accessible via Hwy. 130 due to lava flows. The Kilauea Visitor Center is the best place to obtain information on volcanic activity. Signs indicate safe sites for viewing eruptions. For eruption bulletins, phone (808) 967-7977. For more information: Superintendent, P.O. Box 52, Hawaii Volcanoes National Park, HI 96718. (808) 967-7311.

HOUSE OF FERNS
Hardy amau ferns flourish in the rocky soil on the rim of Halemaumau Crater, Kilauea's main vent. The crater is the legendary home of Pele, Hawaiian goddess of volcanic fires. A lookout on the crater's southeast edge provides a view of the firepit's steaming walls and sulfurous fumaroles.

MOON WALK
A half-mile boardwalk crosses one of the world's most unusual landscapes, an area devastated by the eruption of Kilauea Iki in 1959. Amazingly, plantlife has returned, sending tenacious roots into cracks in the hardened lava. In the background looms Puu Puai, the cinder cone of ash and pumice formed when the volcano blew fountains of lava as high as 1,900 feet.

106

winds, ocean currents and as gifts of migratory birds. They took root at the rate of one new species every 40,000 years. In utter isolation, 2,400 miles from the nearest continent, these early botanical colonizers developed into a unique flora and fauna. Ninety percent of Hawaii's 1,700 native plants are found nowhere else in the world. Residing among the exceptional trees and plants is a beautiful and diverse bird population that evolved from the first winged creatures to find themselves upon the shores. With civilization's intrusion, many of the endemic birds, plants, insects, spiders and snails are now either extinct or endangered. The upland forests of the park offer some protection, and have become the last stand for various embattled species.

PRISTINE POCKETS OF GREEN

Dotting the harsh volcanic landscape are pockets of pristine wilderness, some of them quite large, spared by the volcano and left isolated, surrounded by hardened lava. Called kipuka, such naturally protected areas are ideal habitats for Hawaii's rare birds and vegetation. A hiking trail into the hilly 100-acre Kipuka Puaulu winds upward into a dryland forest through stands of trees—tall ohia and magnificent koa, once the king of the Hawaiian forest. There are occasional benches along the trail so that hikers can pause and be serenaded by a symphony unique to Hawaii—the cheerful notes of the apapane, the little red bird that drinks nectar from the scarlet ohia lehua blossom, the warbling of the iiwi and the police whistle of the omao. At Kipuka Nene, the waddling nene, probably the descendant of some off-course Canada goose, has made a home. The bird has been rescued from the brink of extinction by recent conservation efforts.

Throughout the park, plants that are marvels become commonplace: the hapuu, or tree fern, grows twice as tall as a man, arching overhead in a delicate green canopy; brave amau ferns seem to spring from the lava itself, nesting into the tiniest cracks; and the ohia lehua, rooted in a speck of soil in the midst of the lava desert, bursts into fiery red blossoms as if in memory of the lava that once devoured the land. There are even small, delicate wild orchids and white anemones springing up along walking paths.

The landscape speaks to the spirit about such things as patience, endurance, triumph over adversity, solitude, opportunity and simple hope. But while volcanic eruptions are definitely dramatic, they are only a part of what Hawaii Volcanoes National Park is all about.

Visitors usually arrive wanting to see red-hot lava. But park rangers hope visitors will absorb other marvels as well—the culture, the native plants, and the wildlife that exist no place else on the planet. They would like visitors to walk the park, and this unusual place has some of the most unusual walks in the world. The Kilauea Iki Trail descends into a crater that as recently as 1959 was a lava lake. The ground, in some places, is still warm underfoot from the fires smoldering below. Steam ghosts up through fissures.

The 15-minute walk through Thurston Lava Tube Trail invites the curious to stroll into a tun-

nel that once ran red with magma pumped by Kilauea from the bowels of the earth. Lava tubes, or channels, form when the surface flow cools and the hot interior lava drains away.

Along the Mauna Iki (Footprints) Trail—an easy, paved path in the Kau Desert—are ashen footprints preserved in lava, left behind by the army of Chief Keoua, as it marched in 1790 to do battle with Kamehameha, a rival chief intent on conquest. Kilauea erupted while the soldiers were en route and they perished, leaving behind only footprints made as the men fled over the hot lava. Kamehameha, with this dramatic help from the volcano, triumphed in his wars and succeeded in uniting the Hawaiian Islands into one kingdom.

A boardwalk stretches the length of Devastation Trail across ebony cinders in a landscape completely scorched by the volcano. Among the spatter cones—miniature volcanoes on the lava flow—and white skeletal remains of trees, new life

FIERY FLOOD
Fast-moving lava flows downslope through a stand of ohia trees in the Kalapana section of the park. Eventually the lava will cool and harden, and new ohia seeds, arriving on the wind, will anchor their roots in the cinder field.

The top branches of coastal vegetation make a lofty perch for a noddy tern. Male birds display elaborate nodding gestures to ward off predators. The noddy tern's sooty-colored feathers protect it from the harmful rays of the sun.

is already asserting itself in brave tufts of tawny grass and native wildflowers in colors from scarlet to palest lavender.

One of the strangest vistas in the park is afforded by the trail that skirts the Keanakakoi Crater. The trail begins in the forest, knifes across a hardened lava flow and ends at the crater's lip. Along the way are tree molds, formed when a fast-moving lava flow rushes through a forest. The lava engulfs trees and hardens around them while the trees burn in the center. What's left are stands of eerie black lava sculptures, leafless and lifeless in an onyx desert.

Evidence of volcanic activity is visible from Crater Rim Drive, which circles the edge of the main summit caldera and Kilauea Iki Crater. The Hilina Pali Road offers panoramic vistas of miles of black lava cliffs and the turquoise Pacific below. The Chain of Craters Road descends the slopes of Kilauea to the shoreline section of the park and dead-ends at the latest lava flow.

On its most recent rampage, Kilauea destroyed not only the park's Wahaula Visitor Center and more than 200 homes in and around the town of Kalapana, but also the famous Black Sand Beach at Kaimu. Fortunately the flow was slow, allowing ample time for evacuation. As if in compensation for Kaimu, the capricious volcano has created a beautiful new crescent-shaped black sand beach at Kamoamoa.

FOLLOWING THE STAR MAPS

The first people to encounter this awesome volcanic landscape were Polynesian explorers who followed their star maps, probably sailing northward from the Marquesas Islands in huge voyaging canoes around A.D. 400. The volcanoes must have been erupting at the time, for the voyagers called the new land "Hawaii Ia," Burning Hawaii. Certain that only a divinity could command such powerful forces, they attributed the fires to the work of a tempestuous goddess they called Pele, the keeper of fires and volcanoes. Pele's home was the Halemaumau Pit of Kilauea. She is said to dwell there to this day.

Before every major eruption, people claim to see her, a lovely young lady in red with hair the color of flame, or a ghostly old woman out walking her white dog. At the edge of Halemaumau, in the midst of the sulfuric steam, visitors walking the trail will encounter offerings of flowers or rocks wrapped in shiny green leaves placed there for Pele. Hula dancers come and chant her name as they dance at her portals. Anyone picking ohelo berries, the cranberry-like fruit that grows at the volcano, always throws the first handful into the pit, for the berries, like the scarlet blossoms of the ohia tree,

are sacred to the goddess. A more recent myth maintains that the goddess can be pacified by a bottle of gin. That, too, gets tossed into the crater.

Though there are all kinds of theories about what might appease or even frighten Pele, in the end she always does as she pleases. When she consumed the Wahaula Visitor Center in 1989, she spared an ancient temple of human sacrifice nearby. The lava flows that had stopped at nothing rolled right up to the walls of the temple, parted and went respectfully around it. It can be seen now, an incongruous oasis of stone and trees in a sea of hardened black lava.

Even the national park service pays attention to Pele. In impressive murals at the Thomas A. Jaggar Museum, Hawaiian artist and historian Herb Kawainui Kane has depicted the goddess and her work. She resides with honor, and perhaps amusement, amidst the seismographs, the million-dollar computer, and the battery of high-tech monitoring equipment designed to take her pulse and predict what she will do next. Continuously running videos document her past escapades, her

tantrums and fireworks, her monumental deeds of destruction and creation.

The equipment is linked to the Hawaiian Volcano Observatory next door, where scientists evaluate every tremor. Visitors are almost assured of being able to watch an earthquake as it is actually occurring—in this volatile environment, minor quakes are recorded every day. The innovative museum, designed to be a journey of discovery and imagination, will make an amateur volcanologist out of anyone with even a trace of curiosity.

The information hub for park users is the Kilauea Visitor Center. There is a small museum here, and a theater that features regularly scheduled screenings of a volcano film. Rangers offer advice on the constantly changing conditions in the park, conduct guided hikes and nature walks, and stage special programs and lectures. Because actually seeing a volcanic eruption is the experience of a lifetime, rangers try to make any current outbreaks of lava accessible to the public and, if possible, will conduct walks to the site. There have been times when it

was possible to walk close enough to a sluggishly moving lava flow to poke a stick in it and watch the stick instantly ignite in the 2,000°F lava.

It is a strange world, this volcanic landscape. It has a magnetic and unforgettable effect on all who walk its glistening ebony lava, smell the sulfur from the middle of the earth, touch a scarlet ohia blossom, listen to bird song heard only here and see, if favored, the greatest fireworks show on earth.

TIMEWORN COASTLINE
Waves crash against 60-foot cliffs in the park's coastal section. Countless rivers of lava that stopped and were cooled by the sea formed these towering black headlands. The tireless erosive forces of the waves beat away at the raw volcanic rock, carving and recarving the ancient coastline. The dazzling red pompon blossoms of an ohia lehua tree (left) signal birds and insects to feed on their rich nectar. The ohia is the most common tree in Hawaii, comprising a multitude of hybrids that adapt to the habitat: in Hawaii's humid rain forest the ohia stands as a lofty tree, but in the desert it resembles a stunted shrub.

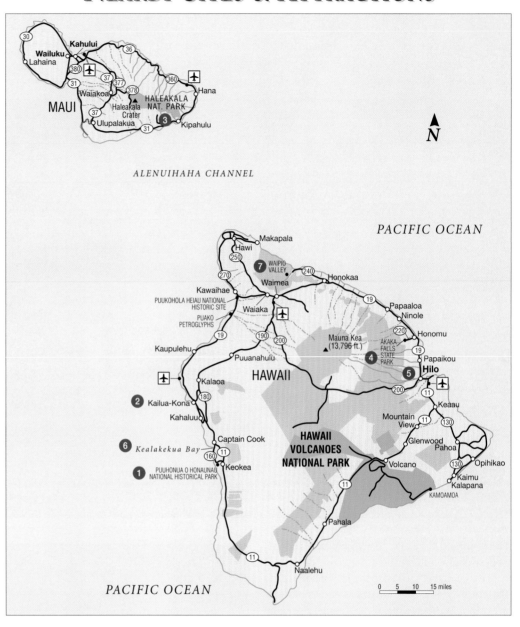

A grimacing sentinel guards Hale-o-Keawe Heiau, the main temple in Puuhonua O Honaunau National Historical Park. These fearsome statues of ancient gods warned people against intruding on the sacred ground. After painstaking research, local crafts-men carved these reproductions from enormous ohia logs.

1 PUUHONUA O HONAUNAU NATIONAL HISTORICAL PARK

From the 16th century onwards, "puuhonua" has meant a place of refuge—an asylum where wrongdoers, vanquished warriors, and those who had broken Hawaii's sacred laws were offered a second chance. Hawaiians believed that the gods reacted violently to the breaking of taboos by unleashing tidal waves, volcanic eruptions, and earthquakes. This sanctuary operated until 1819, holding ceremonies of absolution and protecting the sacred remains of 23 Hawaiian chiefs. The site is the last one of its kind—180 acres of faithfully preserved and restored prehistoric houses and temples, royal fishponds, and palace grounds—set in a lush landscape of plants and coconut groves. Located on the western side of the island on Hwy. 160.

2 HULIHEE PALACE, KAILUA-KONA

This mansion is more suggestive of the English countryside than of the Hawaiian coast. Built in 1837-38 as a summer home by Hawaii's first governor, it is a testament to the elegant tastes of 19th-century Hawaiian royalty. The two-story Victorian manor is now a museum filled with massive furniture elaborately carved from native koa wood, and oil portraits of Hawaiian monarchs. A modest native "pili" grass house stands in the garden. On the North Kona Coast on Alii Drive, off Hwy. 11.

3 HALEAKALA NATIONAL PARK, MAUI

The park's most popular venue is Mount Haleakala— a gigantic, dormant volcano. Its immense crater is 2,720 feet deep and 19 square miles in area. The

Hulihee Palace, a gracious two-story mansion, served as a summer residence for Hawaiian rulers until 1916. The palace is surrounded by a well-tended garden of native Hawaiian foliage.

park's 29,000 acres span from the summit of Haleakala Crater down the volcano's southeast flank to the rugged Kipahulu coast. In an effort to protect the park's fragile ecosystems, the Kiopahulu Valley is closed to the public. Coastal trails wind through lush green forests of ginger, kukui and mango. Hwys. 37, 377 and 378 lead to Haleakala Crater; Hwys. 36 and 360 lead to the Kipahulu coastal section of the park.

4 AKAKA FALLS STATE PARK

Akaka Falls is the centerpiece of this 66-acre arboretum. A circular paved walkway leads to the falls, which plunge 420 feet in a single drop. The walk takes about an hour to complete and passes through vegetation typical of a Hawaiian valley—giant ferns and groves of magnificent torch ginger, bamboo, bird-of-paradise, heliconia, bougainvillea and orchids. Wooden footbridges lead over gurgling streams, and benches along the walkway allow visitors to stop and admire the deep greenery. Located off Hwy. 19, 3½ miles from Honomu.

5 HILO

Situated on a deepwater bay, Hilo is the Big Island's capital city and one of its oldest settlements. An annual rainfall of 133 inches and rich volcanic soil make the region a botanical paradise. Hilo is particularly noted for its flower farms—acres of orchids and anthuriums, including the 30-acre authentic Japanese Liliuokalani Gardens. The Lyman House Memorial Museum, a restored 1839 missionary's house, features a fine collection of period pieces, and is the oldest frame building on the island of Hawaii. An adjoining museum exhibits native Hawaiian arts and crafts as well as mineral and rock displays. Located on the eastern side of the island on Hwys. 200, 11, 19.

6 KEALAKEKUA BAY

Hawaii's dry, sunny western side is the setting for one of its most historic sites on the island. Hikiau Heiau, a well-preserved ancient temple dedicated

to the god Lono, looks out over the beautiful azure bay, into which native Hawaiians believed that Lono would descend from the heavens. Captain James Cook sailed into the bay in 1778. Although relations between the Europeans and the native population were successful at first, Cook was murdered there early in 1779 after a series of misunderstandings and mounting hostilities. A 27-foot marble obelisk commemorates Captain Cook and a plaque marks the spot where Cook met his death. The bay itself has been designated a Marine Conservation District and its underwater park is renowned for its snorkeling and scuba diving. Located on the western side of the island off Hwy. 11.

7 WAIPIO VALLEY

This wild jungle valley with sheer cliffs was once the home of Hawaii's rulers. An overlook affords a grand view of the mile-wide valley, which is rimmed at the sea by a black sand beach. The lush green vegetation that drapes the valley and its many waterfalls and streams give the area its Eden-like reputation. A thriving farming community grew a wide variety of crops on the terraced slopes until the settlement was washed away in 1946 in a tsunami. Lemons, limes, breadfruit, grapefruit, avocados and coffee still grow wild on the overgrown garden terraces. The road down the valley is very steep and treacherous; most visitors opt to descend in a four-wheel-drive shuttle van. Located on the northeast Hamakua Coast on Hwy. 240, off Hwy. 19.

Pink and gray cinder cones stud the floor of Haleakala Crater. The great water-carved basin of Haleakala National Park is large enough to swallow Manhattan. According to legend, the volcano was made by the demigod Maui who snared the sun and held it captive in an attempt to provide his people with more daylight hours.

Framed by a lush tangle of unspoiled tropical growth, Akaka Falls tumble 420 feet over a mossy precipice into a frothy pool. Akaka Falls State Park is on the wet side of Hawaii, at the southern tip of the Hamakua Coast. The region's tremendous rainfall fosters extravagant jungle growth and spectacular waterfalls.

GAZETTEER: *Traveler's Guide to the National Parks*

Mesa Arch, Canyonlands National Park, Utah.

From Katmai and Glacier Bay in the south to Gates of the Arctic and Kobuk Valley above the Arctic Circle, Alaska's 8 national parks safeguard 41.5 million acres of towering mountains, serrated coastlines, glaciers and icefields, mighty rivers, hidden lakes, tundra and forests. Called Alyeshka, the Great Land, by the early Aleuts, the state has more national parks within its borders than any other.

GLACIER BAY

When Captain George Vancouver first explored the Alaskan coast in 1794, Glacier Bay was not even visible. It was buried by an impenetrable shield of glacial ice about 20 miles wide and 4,000 feet thick. Today, the ice has receded 65 miles, revealing a spectacular fjord ringed by rugged mountain ranges. The 3.3-million-acre park encompasses Glacier Bay and the arms of land on either side of it.

The rapid retreat of glacial ice has provided scientists with a unique opportunity to examine plant regrowth. As the ice melted, plant and animal life slowly began to reclaim the exposed land: alder and willow trees now flourish here as well as mountain avens, black cottonwood, dryads and fireweed. The mature forests are located at the mouth of the bay, the area that has been ice-free for the longest period of time. This regrowth of vegetation has lured animals—wolves, bears, mountain goats and bald eagles—into recolonizing the land.

Most visitors come to the park as passengers on cruise ships and tour boats. This affords them the best chance of seeing Glacier Bay's resident harbor seals and the three kinds of whales—minke, humpback and orca—that also visit the bay.

FOR MORE INFORMATION:
Superintendent, Glacier Bay National Park and Preserve, P.O. Box 140, Gustavus, AK 99826. (907) 697-2230.

WRANGELL-ST. ELIAS

The scale of this park puts it in a league of its own. At 13.2 million acres, it is the largest of all the national parks; the states of Massachusetts, Connecticut and Rhode Island could fit comfortably within its

This huge complex of weather-beaten buildings, located in Wrangell-St. Elias National Park, once housed the Kennecott Mining Company.

boundaries. Three major mountain ranges meet in the park—the Wrangells, Chugach and St. Elias—and 9 of the 16 highest peaks in the United States are found here. Four of them are more than 16,000 feet tall. The park has a massive 300-foot-high waterfall where the Chitistone River plunges over a sheer cliff, an active volcano, Mt. Wrangell, and more than 150 glaciers—one of them, Malaspina, bigger than Rhode Island.

Some of the human incursions into this vastness were also made on a large scale. The Kennecott Mining Company set up shop in the Copper River area in 1911, extracting tons of ore from the world's largest copper mine, creating a boom in the process. Gold was discovered too, and for more than 20 years the towns of Kennecott and McCarthy were sites of feverish activity. By the late 1930's the boom was over, and today there are only a handful of people in the towns with the distinctive oxide red buildings. Kennecott is on the National Register of Historic Places.

FOR MORE INFORMATION:
Superintendent, Wrangell-St. Elias National Park, P.O. Box 439, Copper Center, AK 99573. (907) 822-5234.

Resembling an immense ribbon of ice, the tidewater face of Muir Glacier flows into Glacier Bay. There are 16 glaciers in the park, 12 of which regularly spawn giant icebergs—200-square-foot chunks of ice that split off and plunge into the waters of the bay.

KATMAI

This is a park that embodies both the power and the danger of nature, for it is the home of North America's largest protected population of coastal brown bears—2,000 of them—and of 15 active volcanoes, some of them still steaming.

In 1912, a volcanic eruption occurred here that was so devastating it filled a valley with ash and pumice 700 feet thick in some areas. Four years later, during a 1916 expedition, botanist Robert Griggs was overwhelmed when he entered the Katmai Pass: "The whole valley as far as the eye could reach was full of hundreds—no, thousands—literally tens of thousands of smokes curling up from its fissured floor." He named the area Valley of the Ten

Thousand Smokes. Fumaroles—cracks in the surface that send jets of steam spewing 500 to 1,000 feet into the air—covered the valley floor. They are all damped now, but the valley retains an air of desolation.

From the fishing lodge and campground at Brooks Camp, a mile-long trail leads to Brooks Falls, where visitors can see the park's magnificent brown bears as they forage for salmon. There is also a bear viewing platform near the lodge itself. Fishermen enjoy Katmai's network of rivers and lakes, especially in its northwestern quadrant, that teem with trout and salmon.

FOR MORE INFORMATION:
Superintendent, Katmai National Park, P.O. Box 7, King Salmon, AK 99613. (907) 246-3305.

KENAI FJORDS

The smallest of Alaska's parks hugs the coast, taking in peninsulas, fjords, tranquil bays and coves, and islands. The dominant feature of the park is the massive Harding Icefield, 700 square miles of ice about a mile thick. The icefield feeds 30 glaciers, 8 of which extend to the sea.

The narrow strip of land between the fjords and the icefield supports stunted forests of western hemlock and Sitka

A large natural ice sculpture glows in the afternoon light in Kenai Fjords National Park. The park contains Harding Icefield—one of only four icefields in the United States.

spruce. Alpine meadows grow at higher elevations. Mountain goats roam the craggy cliffs; moose, grizzly bears and gray wolverines live in lower Kenai. Humpback, minke and gray whales, porpoises and dolphins, sea lions, harbor seals and sea otters populate the ocean waters. Tufted puffins, kittiwakes, gulls, bald eagles and peregrine falcons nest in the sheer cliff faces of the coast and islands.

FOR MORE INFORMATION:
Superintendent, Kenai Fjords National Park and Preserve, P.O. Box 1727, Seward, AK 99664. (907) 224-3175.

LAKE CLARK

Considered by many to be a microcosm of Alaska, the park's 1.4-million acres encompass great geological diversity: jagged mountains, glaciers, lakes—including 40-mile-long Lake Clark—cascading waterfalls and two active volcanoes. There are forests of Sitka and white spruce, alpine meadows, tundra, and coastal cliffs that contain fossils more than 150 million years old.

Here, the Chigmit Mountains join the Alaska and Aleutian ranges and divide the park into two landscapes: coastal plains, and lake and tundra country. Lake Clark is one of the world's finest sockeye salmon fishing spots.

FOR MORE INFORMATION:
Superintendent, Lake Clark National Park and Preserve, 4230 University Dr., Suite 311, Anchorage, AK 99508. (907) 781-2218.

Brown bears feast on sockeye salmon at Brooks Falls in Katmai National Park. These huge creatures grow 10 feet tall, can weigh more than 1,000 pounds, and are surprisingly agile as they swat, dive and gorge on this high-protein diet in preparation for hibernation.

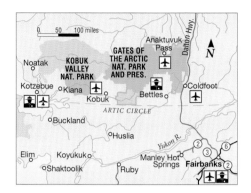

GATES OF THE ARCTIC

In the 1920's, wilderness advocate Robert Marshall described two craggy peaks, Frigid Crags and Boreal Mountain, as the gateway to the far north. The name stuck when the 8.5-million-acre region was designated a national park and preserve in 1980.

Lying entirely north of the Arctic Circle, the park's landscape is dominated by the Central Brooks Range. Its towering granite peaks overlook peaceful, glacier-carved valleys and cast shadows on the Alatna, John, Kobuk, Noatak, North Fork Koyukuk and Tinayguk rivers. The range is the northernmost extension of the Rocky Mountains.

The southern mountain slopes are covered with taiga—a thin forest of stunted black spruce trees. The treeless tundra lies to the north. These plains remain frozen during the long Arctic winter, but during the summer months, the tundra is warmed by the long summer days and comes alive with a profusion of wildflowers—buttercups, lupines and avens—mosses, sedges, lichens and dwarf willows.

The taiga and tundra are home to herds of Western Arctic caribou that migrate through passes in the Brooks Range to their southern feeding grounds in the Yukon basin. Grizzly bears, gray wolves, Dall sheep and foxes also inhabit the region. More than 130 species of birds, including hawks, peregrine falcons, ptarmigans and snowy owls have been sighted in the park.

FOR MORE INFORMATION:

Superintendent, Gates of the Arctic National Park, P.O. Box 74680, Fairbanks, AK 99707. (907) 456-0281.

KOBUK VALLEY

This park's 1.71 million acres sit in a semi-enclosed natural amphitheater, ringed on the north by the Baird Mountains and on the south by the Waring Mountains. The Kobuk River meanders through the broad valley, 25 miles north of the Arctic Circle.

The Endicott Mountains provide a dramatic view for campers in Gates of the Arctic National Park. The mountains are part of the Brooks Range.

Sagebrush, grasses and sedges flourish here along with the plant *Oxytropis kobukensis*, which grows nowhere else on earth. The tundra blends into a stunted boreal forest of spruce trees that reaches its northernmost limit north of the park. Relict plants that flourished during the Pleistocene Epoch, some 2,000,000 years ago, still survive in the Kobuk Valley where the climate approximates Ice Age conditions.

The most unexpected landscape in the park is its expanse of Sahara-like sand dunes. Nestled in a bend in the Kobuk River, the Great Kobuk Sand Dunes cover a 25-square-mile region with 100-foot high dunes. The nearby Little Kobuk Sand Dunes blanket another five square miles.

The Kobuk Valley is a rich cultural storehouse. At a bend in the river, known as Onion Portage, ongoing archeological excavations have exposed layers of earth containing stone tools and artifacts, and housepits from settlements at least 12,500 years old. Seven different cultures may have settled around the portage, hunting herds of caribou as they crossed the river on their annual southward migration. Migrating caribou still swim across the Kobuk River at this point and members of the Kuuvangmiit people live here, practicing traditional ways of hunting and fishing, with few concessions to the modern world.

Caribou tracks cross Great Kobuk Sand Dunes in Kobuk Valley National Park. Geologists believe that the dunes were created about 33,000 years ago.

FOR MORE INFORMATION:

Superintendent, Kobuk Valley National Park, P.O. Box 1029, Kotzebue, AK 99752. (907) 442-3890.

American Samoa

Of all the spectacular scenery scattered throughout the national park system of the United States, none can quite match that of the National Park of American Samoa for exotic splendor. Nestled idyllically among the Polynesian Islands of the South Pacific, this park is a remote tropical paradise lying some 2,300 miles southwest of the Hawaiian Islands.

American Samoa consists of five volcanic islands and two coral atolls. The first European visitor to set foot here was a Frenchman, Louis-Antoine de Bougainville, in 1768. He was followed by American whalers and missionaries, who began visiting in the 1830's. During the 19th century, Britain, Germany and the United States bickered over possession of the islands; the United States secured preferred trading rights in 1878. In 1900, the islands of Tutuila and Aunuu were ceded to the United States, followed closely by the Manua Islands of Ta'u, Ofu, Olosega, and the coral atolls of Rose and Swains islands. The capital, Pago Pago, sweeps around a sheltered harbor on Tutuila, overlooked by a forest-draped mountain, called the Rainmaker. (The island receives an average annual rainfall of 200 inches.)

American Samoa is administered by the United States as a territory. The Samoans elect their own government. In 1988, the National Park Service began negotiations with Samoan village chiefs to lease parcels of their lands for a national park, resulting in the only land-lease arrangement with traditional owners in the system. The park includes land on three islands: Tutuila and the Manua Islands of Ofu and Ta'u. It encompasses about 9,000 acres—1,000 of them underwater—and gives visitors the unique opportunity to experience three distinct environments: rain forest, beach and coral reef. Visitors must first obtain permission from landowners to camp on the islands.

SACRED EARTH
The inhabitants of Polynesia's oldest culture named their land Samoa, which means

Ofu Island, part of American Samoa National Park, has magnificent beaches and one of the best examples of a living coral reef in the Pacific Ocean.

sacred earth. Fittingly, the islands are home to five types of the planet's precious rain forests—lowland, montane, coastal, ridge and cloud. The park portion of Tutuila, the largest island, is covered with a luxuriant cloud rain forest, which descends from the mountaintops to the shoreline, cloaking the island's volcanic peaks in a mantle of vivid green. The rain forest is kept green and lush by the heavy year-round precipitation. The island's park unit—about 2,670 acres of land and some 450 acres of ocean—lies on Tutuila's northern side. A scenic drive meanders through the park region and takes visitors to the picturesque village of Uatia.

The lofty summits of Lata Mountain, American Samoa's highest peak, is located on the island of Ta'u. The mountain's ancient rain forest is shrouded in mist year-round. The park includes about 5,400 acres of land on Ta'u and approximately 250 acres offshore.

Fruit bats are the park's most distinctive mammals. These animals, often called flying foxes because of their foxlike head, can have a wingspan of up to five feet. Flying foxes play an essential role in maintaining the rain forest by spreading seeds and pollinating the bountiful fruit-bearing plants of the rain forest.

BEACHFRONT INHABITANTS
The park is also home to some of the most spectacular shoreline property in the world. Walks along its white-sand beaches wind past plunging sea cliffs, jagged ridges and secluded coves. The blue tropical waters invite visitors to snorkel and to explore the fringing coral reefs. Sea birds abound on these shores: petrels, boobies, noddies, terns, frigates, kingfishers, doves, Polynesian and Samoan starlings and reef herons. Two endangered species of sea turtle, the green and the hawksbill, also call these magnificent beaches home.

The park now encompasses approximately 70 acres of Ofu Island, including what many consider to be one of Polynesia's most stunning white-sand beaches and one of the best examples of a living coral reef in the Pacific Ocean. Divers and snorkelers can view the reef's bounty of brilliantly colored tropical fish—dramatic evidence of the reef's healthy state.

FOR MORE INFORMATION:
Superintendent, National Park of American Samoa, Pago Pago, American Samoa 96799. (684) 633-1031.

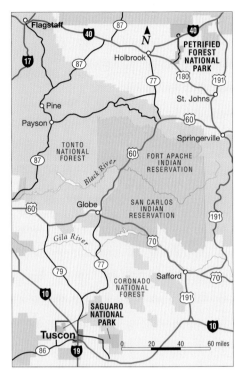

PETRIFIED FOREST

Two hundred and twenty-five million years ago, Arizona was covered by a lush tropical forest of exotic flowers, plants and towering trees. Protected within the confines of the 147-square mile Petrified National Park, the remains of this forest—200-foot-long, rainbow-hued logs—comprise the world's largest collection of fossilized wood.

Some 500 archeological sites in the park also testify to the fact that human beings have been here for at least 8,000 years. Oval pit houses on top of some of the Petrified Forest's mesas housed the Western Pueblo or Anasazi—Navajo for "ancient ones"—the mysterious people who built Cliff Palace at Mesa Verde. During the 800 years from A.D. 500 to 1300, they evolved from primitive pit dwellers to farmers who inhabited settlements like the one called Puerco Pueblo. Here an estimated 75 people lived in an early apartment dwelling of 25 rooms. Nearby is Newspaper Rock, whose surfaces are covered with Anasazi drawings.

The Puerco River divides the park in two. Most of the sites of human habitation and the fossilized trees are scattered through the southern section. The Painted Desert occupies the northern end of the park. Its multihued red, brown and yellow hills are the eroded remnants of the Chinle Formation, a layer of sand and pebbles deposited by ancient waterways. Erosion and weathering continues to mold the landscape of these badlands. Iron oxides in the soil give the desert its distinctive tones.

FOR MORE INFORMATION:
Superintendent, Petrified Forest National Park, P.O. Box 2217, Petrified Forest, AZ 86028. (520) 524-6228.

The variegated patterns found in petrified logs are crystal formations within the wood. In places where insects or rot left cavities, quartz and amethyst crystals have formed.

SAGUARO
Separated by the city of Tucson, the two sections of Saguaro National Park encompass more than 94,000 acres of the spectacular Sonoran Desert.

The western section of the park offers visitors trips into the heart of the dense saguaro forests. The monarch of the Sonoran Desert, saguaro cacti grow up to 40 feet tall and weigh as much as 8 tons. The armlike branches of a mature saguaro are often aflutter with birds, including Gila woodpeckers, purple martins and elf owls, which fly in and out of nests burrowed into the cacti's cool flesh. Longnose bats and white-winged doves can be seen in May and June sipping nectar from the saguaro's white blossoms.

More natural splendor awaits visitors in the larger eastern section. With over 75 miles of trails at their disposal, backpackers of all levels of experience can enjoy the breathtaking scenery. Short loops introduce hikers to the abundant plant and animal life, and longer treks lead them into the scrub oak and Douglas fir forests of the majestic Rincon Mountains.

FOR MORE INFORMATION:
Saguaro National Park, 3693 South Old Spanish Trail, Tucson, AZ 85730. (520)-733-5153 (Rincon Mountain District); (520)-733-5158 (Tucson Mountain District).

Long Logs has the largest concentration of petrified wood in the park. Paiute Indians believed the logs were the arrows of their thunder god; the Navajos thought they were the bones of an ancient giant.

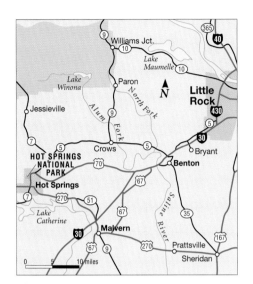

H ot Springs National Park's carefully crafted architecture and well-manicured lawns are reminiscent of days gone by when horse-drawn carriages paraded down the streets.

Legend has it that in 1541, Spanish explorer Hernando de Soto and his men were the first Europeans to take advantage of the waters. French fur trappers made use of the hot springs and left rough log structures as evidence of their visit. When the United States acquired the Arkansas area in the Louisiana Purchase of 1803, the government quickly realized the business potential of the area as a tourist attraction. In 1832, four sections of land surrounding the springs were set aside as a federal reserve—the first one in the United States. The national park was established in 1921.

THE GREAT SPIRIT

Long before the first European settlers arrived, however, the region was sacred Indian ground. The native Americans believed that this was where the Great Spirit resided and that his breath was the steam rising above the water. The heated pools were neutral ground where opposing warriors could bathe together in peace to soothe their aches and pains and work out their conflicts. In more prosaic, scientific terms, it is precipitation that nourishes the springs. Rainwater seeps through the surface cracks in the earth and gradually descends to depths of 4,000 to 8,000 feet. Heated by the earth's deep, internal furnace, the mineral-rich waters then rise back to the surface through faults in the

The elegant spas that line Central Avenue, nicknamed Bathhouse Row, were built during the early 20th century when Hot Springs was a popular resort.

Hot springs cascade over Tufa Terrace, depositing minerals that harden and form porous, milky-colored rock called tufa.

sandstone. The water's average temperature is 143°F; during a typical day, 850,000 gallons gush from the springs.

The high temperatures were thought to cure a variety of ailments, including kidney and liver disorders, eye problems, arthritis, and foot complaints such as corns and bunions. By the end of the 19th century, the majority of the springs were enclosed to prevent contamination of the water.

To accommodate the influx of visitors, enormous bathhouses were built along

Central Avenue, known by aficionados as Bathhouse Row. Underground pipes were installed in the 1890's to convey the scalding water to the bathhouses. These lavish buildings had marble walls, elaborate murals and stained glass windows. The architecture was a wild mix of Spanish towers, Grecian urns, Byzantine design, Mediterranean flair and Georgian sophistication.

Today, only one bathhouse on Bathhouse Row is still in operation: tub and pool baths, steam cabinets, private attendants and whirlpools are all part of the elaborate procedure. Five others are open to the public. Fordyce Bathhouse, one of the most luxurious buildings, has been transformed into the park's visitor center. Its restored architectural features capture the atmosphere of the resort's elegant past.

Hot Springs does have other natural attractions. Of the 150 species of birds found in the park, the most conspicuous are cardinals and mockingbirds. The park is also home to an abundance of squirrels and pigeons; when the sun sets, timid cottontail hares make an appearance, as well as nocturnal opossums and raccoons.

Spring and summer flowers line Goat Rock Trail: purple coneflowers, fire pink, bird's-foot violets, and butterfly milkweed. Southern magnolias stretch in languid columns along Bathhouse Row and periwinkles brighten up the Grand Promenade.

FOR MORE INFORMATION:
Superintendent, Hot Springs National Park, P.O. Box 1860, Hot Springs N.P., AR 71902-1860. (501) 623-1433.

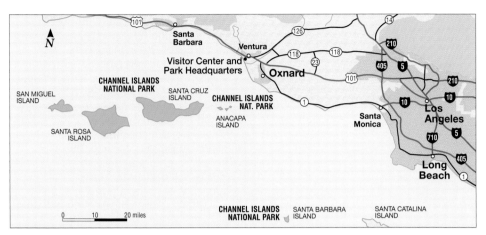

Channel Islands National Park off California's southern coast is a place where different worlds collide. Here the barren and the lush, the desolate and the teeming with life coexist in timeless harmony. Together with the surrounding offshore kelp forests, the park encompasses a chain of five main islands, as well as a number of rocky islets.

Chumash Indians lived here for centuries before the islands were discovered by the Spanish in 1542. The Channel Islands have since been populated by fur traders, Spanish cattle ranchers and the U.S. Navy. Together with Santa Barbara Island—40 miles to the southeast—the islands officially became a national park in 1980.

The Channel Islands are accessible by plane and by boat; landing permits are required for private craft, and charter and tour boats bring visitors to the islands on day trips. Anacapa—the closest island to the mainland—is 11 miles from the coast, and actually consists of three small islets. Each January through March, migrating gray whales can be spotted offshore. The western portion of Anacapa is the chief nesting rookery for the endangered brown pelican and so is closed to the public.

UNDERSEA FORESTS

Encircling the islands are magnificent kelp beds, with nearly 1,000 varieties of undersea life. Kelp is a type of algae that grows at the astonishing rate of two feet per day and can reach heights of about 200 feet. These rich feeding grounds attract a dazzling, colorful display of limpets, anemones, abalones, starfish and larger sea creatures such as dolphins, porpoises, sharks and whales.

The islands are also the breeding grounds for large numbers of pinnipeds; elephant seals deliver their pups on the beaches and harbor seals raise their young in the rocky tidepools. In spring, more than 35,000 seals at a time haul themselves onto the beaches at Point Bennett on San Miguel.

More than 70 species of plants grow on the Channel Islands and nowhere else in the world. Most are hardy species, able to tolerate salt and wind. The best examples of *caliche*—fossilized logs and trunks coated with a white crust of calcium carbonate— are found on San Miguel.

The Channel Islands can be a harsh place to visit. There are only limited facilities and permits are required for camping. Park rangers lead hikes along the islands' nature trails. More adventurous visitors can go scuba diving off Anacapa Island.

FOR MORE INFORMATION:

Superintendent, Channel Islands National Park, 1901 Spinnaker Drive, Ventura, CA 93001. (805) 658-5730.

Sea lions and elephant seals bask at Point Bennett on San Miguel Island (above). They return every year to bear pups, mate and raise their young. Santa Cruz (below), the largest of the Channel Islands, was once used by the U.S. Navy as a bombing range. Today it is a wildlife preserve and a treasure trove of Chumash Indian artifacts.

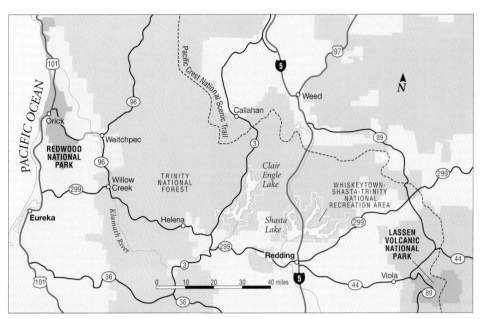

LASSEN VOLCANIC

On May 22, 1915, Lassen Peak exploded, sending an enormous mushroom cloud seven miles into the air over northern California. Three square miles of forest were destroyed as rivers of molten lava moved down the northeastern side of the mountain. Mudflows buried everything before them in a sticky grave of gray-black ooze. Photographer B. F. Loomis captured this outburst of nature's violence on photographic plates. The eruptions continued with decreasing intensity until 1921. Loomis' pictures helped the Lassen area achieve national park status in 1916, saving it from large-scale economic development.

The origins of the park's famous volcanic terrain began 70 million years ago, when the Pacific and North American geological plates collided; in the millennia that followed, western North America experienced tremendous upheavals of the earth's crust. Red-hot lava rose to the surface and volcanoes were born.

Lassen belongs to the famous network of volcanoes, known today as the Ring of Fire, which encircles the Pacific Ocean. The park covers 106,000 acres of volcanic terrain and offers a dramatic landscape of towering lava pinnacles, gaping craters, sulfur vents and the bleak beauty of the Devastated Area.

Despite the chaos and ruin, regeneration and rebirth continue as trees and tenacious grasses sprout on lands laid waste 75 years ago. After it cools, lava decomposes into fertile soil, allowing a wide variety of flora and fauna to flourish. Lush forests, meadows and wildflowers provide a startling contrast to the inferno-like vistas.

Recent monitoring has led scientists to classify Lassen Peak as an active volcano, and there is no doubt that the earth will tremble again in the face of its awesome power. For the visitor, the park's trails present a unique opportunity to witness the forces that continue to shape the planet.

FOR MORE INFORMATION:
Superintendent, Lassen Volcanic National Park, P.O. Box 100, Mineral, CA 96063-0100. (916) 595-4444.

REDWOOD

No visitor to Redwood National Park can fail to be subdued by the enormity of the coast redwoods—the tallest living things on earth. The tree occurs naturally only along the coast of northern California. By 1960, clear-cut logging had dramatically reduced the extent of the state's redwoods. Redwood National Park was established in 1968 to protect some of the remaining stands.

The world's tallest known tree is found in the park, near Redwood Creek: discovered in 1963, Tall Tree rises 367.8 feet into the air and boasts a circumference of 44 feet. On average, coast redwoods reach heights of 200 to 250 feet, and some may be 2,000 years old. That long life span has earned the redwood the nickname of "the everlasting."

Redwood National Park preserves one of the world's major ecosystems. It is protected as a World Heritage Site and an International Biosphere Reserve. Land and sea combine to make the park an ideal location to appreciate the forces of nature and the need for conservation. The park's 63 hiking trails are generally short, giving visitors the chance to visit all of Redwood's environments: forests, mountain meadows, river valleys and seacoast, which provide a habitat for a variety of plants and animals.

FOR MORE INFORMATION:
Superintendent, Redwood National and State Parks, 1111 Second Street, Crescent City, CA 95531. (707) 464-6101.

Bumpass Hell is one of many thermal areas in Lassen. It is named after Kendall Bumpass, who burned his leg in 1864 when he fell through the thin crust covering a boiling mud pot.

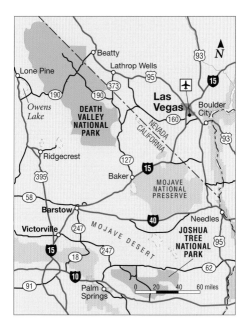

DEATH VALLEY

When Native Americans peered across this vast expanse of dry saltpan, where the sun bakes rock and sand at temperatures that can soar above 120°F, they called it Tomesha, or "ground afire." Attempting to cross through the region on their way to join the California gold rush in 1849, a group of pioneers who barely escaped with their lives were even less flattering, dubbing the wasteland Death Valley. Today that name conjures up an image of a barren stretch of land where life is as rare as rain.

Despite its reputation, this legendary land of burning sun and shimmering heat is surprisingly alive and vibrant. In all, some 900 species of plants have taken root within the confines of the Death Valley National Park, varying as wildly as the magnificent terrain in which they live. As the hardpan changes into rippled sand dunes and snow-capped mountains, beavertail and grizzly bear cactus give way to juniper, mountain-mahogany and piñon pines. Although desolate for much of the year, after each winter rain the valley is transformed by the colors of blooming wildflowers. Tiny desert fivespots, goldpoppies and rare rockladies squeeze up through the sand and limestone, painting the desert in delicate shades of cream, purple, and yellow.

Where there is vegetation, there is wildlife. Ground squirrels, kangaroo rats, pocket mice and jackrabbits feed on plants and insects, and they, in turn, are important staples in the diets of the snakes, kit foxes, coyotes and bobcats that patrol the area. Hungry red-tailed hawks soar overhead—just one of the 230 species of birds that pass through the valley each year.

Visitors to Death Valley must remember that this is wilderness at its most unforgiving. Although the park is equipped with nine campgrounds and three resorts, travelers are advised to bring sufficient water for every member of their party, as well as a reserve supply for their vehicles. Visitors who respect the rigorous demands of this harsh environment will return home with the grandest memories.

FOR MORE INFORMATION:

Superintendent, Death Valley National Park, Death Valley, CA 92328. (619) 786-2331.

JOSHUA TREE

Wedged between the arid Colorado Desert and the cooler Mojave Desert, Joshua Tree National Park lays claim to the best of both worlds. The 794,000-acre park encompasses some of the most beautiful terrain found in California's deserts.

In the eastern section of the park, hearty creosote bushes speckle the rocky landscape with tiny yellow flowers that blossom after each cooling shower, and spidery ocotillo shrubs wave clusters of red blossoms like flags at the tip of each spindly branch. During the day, curious roadrunners can be seen scurrying across the burning desert sands. When the searing sun finally dips behind the horizon, the desert comes alive. Then even scorpions, tarantulas, and wary rattlesnakes make rare appearances in their nocturnal quest for food.

The Panamint Range rises above a salt marsh in Death Valley National Park, above. The region receives some two inches of rain per year.

The western section of the park is located in the Mojave Desert at a higher elevation; its cooler environment supports more plant and animal life than the eastern section. Black-tailed jackrabbits test the warm breeze for the scent of coyotes, bobcats, and other predators. At dusk, burrowing owls hoot softly as they emerge from their underground homes, signaling the start of another busy night in the desert.

Perhaps the most awesome of all the plant life in the park is the magnificent Joshua tree for which the park is named. Because their trunks do not have rings, it is difficult to determine the age of these trees, but biologists estimate that some of them may be approximately 800 years old. This member of the yucca family grows up to 40 feet in height, sports daggerlike leaves at the end of its twisted branches, and stores water in its trunk. Mormon pioneers traveling through the region named the trees for the prophet Joshua because their outstretched branches reminded them of Joshua raising his arms to God.

FOR MORE INFORMATION:

Superintendent, Joshua Tree National Park, 74485 National Park Drive, Twentynine Palms, CA 92277. (619) 367-7511.

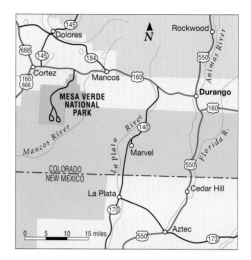

Cliff Palace (above) at Mesa Verde dates back 800 years and has been vacant since the end of the 13th century. There are two kivas in the Balcony House (left). The kiva was an underground chamber used as a gathering place and workshop as well as for religious ceremonies.

On a winter's night in 1888, two cowboys searching for lost cattle on a mesa top instead found a magnificent city tucked below the canyon rim inside an immense cave. They christened it "Cliff Palace." The ruins had been undisturbed for six centuries and were known to only a few native tribes who feared to tread on the property of the mysterious Anasazi.

Cliff Palace is located within Mesa Verde National Park—the first national park set aside to protect manmade wonders. Created in 1906, the park shelters nearly 4,000 archeological sites, which range from early pithouses to vast complexes built into the sandstone cliffs.

The word "mesa" refers to a high, flat-topped block of sedimentary rock, composed primarily of 90-million-year-old shale and sandstone. Mesa Verde (Spanish for Green Table) is made up of a number of smaller mesas, such as Chapin and Wetherill, running north and south covered by stands of piñon and juniper trees.

A GLIMPSE INTO THE PAST

Mesa Verde's multistoried structures bring to life the history and way of life of a people who flourished more than 200 years before the arrival of Columbus. The Anasazi lived in the region from at least A.D. 550 to the end of the 13th century. The peak of their civilization is thought to have been around A.D. 1200, when they built many two- and three-story houses, some with more than 200 rooms. Mesa Verde's most impressive sites—Cliff Palace, Spruce Tree House and Long House—were built at this time. Underground ceremonial chambers, known as kivas, were dug in the courtyards. Curious D-shaped towers were often connected by tunnels to the kivas. Cliff Palace alone boasts 217 rooms and 23 kivas.

Three to four generations after these settlements were built, the Anasazi abandoned their extraordinary dwellings. They left behind baskets, arrows, jewelry and distinctive black-on-white pottery. It is likely that a 20-year drought and the clearing of surrounding forests had depleted local resources, forcing the Anasazi to move on to more fertile areas. About a mile away, a 60-foot carved panel of humans, birds and other animals stretches across the wall above Petroglyph Point Trail.

Under the immense blue canopy of Colorado sky, the deserted cliff dwellings overwhelm the natural surroundings. Balcony House, a village poised in an almost inaccessible gap of precipitous cliff, is reached by climbing a 32-foot ladder. A visit to Balcony House is not for the faint-hearted—the exit is a cramped passageway (at one point only 14 inches wide).

The park, now a World Heritage Site, encloses 52,000 acres of scenic mesa land. Although Mesa Verde is open all year, all but one of the main cliff-dwelling sites and many of the park services are closed in winter; these off-season months, however, are a pleasant and uncrowded time to visit.

FOR MORE INFORMATION:
Superintendent, P.O. Box 8, Mesa Verde National Park, CO 81330. (970) 529-4465.

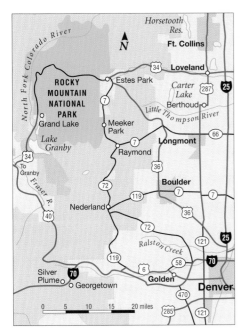

Visitors to Rocky Mountain National Park often sight foraging mule deer.

R ocky Mountain National Park's 265,753 acres enclose 2,200 miles of diverse landscape, ranging from the grassy meadows and pine forests of the lower elevations to the tundra and windswept tops of the highest peaks. This natural reserve is a paradise for climbers and photographers alike.

Established in 1915, the park straddles the Continental Divide, preserving a portion of the southern Rocky Mountains. The range rose up some 40 to 60 million years ago and its peaks were shaped through the combined forces of streams and glaciers. Because of their prominence, two of the park's highest summits—Longs Peak and Mount Meeker—were known to Arapaho Indians as the "Two Guides."

A HIGHWAY IN THE SKY

In Rocky Mountain each season has its unique attractions and every night is ideal for gazing at the multitudes of glistening stars. Trail Ridge Road traverses the park from east to west—a 48-mile journey through the park's layered terrain. The route, which is open from Memorial Day to mid-October, extends for 11 miles through the alpine tundra zone, making it the highest continuous paved highway in the country. But the park's 355 miles of hiking trails are the ultimate way to experience the incredible contrasting beauty.

Dream Lake, Goblin's Forest and Nymph Lake are a few of the irresistible destinations. In the north, Mummy Range commands one-third of the park and is one of the best places to spot bighorn sheep. The Diamond on the East Face of Longs Peak poses a challenge for experienced climbers.

The park supports a multiplicity of distinct worlds. In the meadows, wetlands and mixed forests of the Montane Life Ecosystem, foxes and red-tailed hawks stalk vulnerable ground squirrels and chipmunks; American elk roam freely; Abert's squirrels (which resemble rabbits) feed off ponderosa pines. Here are found purple and violet wildflowers, blue columbine and, at lower elevations, prickly-pear cacti.

The Subalpine Ecosystem is a cousin to the forests of northern Canada. Bog orchids and blueberry bushes sheathe the black bear's retreat, which is also home to whiskered snowshoe hares and shrill jays. Wildflowers grow in abundance near subalpine creeks; the obvious favorites are the elephantellas. Their stems burst with dozens of purple or pink blossoms, each a tiny replica of an elephant's head.

THE ALPINE ECOSYSTEM

The Krummholz ("crooked wood" in German) is located at the treeline border. Centuries-old spruce and fir trees stand less than a foot high, stunted by the extreme climate. Above the treeline, arctic conditions prevail, but a surprising assortment of vegetation thrives on the chilly tundra. Even above 12,000 feet, low-growing alpine flowers burst into overwhelming color displays in July and August. The tundra surface is fragile and plants may take years to recover if trampled.

In addition to hiking and climbing, horseback riding, fishing, camping and skiing are all possible in Rocky Mountain. The uncrowded routes lend themselves to solitude, despite the fact that the park hosts as many visitors as Yellowstone and is only one-eighth the size. However Rocky Mountain's ruggedness ensures that it will remain a wilderness. What seems so constant and eternally fixed, though, is actually in a perpetual state of change.

FOR MORE INFORMATION:

Superintendent, Rocky Mountain National Park, Estes Park, CO 80517. (970) 586-1206.

More than 150 crystal-watered lakes dot the park, ranging from cold, glacier-scoured tarns, to low-lying pools rich in fish, waterfowl and other wildlife.

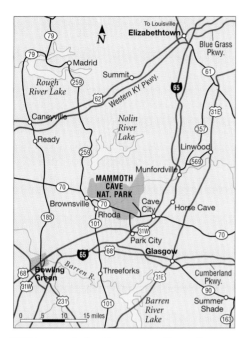

Frozen Niagara, Mammoth's largest flowstone, resembles a tumbling waterfall. However, formations like this grow by only a cubic inch every 200 years.

Beneath the 80-square-mile surface of the lush forests of a quiet Kentucky plateau lies an intricate labyrinth of passages, tunnels and cavities. Entombed in absolute darkness, this underground park has five levels of mapped, interconnected passageways, totaling more than 330 miles in length, making Mammoth Cave the world's longest known cave system.

Although known to Native Americans for several thousand years, the caves were not exploited until the War of 1812, when deposits of calcium nitrate were used to produce saltpeter, an essential ingredient of gunpowder. Systematic exploration of the caves started in 1839, when the slave Stephen Bishop began to discover and chart some 20 miles of passageways, including underground Echo River. Since Bishop's time, spelunkers (cave explorers) have continued to discover new appendages to this ever-growing labyrinth.

CARVED BY WATER
Standing in majestic Mammoth Dome—a 192-foot chamber that is the climax to two of the park's guided tours—it is hard to believe that all of Mammoth Cave's tunnels began as tiny cracks in the limestone some 230 million years ago. As surface water drips through these cracks, it mixes with carbon dioxide and decaying vegetation to form a mild acid that eats away at the limestone. What began as tiny cracks widen into the likes of Echo River, 20 feet wide in some spots and 25 feet deep in others.

The steady drip of mineral-rich water from the surface not only carves the cave's tunnels, it also creates magical forms in the caves themselves. Travertine, formed when calcium and bicarbonate are precipitated out of the water, is responsible for the stalactites and stalagmites. As water seeps down vertically through the limestone, it picks up minerals that cause these travertine formations to take on spectacular yellow, red, brown and black hues of the minerals. The stalactites and stalagmites sometimes join to form columns running from floor to ceiling.

Where mineral-rich water has flowed over a limestone surface, spectacular flowstones are created. Frozen Niagara, near the park's southeast entrance, is Mammoth's most spectacular flowstone. This tumbling river of travertine deposits seems to have been stopped in mid-course.

GARDENS OF STONE
Native Americans once delved into the caves to mine gypsum—a white, or sometimes brownish, mineral that adorns the drier cave walls. Water carries gypsum crystals through the limestone, allowing them to escape from microscopic pores. The water evaporates, leaving a gypsum crust on the surface of the wall. The pressure of growing crystals pushes out "snowballs." Other gypsum formations resemble plant stems or needlelike crystals, which burst open to reveal delicate "flowers." A walk through the Snowball Room or Cleveland Avenue reveals these gypsum gardens.

After a million years of evolution in murky blackness, Mammoth Cave's 30 species of permanent cave dwellers have lost their sight and their need for pigment. Completely translucent or startlingly white, these blind fish, crayfish, spiders and beetles are at home in Mammoth's 54°F temperature and 87 percent humidity, but can no longer survive outside the lightless environment. For food, they rely on organic matter washed in during spring flooding or brought in by other animals, including four species of bats and crickets with long, ultrasensitive antennae.

Mammoth is America's second-oldest tourist attraction (after Niagara Falls); it became a national park in 1941, a World Heritage Site in 1981, and an International Biosphere Reserve in 1990. The park is open to visitors all year long, but in an environment where a footprint can remain for a millennium, the park restricts visitors to 12 miles of passageways on guided excursions.

These tours range from the one-and-a-quarter-hour Historic Tour to the six-hour Wild Cave Tour. For the experienced spelunker, permits are available to explore nearby Ganter Cave. On the surface, 70 miles of woodland trails reveal scenic overlooks and the park's abundant white-tailed deer population.

FOR MORE INFORMATION:
Superintendent, Mammoth Cave National Park, Mammoth Cave, KY 42259. (502) 758-2328.

124

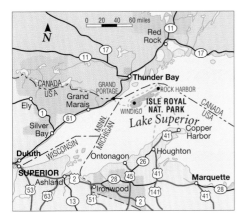

S tand on the shore of Isle Royale, with the cold, dark waters of Lake Superior lapping at your feet, and listen for the haunting cry of the timber wolf. It is a reminder that this national park's 571,790 acres of glacier-scoured basalt ridges, bog, lakeland and thick coniferous forest preserve a unique and untamed wilderness.

Situated 15 miles from the Canadian coast, and 50 miles from the nearest point of its home state of Michigan, Isle Royale is the largest island in the largest freshwater lake in the world. One of the most secluded national parks in the country, it is accessible by boat from Houghton or Copper Harbor in Michigan, and from Grand Portage in Minnesota. Seaplanes make the trip from Houghton. There are no public roads on the island; to explore the raw beauty, visitors must take to the park's 166 miles of rugged trails and canoe routes, which move from lake to lake by 16 portages of various lengths and difficulties. These routes crisscross the 45-mile length and 9-mile width of the island's rippled topography, revealing its long coves, fjord-like inlets and the surrounding 200 scattered islets.

This ridge-and-valley landscape was formed about 1.2 billion years ago as waves of lava poured forth from cracks in the earth's crust. Subsidence then tilted the layers of hardened lava near the rim of what is now the Superior Basin, forming long, roughly parallel ridges and valleys. Greenstone Ridge, which forms the spine of Isle Royale, is the most prominent of these ridges. The whole region was then scraped and eroded by the slow movement of four glacial periods. The island has only existed in its current form for the last 10,000 years—a mere moment in geological terms.

THE WILDERNESS WORLD

The park was formally established on March 3, 1931, and in 1981 it was declared an International Biosphere Reserve. Even a short walk along one of the trails will reveal many of the island's 700 species of plant life, including 32 types of orchids. Because of its isolated nature, Isle Royale has proven to be an excellent environment to study the complex interrelations among its diverse animal species, most notably the moose and timber wolf.

Sometime early in this century, moose either swam or walked to the island across the winter ice. They felt at home in the island's multitude of cedar bogs and swamps, many of which were created by the industrious beaver. Today, moose still number in the hundreds and have been the main source of food for the timber wolves that came to the island during the exceptionally cold winter of 1948-49.

Wolves and moose replaced the caribou, lynx and coyote that roamed Isle Royale around the turn of the century. The island is also home to muskrat, snowshoe hare and red fox.

A cow moose, browsing for food on Isle Royale's Stoll Trail, is part of a population that originally swam or migrated across winter ice from Canada, some 15 miles distant.

A LAND RENEWED

Today 100 percent of the park's land area is legally protected, but the island is far from being a pristine remnant of untouched wilderness. Instead, Isle Royale has felt the influence of both human and natural forces. Around 2000 B.C., the island became the site of North America's first copper mines. The island is one of the few places in the world where copper occurs in pure form and Native Americans came here in summer to dig for this shiny metal. Mining companies resumed the search for copper during the 19th century, leaving behind quarries and abandoned equipment.

Isle Royale once boasted a thriving commercial fishery, harvesting lake trout, whitefish and herring. However, fishing on the Great Lakes declined during the 20th century. Edison Fishery in Rock Harbor houses a living history program.

Nature's resilience has repeatedly turned disasters into opportunities for renewal. In 1936, a fire near a lumber camp burned a quarter of the island's forests. Burned areas have since become rich brushland and have actually saved the moose population from starvation by rejuvenating its food supply.

FOR MORE INFORMATION:
Superintendent, Isle Royale National Park, 800 E. Lakeshore Drive, Houghton, MI 49931. (906) 482-0984.

Rock Harbor Lighthouse signals the approach to Isle Royale's main point of entry. Rock Harbor provides easy access to hiking trails, boat tours and visitor services.

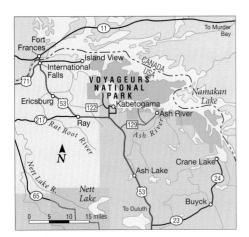

Gold Portage guides canoeists around the rapids at the base of Kabetogama Peninsula. For the voyageurs, portaging meant hoisting back-breaking loads of furs.

Although most visitors get around Voyageurs by motorboat, the wonders of Minnesota's only national park reveal themselves best to those who quietly paddle a canoe on one of the park's 30 lakes. One-third of Voyageurs National Park's 217,892-acre expanse is covered by water and most of its 900 or so heavily wooded islands can only be reached by boat. This island-speckled aquatic network, nestled against the Canadian border, once formed a link in the historic fur-trading route. The park takes its name from the resourceful French-Canadian canoemen (voyageurs) who guided 26-foot birch-bark canoes laden with up to 3,000 pounds of animal pelts from the isolated outposts of Canada's interior to trading posts such as Grand Portage, at the head of the Great Lakes, and Rainy Lake, in what is now Voyageurs National Park.

The strength and stamina of the compact and wiry voyageurs were legendary. With perfect rhythm, to the accompaniment of boisterous *chansons* (songs), the canoe was propelled by 50 strokes a minute for up to 16 hours in a day. To travel the onerous overland trails, or portages, that linked lakes and rivers, the eight crewmen had to carry tremendous loads, attached to the forehead by a leather strap.

By the 1840's European fashion trends favored silk hats over fur and the demise of the voyageurs was sudden. This land of hardwoods and conifers soon became the site of extensive logging operations.

A WILDERNESS SANCTUARY

Touring the region by seaplane, Charles Lindbergh once remarked, "The area is so beautiful and extraordinary that it seems to me it would be a tragedy to miss the opportunity of establishing it as a national park." Because of its wealth of timber—willows, aspens, white spruce, red and white pines—logging was a major industry until 1975 when the area became a federal reserve. Voyageurs is now a permanent sanctuary not only for the trees, but also for many species of wildlife.

Birds abound within the park; its estimated 240 species include ospreys, cormorants, loons, gulls and red-necked grebes. Along the shore, great blue herons wade gracefully in search of crayfish or frogs. At least 14 pairs of majestic bald eagles are known to nest in Voyageurs. After white-tailed deer, the most commonplace mammal is the industrious beaver. Moose can sometimes be seen browsing in shallow bays or bogs for a mouthful of aquatic plants. Fishermen rarely cast their lines in vain—delicious walleye, northern pike and smallmouth bass are in abundance.

Together with Michigan's Isle Royale National Park, Voyageurs is one of the small scattering of places in the continental United States that boasts a population of the endangered eastern timber wolf. The much-maligned silvery-black beast leads an invisible existence, and poses no threat to humans. Its spine-tingling howl can sometimes be heard on moonlit nights.

Thick stands of aspen, pine, spruce and white birch cloak the rocky islands and rugged Kabetogama Peninsula. The forest floor supports swarms of wild fruit, including raspberries, blueberries, strawberries and juneberries. The extensive bogs are graced with fragrant honeysuckle, pink-flowered cranberry stems and drooping red spoonleaf moss. Winsome marsh marigolds and lady's-slippers appear almost as soon as the last snows have melted, accompanied by ground-hugging wild ginger.

FOUR-SEASON PARK

The primitive campsites on the park's secluded islands are open year-round. There are few hiking trails, as most sites are reached by water. Access is limited only during freeze-up (mid-November to mid-December) and thaw-out (April). In winter, the frozen lakes are ideal for snowmobiling, cross-country skiing, ice fishing and snowshoeing. A seven-mile ice road, allowing cars to enter the park over frozen Rainy Lake, begins at Rainy Lake Visitor Center—the only one of the park's three visitor centers that is open throughout the year.

Outnumbered by motorboats and houseboats, the modest canoe is still the ultimate way to savor the outdoors. The abundance of wildlife in the park is visible to those who paddle softly, outpaced by the speeding bright darts of dragonflies. The echoing cries of the loon are ample reward for modern adventurers following the paths of the voyageurs.

FOR MORE INFORMATION:
Superintendent, Voyageurs National Park, 3131 Highway 53, International Falls, MN 56649-8904. (218) 283-9821.

Hundreds of forest-cloaked islands, most of them unnamed, wait to be discovered in Voyageurs National Park. The area was an important logging site until 1975.

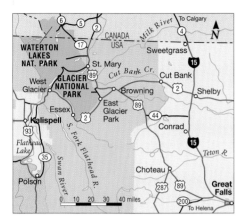

P erched on the Continental Divide and straddling the border between the United States and Canada, Glacier National Park's 1,013,572 acres preserve an unmatched slice of Rocky Mountain scenery. Alpine glaciers, 200 shimmering lakes, luxuriant forests and an extraordinary diversity of wildlife are among the park's attractions for serious hikers and motorists alike.

Officially, Glacier National Park is the southern portion of the Waterton-Glacier International Peace Park. North of the border, Waterton Lakes National Park is Glacier's Canadian sister. The two parks were linked in 1932 to promote goodwill between the two countries.

RIVERS OF ICE

Glacier takes its name from the great rivers of ice that gouged and shaped its landscape. During the four distinct periods of glaciation, only the highest peaks were not covered by ice. The last of the glaciers retreated some 10,000 to 20,000 years ago. Testimony to the work of these massive land sculptors is visible throughout the park in the form of U-shaped valleys, saddle-horn peaks, precipitous basin walls and lofty "hanging valleys." The knife-edged Garden Wall, located on the Continental Divide, was formed when two glaciers scraped and gouged both sides of a long ridge. Fifty small glaciers are reminders of the power of moving ice. The two most notable are Grinnell, nestled on the eastern side of the Garden Wall, and Sperry, high above Lake McDonald.

Yet Glacier is more than spectacular mountain scenery. The Continental Divide separates the park into two climatic environments, marked by heavy rainfall

St. Mary Lake is one of the largest of Glacier's 650 lakes. Ten miles in length, it lies in a U-shaped valley created by a glacier that moved down from the Continental Divide.

Cream-colored beargrass, Glacier's unofficial flower, adorns Logan Pass, 6,646 feet above sea level. The flower—a type of lily—grows throughout the park.

and moderate temperatures on the western side, with drier conditions to the east. Its landscape includes dry grassland on the eastern foothills—lush forests of lodgepole pine, Douglas fir, quaking aspen and red cedar; stands of stunted alpine trees; and fragile arctic tundra.

The lower altitudes are home to moose, white-tail and mule deer, chipmunks, pine martens, badgers and coyotes. Higher elevations are the domain of the sure-footed

mountain goat and Rocky Mountain bighorn sheep. More than 200 bird species soar through the park, including rare bald and golden eagles, some of whom arrive in spring to nest in the park.

HOME OF THE BEAR

The park is famous for its population of black and grizzly bears. Several hundred of the remaining grizzly bears in the U.S. outside of Alaska live in and around Glacier and Waterton parks. These giants can reach 600-800 pounds in weight, but live mainly on grass, berries and roots.

Glacier's more than 700 miles of maintained footpaths lead to spots such as Heaven's Peak and Dawn Mist Falls. These trails present ample opportunities for hiking, horseback riding, and in winter, cross-country skiing. The glacier-fed lakes offer superb boating and fishing, but their low temperature may discourage swimmers!

Naturalist John Muir once said that it would take a month to see all of the park's wonders, but a day on any of the trails will provide a good sampling. To appreciate Glacier's full glory, cross the Continental Divide from west to east by way of the 50-mile Going-to-the-Sun Road—completed in 1932 and considered one of the world's most spectacular highways. This avenue of natural splendor will stir the soul of even the most casual traveler.

FOR MORE INFORMATION:
Superintendent, Glacier National Park, West Glacier, MT 59936. (406) 888-5441.

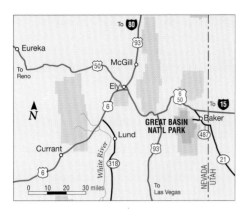

A gnarled bristlecone pine grows on the slopes of Mount Washington. These trees, the oldest on earth, can withstand even the harshest winter conditions.

Great Basin National Park, established in 1986, preserves a diverse environment including palatial limestone caves, Nevada's only glacier, and stands of bristlecone pine, the world's oldest tree.

The Great Basin is a huge dry region of the western United States, which consists of 90 alternating valleys and mountain ranges. It stretches from the Wasatch Mountains in Utah to the Sierra Nevada range in California. The encircling mountains mean that rivers and streams do not drain into the ocean, but soak into the ground or accumulate in landlocked lakes. In an otherwise dry and dusty environment, the mountains capture enough moisture to sustain ecosystems which are so rich as to be unimaginable on the plains below.

The 77,109-acre Great Basin National Park is one of the youngest in the nation. Due to its age and great distance from major population centers—Salt Lake City and Las Vegas are 340 and 250 miles away respectively—the park is rarely crowded. Many of Great Basin's visitors comment that they see more animals than people while hiking the park's 65 miles of trails.

A JOURNEY INTO THE SKY
A visit to Great Basin usually begins at the Lehman Caves, a quarter-mile-long subterranean landscape of limestone and marble chambers carved by water seeping through cracks in the rock. Mineral-rich water then created fantastic stalactites and stalagmites, columns, flowstones, rare shields and clusters of snow-white needles.

A 12-mile highway known as Wheeler Peak Scenic Drive (closed in winter) takes visitors into the heart of the Snake Range, and leads to the top of Wheeler Peak—at 13,063 feet, the second-highest summit in Nevada. As the road climbs, the arid

Wildflowers cling to life in stony Wheeler Cirque, a glacier-carved valley below Wheeler Peak. At the top of the valley is Great Basin's last glacier, the Wheeler Icefield.

sagebrush of the desert floor sinks away below, and piñon-juniper woodlands and aspen trees start to appear along with clumps of manzanita shrubs and mountain mahogany, which grow to tree height. At 9,000 feet, Douglas fir and spruce trees complete the transformation from the Nevada Desert to this island of northern vegetation. Subalpine forests of limber pine, spruce and aspen are interspersed with meadows filled with wildflowers.

The road ends at the Wheeler Peak Campground—one of four campgrounds in the park—and the rest of the trip to the summit must be accomplished on foot.

On the way, ice-cold streams twist and tumble through the forests, which are home to many of Great Basin's numerous mule deer. Sparkling blue alpine lakes are fed by the rains and meltwaters from Nevada's only glacier. The glacier is nestled in a great U-shaped basin at the foot of the 2,000-foot cliffs on Wheeler's northeast face.

THE WORLD'S OLDEST TREES
At the 10,000-foot elevation point grows one of the park's three groves of tenacious bristlecone pines—*Pinus longaeva*, or "long-lived pines." These gnarled and twisted survivors are the world's oldest living tree species. With their gray, wind-sculpted trunks, bristlecones may appear dead, but they cling to life, almost oblivious to the passage of time. The trees adjust to changes in moisture, and the dense, resinous wood prevents rot. Many of these venerable trees are more than 4,000 years old. At the snowy summit of Wheeler Peak, the solitude and isolation of Great Basin National Park are at their most pronounced. On a clear day, the view can extend for up to 140 miles in any direction—the most allowed by the earth's curvature.

FOR MORE INFORMATION:
Superintendent, Great Basin National Park, Baker, NV 89311. (702) 234-7331.

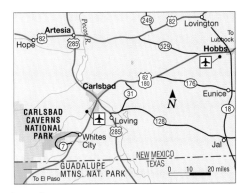

The Guadalupe Mountains rise up above the Chihuahuan Desert, a dry, windswept plain of cacti, mesquite and scrub that seems to contain very little life. But there is more here than meets the eye. For beneath the desert, at the base of the mountains, sits Carlsbad Caverns, a series of enormous caves that has stunned visitors with the unmatched splendor of its rock formations since it was designated a national park in 1930.

The mountains were once a horseshoe-shaped limestone reef on the shores of a large inland sea. When the sea evaporated, the mountains were buried under deposits of sediment, but uplift and erosion uncovered them again. Hydrogen sulfide gas, slowly emitted from petroleum deposits buried deep beneath the limestone, dissolved the limestone and hollowed out enormous underground chambers and passageways.

DECORATION AND DISCOVERY
About 500,000 years ago, the cave filled with air. When mineral-rich water, seeping down from the surface, reached the cave chambers, it partially evaporated, depositing its load of dissolved limestone. The slow build-up of limestone created the stalactites, stalagmites, popcorn and flowstones that represent the park's greatest treasures.

The caverns were discovered in the late 1800's, when settlers spied a column of bats seemingly rising from the ground. Tracing the column to its source, they discovered the mouth of a cave. At that time, the cave's bat population numbered many millions. Today, Carlsbad is home to about 1,000,000 Mexican freetail bats. The nightly bat flight, in which up to 5,000 bats a minute issue from the cave with a roar of fluttering wings to hunt for insects, continues to this day. An amphitheater built at the cave entrance allows park visitors to witness this awesome display.

The proliferation of bats attracted miners, who in 1903 began to extract bat guano. During the next 20 years more than 100,000 tons of this rich fertilizer were extracted from the cave. One of the miners, Jim White, began exploring the caverns in his spare time. Few people believed his descriptions of the size of the caverns and the limestone wonders they contained until White convinced a photographer to venture down into the caves with him.

By 1923 the fame of the caves had spread across the nation. Reports of its wonders led to Carlsbad Caverns being proclaimed a National Monument in 1923. The region was elevated to national park status seven years later.

CHAMBERS IN THE EARTH
Although more than 25 miles of caverns have been explored and mapped, only three miles are open to the public. From the Bat Cave near the entrance to the park, visitors descend through the Main Corridor and Scenic Rooms, into the Big Room, which contains the Hall of the Giants. There are two color-coded tours: the three-mile Blue Tour, and the one-and-a-quarter-mile Red Tour. The Blue Tour takes in the lunar spookiness of the Green Lake Room, festooned with thousands of fragile stalactites. Stunning crystal formations such as spindly stalks of stone, called helictites, extending in every direction can be found in the Queen's Chamber.

The Big Room often leaves visitors with the feeling that mere words cannot do justice to its massive proportions: the chamber is 1,800 feet at its longest, 1,100 feet at its widest and 255 feet at its highest. It is the largest underground chamber open to the public in the Americas. It frequently takes visitors more than an hour to walk around its perimeter. Appropriately, this is the home of the towering Giant Dome—a 62-foot stalagmite.

Will Rogers once called Carlsbad Caverns, "The Grand Canyon with a roof on it." Almost 750,000 people come here annually, to be overwhelmed by the scale of both time and space permanently on display in this gallery of stone masterpieces.

FOR MORE INFORMATION:
Superintendent, Carlsbad Caverns National Park, 3225 National Parks Highway, Carlsbad, NM 88220. (505) 785-2232.

Carlsbad Caverns' beautiful rock formations were built up over many thousands of years as dissolved minerals were deposited by water. In some parts of the caves, this process still continues.

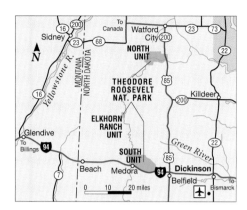

Long before people roamed the grasslands of the Great Plains, wind, water and fire worked together to create the buttes, canyons and rock pillars that form North Dakota's Theodore Roosevelt National Park. This rugged terrain, known simply as the North Dakota Badlands, sparked a future president's passionate interest in conservation and still casts a spell over roughly 475,000 visitors each year.

Named for President Teddy Roosevelt in 1947 and given national park status in 1978, the park preserves only a small part of the extensive Badlands. The park consists of three separate units, which are joined by the meandering Little Missouri River. Largest is the South Unit, containing two-thirds of the park's 70,416 acres. The North Unit lies approximately 45 miles north by road—or three days by canoe. Between the two areas is the tiny Elkhorn Ranch Site, Roosevelt's principal home and the base of his cattle business a century ago.

Theodore Roosevelt came to the Badlands in 1883 to bag a buffalo. Taken by its wildness, he returned as a cattle rancher until bad weather and overgrazing killed his operation. The years he spent here saw the disappearance of the great buffalo herds and taught him how easily humans can upset nature's delicate balance. As 26th president, Roosevelt would pass on the lesson he learned in the Dakota Territory, establishing five national parks in an era when such foresight was rare.

BIRTH OF THE BADLANDS

The Badlands are composed of layers of soft clays and siltstones, first deposited onto a sea-level delta. When the Rocky Mountains were uplifted some 65 million years ago, streams and rainfall began to wash more eroded material down onto the Plains.

Then, the great continental ice sheets slowly inched their way across the continent, altering the course of the Little Missouri River, which once flowed lazily north to Hudson Bay, causing it to veer eastward to join the Missouri River.

Following a steeper route, the river sliced canyons through the rock.

Over the last two million years, rivers and streams have dissected and eroded this land, carving out buttes and valleys. Rain, running over tough sandstone, assaulted the soft rock beneath to form thousands of strange rain pillars; wind has ceaselessly sandblasted the pliant rock, molding smooth shapes here and complex patterns there. Fire, ignited in layers of lignite coal—the remnants of prehistoric forests—has baked the clay crowning many hills a vivid brick-red. Hard gray clay produced from volcanic ash 55 million years ago has formed a slick shield, impenetrable to most plant life. Rainwater forced away from this hard terrain continues to cut channels through softer rock, constantly deepening the gullies and ravines. Painted Canyon Overlook, in the South Unit, presents an unmatched view of this landscape.

Ranchers used horses to gain mastery of this punishing terrain and wild descendants of their steeds can be seen grazing along the paved 36-mile Scenic Loop Drive circling the South Unit. About 500 bison live in the park, along with deer, elk, pronghorn antelope, prairie dogs, bighorn sheep and countless birds. After a spring rain, wildflowers line the park's network of trails.

The North Unit attracts fewer visitors but offers some of the most spectacular scenery in the park. The geology textbook comes to life on the 14-mile scenic drive from the entrance to Oxbow Overlook. At the foot of flat-topped cliffs, where a few longhorn cattle roam, can be seen slump blocks—massive dome-shaped hills that, over the centuries, slid intact to the valley floor. They are easily identified by their tilted rock layers.

When General Alfred Sully came here to battle the Sioux in 1864, he described the Badlands as "like hell with the fires out." Visitors today have kinder things to say. The hunched and craggy bluffs and deep canyons of the national park offer hiking, backpacking and horseback riding in abundance. The park's two primitive campgrounds—Squaw Creek in the North Unit and Cottonwood in the South Unit—are open all year round.

Visitors who leave their cars will experience closeup the many delights this park offers the senses. The spicy smell of sagebrush, the hysterical barking of coyotes, the whisper of wind, a sudden flight of grouse. Crowds are a rarity here, so one can savor the lonely majesty of the Badlands just as Roosevelt did more than a century ago.

FOR MORE INFORMATION:
Superintendent, Theodore Roosevelt National Park, P.O. Box 7, Medora, ND 58645. (701) 623-4466.

The banded sediments exposed in Painted Canyon provide a kaleidoscope of colors: pinks, reds, blacks, ochres, browns and yellows.

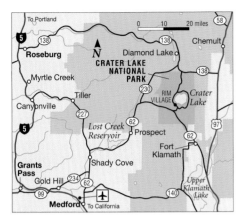

Crater Lake lies in the caldera of Mount Mazama. The explosion of the mountain almost 7,000 years ago scattered ash over what are now eight states and three Canadian provinces.

The sight that greeted a group of weary prospectors, who had puffed their way to the top of a mountain in the Cascade Range in June of 1853, must have made them gasp in astonishment. A vista of dreamlike perfection lay before them: the rim of rock at their feet plunged like a steep-sided bowl to a huge lake of incomparable blue. They called it Deep Blue Lake, but the world knows it as Crater Lake, centerpiece of the 183,227-acre Crater Lake National Park.

Sometime before 5,700 B.C., a series of violent eruptions of the massive Mount Mazama climaxed in an explosion 42 times more powerful than the eruption of Mount St. Helens in 1980. Enormous outflows of rock, ash and lava from the volcanic core created an enormous hollow within. Finally the mountain itself collapsed, leaving a huge pit, or caldera, some six miles wide and 4,000 feet in depth. Over the centuries it filled with rainwater and melted snow to form the deepest lake in the United States and the seventh deepest in the world.

THE BLUE LAKE

No streams or rivers feed Crater Lake and it held no fish until they were introduced in the late 19th century. The absence of dissolved minerals and organic matter in the water gives it an incredible clarity. Sunlight penetrates so deep that green algae grow hundreds of feet below the surface. But most sensational is the lake's effect on color. Longer wavelengths of red, yellow and green are absorbed at a certain depth, but water molecules scatter some of light's shorter blue wavelengths back up to the lake's surface and give the surface its intense blueness. It is no wonder that the lake was sacred to early Indians.

They believed that the lake was created by spirits fighting so fiercely that mountaintops smashed, raining hot rocks on villages and creating rivers of fire. The Indians dared not gaze upon its blue waters or speak its name. The same sense of awe

gripped Kansas schoolboy William Gladstone Steel in 1870. He read about the lake in a newspaper wrapped around his school lunch and became obsessed. After seeing it for himself, he devoted his life to creating a national park here and succeeded in 1902.

AROUND THE RIM

The 33-mile paved Rim Drive allows the visitor to circle the caldera in about half a day, perhaps stopping to picnic amid the wildflowers of Vidae Falls. In summer, visitors can tackle the steep mile-long trail to Cleetwood Cove, where they can board a boat for a guided tour of the lake. They can camp out in the shadow of lodgepole pines surrounded by Steller's jays at Mazama in the south, near a canyon gouged by icy Annie Creek. Snow blankets all of the 140

Dikes of hardened lava on the caldera slopes have resisted centuries of erosion.

miles of trails from October to June, closing the Rim Drive but making possible cross-country skiing and snowshoeing.

Evidence of the Mazama's great eruption lies throughout the park. At the Pinnacles in the park's southeast corner, spires of hardened ash—pipes from which gas escaped through piled ash—rise like a forest of dunce caps. Ignoring the violent history of this place, colorful dwarf monkeyflower thrives north of the lake in a plain of volcanic ash called Pumice Desert.

In Crater Lake, the "sails" of the ghostly Phantom Ship near the lake's south edge pierce the placid blue water to the height of a six-story building—the remnants of a dike of hardened lava. Black garter snakes have evolved to blend with the dark lava of Wizard Island, a cinder cone formed by a lesser eruption after the great collapse.

Under a full moon, the still lake mirrors perfectly the rocky caldera rim. When William Steel rowed out into the center in 1886, he spoke for all who followed when he later wrote of this experience: "I was an atom in the center of an enormous sphere ... Did ever human eye behold such a sight?"

FOR MORE INFORMATION:

Superintendent, Crater Lake National Park, P.O. Box 7, Crater Lake, OR 97604. (503) 594-2211.

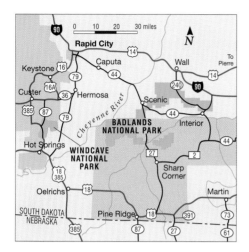

BADLANDS

This park houses a 100-mile-long geological curiosity, known simply as "the Wall," which extends across the arid plains of South Dakota. The dramatic contours of its ridges, buttes, spires and gullies cut through multicolored layers of rock. The Oglala Sioux named this tortured landscape mako sica, which means "land bad."

The Badlands are the heavily eroded remnants of layers of sediment that were first deposited by rivers that flowed across the region about 30 million years ago. Although annual rainfall is only about 16 inches, summer downpours continue to alter the face of the land at a fantastic pace.

Badlands National Park, established in 1978, occupies 244,300 acres of this terrain. The North Unit of the park offers many short and accessible trails, which quickly

The soapweed, or yucca, is one of the most common of the more than 300 varieties of plants and wildflowers that flourish amid the eroded buttes and ridges of the Badlands.

Wind Cave's grassland provides ample grazing for about 350 bison. Hunted almost to extinction in the 19th century, the bison was reintroduced to the park in 1913.

give visitors a feel for the serrated hills of the Wall; the wilder South Unit has few roads and no hiking trails. Today, its prairie grassland is home to a few Rocky Mountain bighorn sheep.

Erosion in the Badlands has exposed some of the world's richest fossil beds. These yield an accurate picture of life during the Oligocene Epoch, some 25-34 million years ago, when creatures such as the mesohippus, a collie-sized relative of the horse, roamed the region.

In more recent times, the Badlands belonged to the Oglala Sioux, who dominated the prairies until the influx of white settlers in the mid-19th century. Stronghold Table, in the park's South Unit, is sacred ground to the Sioux.

FOR MORE INFORMATION:

Superintendent, Badlands National Park, P.O. Box 6, Interior, SD 57750. (605) 433-5361.

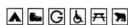

WIND CAVE

Nestled along the southeastern edge of the Black Hills of South Dakota, Wind Cave National Park could be described as two parks in one. A glance across the 29,292 acres of sun-swept prairie gives little indication that beneath its surface lies a limestone labyrinth of passageways, formed by uplift and the dissolving action of water over the last 350 million years.

Prairie grassland covers about 75 percent of the the park, and the Black Hills form an island in this sea of grasses. Many eastern and western species of animals and plants coexist here at the limit of their ranges. The park offers the chance to see animals such as the pronghorn antelope and coyote in their natural habitats. Wind Cave is also one of the best places in the country to see up close the seemingly docile but unpredictable bison.

THE UNDERGROUND PARK

Legend has it that in 1881 two hunters heard a loud whistling noise and found it coming from a hole in the ground, accompanied by a tremendous wind. Tales of the strange phenomenon spread and explorers soon made forays into the cave's depths.

The cave is relatively dry, so stalagmites and stalactites are rare. Instead, the cave boasts the world's largest collection of boxwork, a thin honeycomb-shaped structure made of calcite that protrudes from walls and ceilings. Frostwork—delicate crystals of calcite and aragonite—is plentiful here. To date, nearly 64 miles of passageways have been documented, but miles of corridors await their first human visitors.

FOR MORE INFORMATION:

Superintendent, Wind Cave National Park, RR1, Box 190-WCNP, Hot Springs, SD 57747. (605) 745-4600.

T he 50-mile chain of the Guadalupe Mountains rises from the floor of the Chihuahuan desert in west Texas, its imposing mile-high summits running in a north-south direction. El Capitan, the most prominent of the peaks, towers above the plains, an implacable sovereign watching over the 86,416-acre kingdom that is Guadalupe Mountains National Park.

The Guadalupe Mountains are the remnants of an ancient inland sea that covered much of Texas and New Mexico some 250 million years ago. Countless numbers of algae and sponges formed a huge barrier reef. Gradually the sea evaporated and the reef was buried by sediment. The reef resurfaced 100 million years ago when a gigantic uplift altered the landscape. The timeless forces of erosion have molded the mountains since then, combining with high-altitude moisture to produce the park's unique ecosystem. The arid desert gives little hint of the stunning contrasts that lie just a few hours' hike up the mountain slopes.

FROM DESERT TO FOREST

There are three distinct sections to Guadalupe Mountains National Park—the desert, the canyons and the highlands—all of which contain their own unique attractions and surprises. The desert is home to the agave, or century plant. Growing to a height of a one-story building, this strange plant grows for approximately 35 years then blooms and dies.

The park's canyons are oases of lush vegetation that startle hikers who come across them after only just leaving the desert floor. McKittrick Canyon, in the park's northeast corner, has been described as "the most beautiful spot in Texas." High cliffs shelter the canyon from the sun and a perennial spring allows an incredible range of plants to flourish, including ponderosa pine, walnut, maple, oak and the rare Texas madrone.

Guadalupe's biggest surprise lies 2,500 feet above the desert, in the Bowl, a large, heavily timbered basin. It is unusual to find a hardwood forest growing atop a west Texas mountain; and the Bowl's Douglas fir, pine and oak trees are a relict of a time when the climate of the entire region was much cooler and moister. The Bowl plays host to mule deer, elk, mountain lions and black bears.

APACHE AND STAGECOACH

The Guadalupe Mountains were historically the domain of the Mescalero Apache, a nomadic people who fiercely resisted the arrival of explorers and pioneers. A long and bitter conflict took place between the Apache and the U.S. Army. The area was also a link in the first transcontinental mail route. Near the Pine Springs campground lies the remains of a stagecoach station set up in 1857 by the Butterfield Overland Mail Line to link East and West. Guadalupe Mountains was officially designated a national park in 1972, largely through the efforts of two local landowners, geologist Wallace Pratt and Judge J.C. Hunter.

The park's 80 miles of trails allow visitors to experience the different worlds of Guadalupe firsthand. Under the watchful eye of El Capitan, visitors gain privileged access to a secret world, disguised by the desert and hidden on the slopes of the mountains.

FOR MORE INFORMATION:

Superintendent, Guadalupe Mountains National Park, HC60, Box 400, Salt Flat, TX 79847-9400. (915) 828-3251.

McKittrick Canyon cuts through the Guadalupe Mountains—formerly an oceanic reef—and provides a perfect glimpse into its past.

The dunes of the Chihuahuan Desert seem barren and empty of life, but they support agave, prickly pear and numerous small lizards and rodents. Guadalupe Mountains National Park preserves a small area of desert.

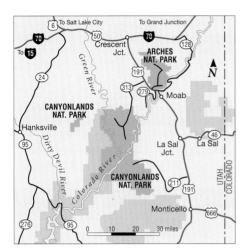

Landscape Arch, one of the longest natural stone spans in the world, is no more permanent than the desert cottontail that darts beneath its 306-foot span in high-tailed retreat from a coyote. Here lies the paradox of Arches: its beauty is found in that which can no longer be seen. The missing rock allows the arch to exist, but the passage of time will continue both to make and unmake all that is great at Arches.

FOR MORE INFORMATION:
Superintendent, Arches National Park, P.O. Box 907, Moab, UT 84532. (801) 259-8161.

The Loop is the most pronounced of the many S-shaped bends, or meanders, in the canyons of the Colorado River.

ARCHES NATIONAL PARK

It is as if nature bent over backwards on a Utah plateau to create Arches National Park. The world's greatest concentration of natural stone arches—more than 1,800—towers above a surreal landscape, casting arcaded shadows on the twisted piñon and juniper trees studding the parched soil. To gaze upon them is to consider the miraculous. But Utah rain, wind and frost are no miracle workers, just patient sculptors shaping this 77,379-acre rock museum from layers of entrada sandstone—a work commissioned about 100 million years ago.

The first American surveyors to see Utah's desert skies framed by stories-high arches might have thought they were in the presence of America's answer to Stonehenge. Geologists soon proved that the arches and monumental spires were the deteriorating remnants of sandstone blocks, fractured into long, roughly parallel, vertical "fins" as underlying salt domes were forced up through them millions of years ago. As the sandstone buckled, frost and running water worked into cracks and pores in the softer sides of some fins—eroding the stone, dissolving the salt domes and creating alcoves. Further erosion turned hollows into windows, and windows into arches.

FRAGILE BEAUTY

Delicate Arch is perhaps the most pristine example of an arch freed from stone by erosion. Majestically perched on the rim of a sandstone bowl, the arch has an opening height of 35 feet. From afar, it looks as delicate as the desert primroses clinging to the stone crevices nearby. And it is that delicate, for today's arch is tomorrow's rubble.

Although dwarfed by neighboring formations, Delicate Arch is one of the best known landmarks in Arches National Park.

CANYONLANDS NATIONAL PARK

Spread over the dramatic landscape of Canyonlands National Park is a veritable geological museum of arches, jagged cliffs, spires and sheer-walled canyons. Over millions of years, erosion has carved layers of sandstone to form this wilderness of rock configurations. The Green and Colorado Rivers meet here, in a deep canyon that plunges more than 2,000 feet below the top of Island in the Sky mesa. The river canyons split the park's 337,570 acres into a Y-shape, creating three distinct sections.

To the north, Island in the Sky offers matchless views of the park. White Rim Road circles the edge of the Island for about 100 miles, the habitat favored by the park's bighorn sheep. Here the vegetation is sparse, the land arid and sometimes unbearably hot.

To the west, the Maze is Canyonlands at its most untamed. The traveler who braves its crude trails will be rewarded by a silent, still world where nature is wide open and inviting. At the edge of the Maze, on the walls of Horseshoe Canyon, a richly detailed collection of rock paintings known as the Great Gallery presents a tantalizing, 2,000-year-old vestige of Native American culture.

To the east, the Needles comprises a startling array of sculpted rock spires, arches, canyons and potholes. The dominant formations—the needles themselves—are rock pinnacles banded in orange and white, massive sandstone spires created by erosion and fracturing.

FOR MORE INFORMATION:
Superintendent, Canyonlands National Park, 125 West 200 South, Moab, UT 84532. (801) 259-7164.

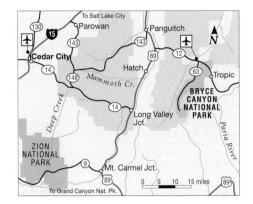

Sheer limestone cliffs tower above hikers as they enter the Wall Street section of Bryce Canyon's Navajo Loop Trail.

Bryce Canyon's ever-changing appearance has always sparked flights of imagination. Legend has it that when the Paiute Indians first mounted the Paunsaugunt Plateau, the top step of a colossal staircase descending from southern Utah to the Grand Canyon, they discovered the escarpment cavity and saw within "red rocks standing up like men in a bowl-shaped recess." Mormon settler Ebenezer Bryce gave his name to the spire-spiked canyon in the 1870's.

THE CARVING OF A PLATEAU

Like much of the Colorado Plateau, the 35,835 acres that is now Bryce Canyon National Park were once covered by a warm, shallow inland sea. About 60 million years ago, the sea receded and layers of sediment began to accumulate on the seabed. Later, movements of the earth's crust created the plateau almost two miles above sea level, fracturing the hardened sedimentary layers into blocks—like the Paunsaugunt Plateau—along fault lines in the rocks.

Bryce Canyon is only the largest of a number of horseshoe-shaped gorges formed through the steady erosion of the eastern edge of the Paunsaugunt Plateau. The edge of the plateau is rapidly eroding because it is fraught with vertical cracks known as joints. Bryce Canyon is the yawning heart of this zone. Rain, snow and ice have colluded for millions of years to break down and wash away its soft sedimentary rock. Slope debris loosened during winter freeze-thaw cycles is carried in the runoff, cracking and widening joints and eventually creating deep gullies and the strange rock pillars that are known as hoodoos. What remains is six square miles of natural amphitheaters populated by an upstanding cast of castellated stone characters. These rainbow-hued hoodoos inspire visions of everything from Queen Victoria and sinking ships to "platoons of Turkish soldiers in pantaloons."

Established in 1928, the park today hosts more than one and a half million visitors each year. Sixty-one miles of trails offer short and long hikes along the terra-cotta-colored rim, down the oxide-tinted canyon and through the shadowy diffusion of its maze-like floor. The closely packed towers of Silent City, a decibel-depleted floor maze, are actually a series of gully walls, some of which reach heights of more than 200 feet. The natural sound levels of the park are like those in a recording studio.

Other trails guide visitors to hoodoo formations with names such as Thor's Hammer, Gulliver's Castle and Queen Victoria. The rugged 22-mile Under-the-Rim Trail is a two-day odyssey from Bryce Point in the north to Rainbow Point in the south, guiding visitors not only through the ranks of eroded pillar, pedestal and toadstool forms, but also through some of the park's richly forested areas.

Those who descend to the bowels of the canyon are warned that the return trip uphill is strenuous, especially as the oxygen content of the air lessens at 7,000 to 9,000 feet. Drinking water is a suggested trail companion for all hikers.

On the plateau itself, a surprising variety of habitats supports forests of juniper, ponderosa pine and Douglas fir. The barren, wind-blasted pink cliffs at Rainbow Point are the park's highest elevation.

Here, only the hardy bristlecone and limber pines can flourish. Some 164 species of birds have been seen in the park area. Bryce Canyon National Park is also home to mule deer, ground squirrels, chipmunks, marmots, bobcats, coyotes and even the elusive cougar. Efforts are being made to re-establish the endangered peregrine falcon and the threatened Utah prairie dog, both native to the region.

THE VIEW FROM THE TOP

Bryce Canyon's scalloped beauty can also be captured from the 35-mile road that runs along the edge of the plateau. Park lookouts offer visitors stunning views.

As the sun rises any place along the rim between Fairyland and Paria Points, the changing light of day seems to work on the landscape like a temperamental painter who keeps changing the color to suit his mood. Then, with the fall of night, the silhouetted hoodoos close their ranks and stand watch in stony silence.

FOR MORE INFORMATION:

Superintendent, Bryce Canyon National Park, Bryce Canyon, UT 84717. (801) 834-5322.

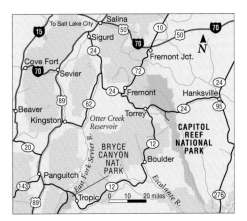

The Navajo Indians named it the "Land of the Sleeping Rainbow," and there has not been as succinct or exquisite a description since. The layers of multicolored sandstone, buckled over one another in soft waves along what is known as the Waterpocket Fold, prompted early travelers to call this barrier of parallel ridges a "reef." The rounded domes of the 1,000-foot-thick Navajo sandstone layer inspired comparisons with the Capitol building in faraway Washington. Capitol

Reef National Park, established in 1971, preserves 241,904 acres of a geological marvel that stretches for 100 miles across arid south central Utah.

Pierced by only a few canyons, the Waterpocket Fold imposes an isolation almost as complete as the Great Wall of China. However, humans have played no part in the making of this boundary. The stark, forbidding landscape of Capitol Reef was one of the last explored territories in America. Only in 1962 was the first paved road constructed through the region.

A WRINKLE IN ROCK

The shifting and collision of continental plates 65 million years ago may have caused the uplift of the Colorado Plate in the same extraordinary process that formed the Rocky Mountains. In the Capitol Reef area, the crust wrinkled, causing newer layers of sedimentary rock to fold over layers of ancient rock in an S-shape—the only place in the contiguous United States where this kind of rock formation exists.

Over the succeeding millennia, erosion wore down the rock layers at varying rates—depending on the hardness of each layer—to create the park's spellbinding peculiarities. These include brilliant multi-colored cliffs, towering spires, serpentine canyons, huge white domes, sylphlike arches and looming monoliths. The Fold itself takes its name from shallow, eroded depressions in the sandstone, known as waterpockets. Scarce rainwater accumulates in them, helping many creatures to survive in the arid environment.

At the north end of the reserve, Cathedral Valley is identified by its impressive, 500-foot, toothlike pillars of luminous sandstone. Dazzling phantom shades of maroon and golden-brown flit across this forsaken terrain. Until just a short while ago, Cathedral Valley was essentially unknown to the outside world; today only a few primitive, unpaved roads permit the visitor to unlock its barren secrets.

DESERT OASIS

Water is vital to sustain life in Capitol Reef's moisture-starved environment. For about 600 years, the Fremont Indians farmed and hunted in the vicinity of the life-giving waters of the Fremont River, until their disappearance around A.D. 1200. They left behind beautiful pottery and finely crafted figurines, pit houses fashioned from wood and brush, and petroglyphs and pictographs on cave walls.

Mormon settlers entered the region during the 1880's. One of their communities came to be known as Fruita because of

Grand Wash, a narrow canyon, cuts through Capitol Reef.

Cherry, plum, peach, pear and apple orchards still flourish around the old Mormon settlement of Fruita. Visitors can pick fruit here in season.

its resplendent orchards. These are located near the park's visitor center, and visitors can still pick fruit here.

The Fremont's moisture ensures more than human-introduced beauty. Its banks support lush groves of cottonwood, tamarisk and singleleaf ash trees, along with native wildflowers such as scarlet bugles, gilia, blue lupine and skyrockets. The sweet-smelling blossoms and greenery are an oasis in the midst of the sweeping, desolate panorama that begins only a few hundred yards away. Away from the river, hardy flowers flourish in the most unusual places, and robins, warblers and orioles are a common sight. Golden eagles make their nests on the high ledges of the Wingate Sandstone, and hundreds of migratory bluebirds grace the skies. Ring-tailed cats, foxes, nighthawks and a host of other creatures appear as night falls.

The park draws more than 700,000 visitors each year. The Capitol Reef Scenic Drive affords an easy introduction to the landscape of the Fold. There is a network of 15 maintained trails, and the backcountry offers many unmarked or little-used hiking routes. The difficulties of trekking through arid backcountry should never be underestimated, though wilderness backpacking through Lower Muley Twist Canyon and Halls Creek Narrows in the southern portion of the park is an unforgettable experience. Other rewarding destinations include Cassidy Arch (possibly the canyon hideout of the outlaw Butch Cassidy), Strike Valley Overlook and Golden Throne, site of a majestic cluster of sandstone domes.

FOR MORE INFORMATION:

Superintendent, Capitol Reef National Park, HC 70 Box 15, Torrey, UT 84775. (801) 425-3791.

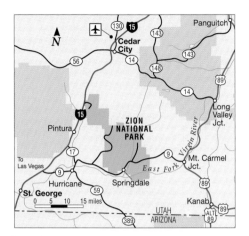

High above the park's campground, sunset drenches Zion's sandstone cliffs in a golden light.

The mighty sandstone cliffs and plunging canyons of Zion National Park have inspired feelings of reverence since the Anasazi and Paiute Indians occupied this corner of southwest Utah. The region was named by a Mormon settler who called it "Little Zion" because he was so taken with the "natural Temples of God" in what is now Zion Canyon.

Established in 1919, Zion National Park is a 146,551-acre world of canyons, grottoes, buttes, mesas, and stunning rock sculptures, all testifying to the power of erosion. At its heart is Zion Canyon, a deep gorge whose sheer cliffs plunge 2,000 feet to the canyon floor. Zion's collection of geological marvels has been carved over great spans of time by the North Fork of the Virgin River, a deceptively placid stream that runs southward through the park.

SCULPTED SANDSTONE

The canyon walls are made up of layers of limestone, sandstone, shale and volcanic ash, the most important section of which is the 2,000-foot-thick Navajo Sandstone. This layer of mineral-rich sedimentary rock, once the shifting sand dunes of a desert, was deposited some 150 million years ago. The soft, easily eroded Navajo Sandstone has been no match for the scouring power of the Virgin River. Each year, the river picks up and carries almost one million tons of loosened rock debris. Combined with the steep gradient—dropping almost 80 feet per mile in some spots—this has acted like sandpaper, scouring the canyon, and undercutting the sandstone of its banks.

The impressive natural sculptures left behind suggest enormous thrones, temples and altars. The subtle reds and whites of these awe-inspiring sheer cliff walls are caused by mineral deposits in the sandstone. After a rainfall, when waterfalls stream off the cliffs in crystal showers, the colors attain their greatest beauty.

For most visitors, the Zion-Mount Carmel Highway and the Zion Canyon Scenic Drive provide the best introduction to the park's marvels. The first begins at the park's East Entrance and follows the canyon carved by Pine Creek, a tributary of the Virgin. Highlights of this route include the Checkerboard Mesa, a colossal wall of sandstone grooved and cracked into rectangular patterns, and the Great Arch, a blind arch created when water undercut a section of the canyon wall.

The park's centerpiece is the Zion Canyon Scenic Drive, a six-and-a-half-mile route through the gorge of the Virgin River. The road passes Mountain of the Sun, Lady Mountain, the Great White Throne, Angel's Landing, Weeping Rock, and ends at the Temple of Sinawava, named for the coyote-spirit of the Paiute Indians.

Paved routes total some 23 miles, but Zion also boasts a network of 10 wilderness trails, totalling 116 miles in length, which guide visitors into the wild heart of the park. Gateway to the Narrows Trail probes a 12-mile erosion-enlarged cleft in the rock that is 2,000 feet deep but barely 20 feet wide. In the park's northwest corner, the La Verkin Creek Trail runs from Kolob Canyons Visitor Center to Kolob Arch— at 310 feet in length, the world's largest free-standing arch. The five-mile round trip

hike on the Angel's Landing Trail ascends 1,488 feet to reveal a spectacular view of Zion Canyon and the Great White Throne.

LIFE IN THE CANYONS

Each year about two and a half million visitors are drawn to Zion's stunning water-carved rock sculptures. The sheltered canyon floors nourish lush communities of wildflowers, and along river banks flourish groves of cottonwoods, box elder, willow and ash. The changing color of their leaves is a vivid seasonal counterpoint to the many-hued rock sentinels. More than 270 bird species have been recorded, including roadrunners and Gambel's quail. Cougars live in the park but are rarely sighted; bighorn sheep were reintroduced in 1970.

Although erosion continues to alter the landscape at a remarkable pace, the thoughts of geologist Clarence E. Dutton about the area in 1880 remain true to this day: "Nothing can exceed the beauty of Zion...in the nobility and beauty of the sculptures there is no comparison."

FOR MORE INFORMATION:

Superintendent, Zion National Park, Springdale, UT 84767-1099. (801) 772-3256.

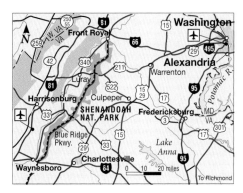

Named for the blue haze of humid air that blankets them, the Blue Ridge Mountains are a section of the larger Appalachian range.

Perched atop the Blue Ridge Mountains of Virginia, Shenandoah National Park is a living museum of rebirth and renewal. When the park was established in 1935, the hardwood forests that originally cloaked these ancient mountains had been severely depleted by decades of farming and logging. The park gave nature a second chance. Today, the peaceful forests, carpeted with wildflowers, furnish proof of its recuperative powers.

Whoever coined the term "old as the hills" probably had the Blue Ridge Mountains in mind. These granite monoliths were formed about one billion years ago. Later they were covered up, first by thick layers of volcanic basalt and then by layers of silt and sediment. The mountains were born when movements in the earth's crust uplifted a series of long, parallel ridges, which stretch from Alabama to Newfoundland. They are known as the Appalachian Mountains. The forces of erosion exposed the hard granite underneath.

Shenandoah lies in the zone of hardwood forest that once covered almost all of the northeastern United States. This natural deciduous forest included oak and hickory trees, but was dominated by the majestic American chestnut tree. Sadly, the chestnut trees have been wiped out, victims of logging and of chestnut blight.

The forests that cloak the Blue Ridge Mountains were never uniform in character. During the ice ages, the great glaciers never reached as far south as Virginia. But they influenced the climate of the region, encouraging the growth of coniferous forest, especially at higher, cooler elevations. Today, substantial stands of balsam, hemlock and spruce grow alongside Shenandoah's hardwoods. Throughout the park, the shady understory of these trees shelters a rich community of smaller trees, shrubs, wildflowers and mosses.

The Shenandoah Valley was first explored and settled by Europeans in the late 17th and early 18th centuries. Settlers cleared the land for farming, greatly affecting the balance of plant and animal life in the region. Removal of tree cover damaged the soil and led to erosion. Within 200 years, the cougar, wolf, elk and bison had almost completely vanished from the area. By the late 19th century, logging, agriculture and industry had practically exhausted the region's resources.

In the early part of this century, a movement grew to establish Shenandoah as a national park. Land was purchased by the state of Virginia and donated to the United States government. As a result, 465 families had to move. These mountain people were relocated in seven new settlements.

THE FOREST RETURNS

In the decades since the park's establishment, Shenandoah has returned to its former glory. Forest now covers more than 95 percent of the park's 195,403 acres. Amid towering hardwood trees and rocky hollows live 1,200 species of plants, 200 kinds of birds, and countless reptiles, amphibians, fish and insects. Hikers strolling beneath mighty oak, pine, maple and hickory trees might chance upon jack-in-the-pulpit or a rose azalea in full bloom. Near the Skyland resort—the highest point on the scenic Skyline Drive—lies the Limberlost, a grove of 500-year-old hemlock trees spared by loggers. Big Meadows, a three-square-mile field, was probably cleared in pre-colonial times. Today, it is kept open by park officials to allow grasses and berries to grow. Each year, two million visitors come to Shenandoah to witness the rejuvenation of its natural environment. The 105-mile Skyline Drive is perhaps the park's most famous attraction. Running north-south along the top of the Blue Ridge, the route winds all the way through the park's 70-mile length. Seventy scenic overlooks and numerous parking areas encourage visitors to stop and linger. Speed is limited to a leisurely 35 miles per hour. Most of the park's 500 miles of interconnecting trails are easily accessible from Skyline Drive. Bearfence Mountain Trail ascends 275 feet to reveal a spectacular 360-degree view of the Shenandoah Valley and the Appalachians. The park also contains a segment of the Appalachian Trail, a hiking route extending from Georgia to Maine.

As visitors drive along Skyline Drive or walk one of the trails, the miracle of renewal speaks out from every tree, plant and animal in the park. Shenandoah is a land of the past, revived and thriving in the present.

FOR MORE INFORMATION:

Superintendent, Shenandoah National Park, Route 4, Box 348, Luray, VA 22835-9051. (540) 999-3500.

Virgin Islands

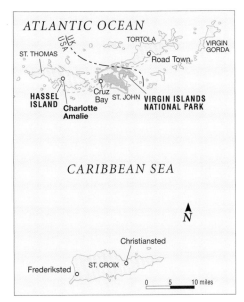

The island of St. John, in the U.S. Virgin Islands, lives up to the travel-brochure phrase "tropical paradise." About half of the island is home to Virgin Islands National Park, a 12,909-acre preserve—5,650 acres of it beneath the sea—established in 1956. The park ranks as one of the smallest national parks, but more than makes up for this in its diversity. On land, lush subtropical vegetation cloaks hills once planted with sugar cane. Under the sea, the park's coral reefs support complex communities of animals and plants.

When Columbus caught sight of the islands in 1493, he was so struck by their beauty that he named them after the 10,000 Virgins of St. Ursula. In Columbus' day, the islands were populated by members of the fierce Carib tribe. Control of the islands then passed into the hands of English, Dutch, French and Danish pirates and adventurers. In 1718 Danish colonists began to clear the islands' forests and set up sugar plantations. The plantations prospered until 1848, when Denmark abolished slavery. The islands remained under Danish rule until their purchase by the United States in 1917.

It is possible to drive through the park in a day. However, walking one of the island's trails, past the ruins of an old plantation or a cobblestone road overgrown with plant life, is one of the best ways to experience its riches. The hilltops reveal sweeping panoramas of the bays and glistening beaches below. The partly restored Annaberg Sugar Mill ruins nestle on a hill overlooking Leinster Bay. Built of coral blocks, as well as bricks imported from Denmark, the mill produced sugar, molasses and rum for export. The bay offers some of the park's best snorkeling.

Despite its small size, the park supports more than 800 species of subtropical plants, including mangoes, soursop, teyer palm and tamarind. The vegetation has almost completely reclaimed land once planted with sugar cane, cotton and indigo.

St. John's varied animal life is one of the reasons the park was named an International Biosphere Reserve in 1983. More than 100 bird species visit the island, including the yellow breasted bananaquit—the official bird of the Virgin Islands—and the pearly-eyed thrasher, known locally as the "trushee." Along the shore, brown pelicans and frigate birds soar above the waves in search of fish. Bats are the only mammals indigenous to the island; donkeys and mongooses were introduced in colonial times.

THE WORLD OF THE REEF

The other half of the park lies under the waves. The white beaches that ring the bays are an invitation to snorkel or scuba dive into an underwater world of intense colors and fascinating shapes.

Coral reefs are communities of tiny, tentacled creatures known as polyps, which measure only a fraction of an inch apiece. Polyps secrete calcium carbonate that forms into a tubular limestone casing around them. Thousands of polyps together create the coral reef formations. These formations grow slowly and are easily damaged: even the fastest grow only two or three inches each year, and a large piece of brain coral may take half a century to reach the size of a basketball.

A swim among the coral yields a spectacular display of color. Reds, yellows, blues and greens vie for prominence among the shallow-water elkhorn and staghorn coral. At the outer edges of the reefs are found brain and star corals, as well as plantlike sea plumes, sea whips and sea fans. Along the bottom live sponges, conch and starfish. Recesses in the coral are the domain of lobsters, crabs, octopuses, spiny sea urchins and the shy moray eel.

Schools of glittering fish of every shape and size dart over the reefs. The most common are the brightly colored parrotfishes, snappers, grunts, surgeonfishes and wrasses. Fishing is permitted along most of the coast, except for Trunk Bay and certain beaches designated as swimming areas. The crescent-shaped bay is considered to be among the world's 10 most beautiful beaches. Its white coral sands invite visitors to swim, snorkel along a marked underwater nature trail, or simply enjoy the sense of harmony between land and sea. A delicate balance exists between these two forces, making the park a unique environment.

FOR MORE INFORMATION:

Superintendent, Virgin Islands National Park, 6310 Estate Nazareth #10, Charlotte Amalie, VI 00802. (809) 775-6238.

A ruined sugar mill at Peace Hill on the island of St. John stands amid former plantation land now returned to subtropical jungle.

Turk's cap cactus flourishes today at peaceful Ram Head, where in 1733 leaders of a slave rebellion leaped to their deaths to avoid capture by Danish colonial forces.

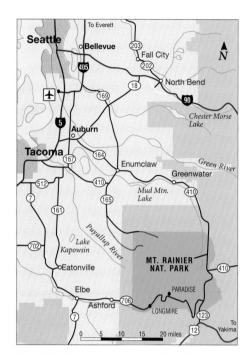

V isible on the horizon for a hundred miles, the majestic presence of Mount Rainier has captivated the imagination of visitors to this part of Washington ever since the volcano was named by Captain George Vancouver in 1792. Set amid 235,404 acres of dense forests, alpine meadows and imposing glaciers, the snow-capped mountain takes center stage. At 14,410 feet, it ranks as the highest peak in the Cascade Range and the fifth-highest in the United States. Wreathed by clouds, the peak towers over everything in the region, justifying its Indian name of Tahoma—The Mountain.

The mountain is part of the chain of volcanoes running along the Pacific coast known as the Ring of Fire. Over the last million years, powerful volcanic eruptions created Mount Rainier by forcing molten rock upwards through a fissure in the earth's surface. These cataclysmic forces also helped to shape the surrounding land. Thousands of lava flows have blanketed the area, forming ridges and filling in valleys. Mudflows have created the rivers, ridges and valleys in the surrounding countryside. Ash and pumice have blanketed the land, enriching the soil and encouraging the growth of trees and plants.

Twenty-five major glaciers carpet Mount Rainier's slopes—the largest single area of ice in the 48 contiguous states. Glaciers form when the amount of snow that falls in a given year exceeds the amount that melts. The weight of the snow forces the air out and compresses the snow into ice. The movement of the glaciers has inexorably eroded and shaped the valleys, which radiate down the mountain slopes. In summer, the four-mile Nisqually Glacier advances downhill one foot each day.

The park receives an abundance of rain and snow, particularly on the western side of the mountain. The heavy moisture encourages a profusion of wildflowers, mosses, ferns and trees. Dense forests of Douglas fir, red cedar and hemlock predominate on the lower slopes. Many trees in the park reach 250 feet in height and some are well over 500 years old. At higher elevations, the trees are smaller and less dense. Starting at about 6,500 feet, there are few trees, but patches of alpine wildflowers—phlox, white anemone and Tolmie saxifrage—cling to windswept meadows.

THE SLOPES OF PARADISE

A drive along the 80 miles of paved roadways that snake through the park is a good way to experience the park's different landscapes. The most famous trip is the carefully engineered 13-mile route that ascends 2,600 feet to the alpine meadow known as Paradise. The view of Mount Rainier from the flower-speckled meadow prompted the wife of settler James Longmire to exclaim, "this must be what Paradise is like!" The name has stuck, and the area is still the park's most popular attraction.

In the shadow of Nisqually Glacier, the Paradise Visitor's Center is the starting point for many of the 300 miles of nature trails and hiking paths that crisscross the mountain. A colorful pageant of wildflowers unfolds every summer as the paintbrush, firewood, asters, lupines and mountain goldenrod come alive. In winter, an average of 620 inches of snow makes Paradise a center for cross-country skiing, snowshoeing and other winter activities.

More adventurous hikers will relish the challenge of the Wonderland Trail. This 93-mile trail encircles Mount Rainier along a path that rises and falls a dizzying total of 20,000 feet. This mountain circuit takes two weeks to complete.

This sleeping giant's exterior hides an interior of potential violence. Like its neighbor Mount St. Helens, Mount Rainier will probably erupt again.

FOR MORE INFORMATION:
Superintendent, Mount Rainier National Park, Tahoma Woods, Star Route, Ashford, WA 98304-9751. (360) 569-2211.

The still waters of Reflection Lake perfectly mirror the mighty bulk of Mount Rainier. Like most of the park, the lake was carved out by local glacial movement.

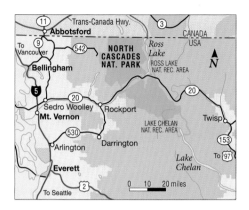

The Nooksack River has its source in the East Nooksack Glacier, one of the more than 300 glaciers in North Cascades National Park.

Like a turbulent ocean of stone, the hundreds of peaks of the North Cascades range present an awesome natural barrier. Explorers, fur traders and prospectors all tried to find a passage through these glacier-clad monoliths, and the names they gave some of them—Mount Fury, Mount Despair, Forbidden Peak, Mount Torment, Mount Terror—are testimony to the hardships of travel in this high frontier. Alexander Ross, a trader working for the Pacific Fur Company in 1814, commented: "A more difficult route to travel never fell to man's lot." Largely isolated from civilization even today, this untamed land has come to be known as the "American Alps."

North Cascades National Park is a rugged wilderness preserve established in 1968, encompassing 684,000 acres of the North Cascades range. The park includes the North and South Units of North Cascades National Park as well as the Ross Lake and Lake Chelan National Recreation Areas.

A GEOLOGICAL JUMBLE

The mountains were formed through a long and complex process of folding and faulting caused by movements in the earth's crust. Volcanic activity pushed new rocks to the surface, while prehistoric seas laid down layers of sediment. The appearance of the mountains today is largely the work of the great glaciers that once covered this part of North America. Glaciers carved wide, U-shaped valleys and left jagged ridges of peaks. Meltwater from the many glaciers that circle the mountains trickles into creeks and streams. They then cascade over the waterfalls, giving the range its name. This process contributes to the steady erosion of the landscape, but also enriches the verdant floors of the valleys.

From the lush river valleys to the desolate tips of the ice-clad peaks that jut more than 8,000 feet into the sky, North Cascades National Park's ecosystem is varied and vibrant. At low levels, the well-watered western slopes support forests of hemlock,

Douglas fir and red cedar, and a rich variety of shrubs. Wildflowers are at their best in the subalpine meadows, also the home of black bears, mule deer and hoary marmots. At high elevations, the tiny krummholz ("crooked wood") trees cling to life alongside yellow heather, moss campion, spreading phlox and 160 species of lichen.

This unspoiled region draws a half-million visitors a year, all of them eager to view nature at its most formidable and fascinating. The park is a paradise for hikers, backpackers and mountaineers. Visitors can hike on any of the 350 miles of trails. These range from the gentle one-mile

White and pink heather in an alpine meadow provide a colorful counterpoint to craggy Mount Challenger and slightly lower Whatcom Peak.

Thunder Woods Nature Trail to the grueling 35-mile Chilliwack River-Copper Ridge Loop in the North Unit.

Although very few roads enter the wild heart of North Cascades, the North Cascades Highway, along the Skagit River Valley, which divides the park's North and South Units, is known as "the most scenic mountain drive in Washington." Other drives include the unpaved Cascade River Road, which twists and turns through the South Unit before ending up between 8,200-foot Johannesburg Mountain and 8,894-foot Boston Peak. A ferry trip on Lake Chelan—the third deepest lake in the United States—is one of the few ways to reach Stehekin, a remote community on the North Cascade mountains' drier, sheltered eastern side.

FOR MORE INFORMATION:

Superintendent, North Cascades National Park, 2105 State Route 20, Sedro-Wooley, WA 98284. (360) 856-5700.

INDEX

PICTURE CREDITS

Cover photograph by Tom Bean
2 James Blank/Masterfile
5 Barbara von Hoffmann/Tom Stack
  & Associates

ACADIA
8, 9 Carr Clifton/AIIStock
10 Kerry T. Givens/Tom Stack & Associates
12 (lower left) Kennan Ward/Natural
  Selection
12,13 Carr Clifton/AIIStock
13 David Cavagnaro/Natural Selection
14,15 Ric Ergenbright
15 (upper right) Huston Westover/f/Stop
  Pictures
16 (left) Kennan Ward/Natural Selection
16 (right) Courtesy Maine Office of Tourism
17 (lower left) Robert Perron/f/Stop Pictures
17 (right) Don DeFeo, courtesy Wendell
  Gilley Museum

GREAT SMOKY MOUNTAINS
18,19 Marc Muench
20 (upper left) Michael Collier
20 (lower right) Pat O'Hara
22 (upper left) Michael Collier
22 (center) Michael Collier
22, 23 Daniel J. Cox/Natural Selection
24 (upper lest) Michael Collier; permission
  of Lloyd Owl/Qualla Arts & Crafts Mutual
24, 25 Lewis Portnoy/The Stock Market
25 (upper right) Anthony Mercieca/Natural
  Selection
26 J.A. Kraulis/Masterfile
27 (top) Courtesy Biltmore Estate
27 (bottom) Courtesy Museum of Appalachia

EVERGLADES
28, 29 Glenn Van Nimwegen
30 Glenn Van Nimwegen
32 Glenn Van Nimwegen
33 (upper right) Glenn Van Nimwegen
33 (lower left) Glenn Van Nimwegen
34 (upper left) Glenn Van Nimwegen
34 (lower left) Glenn Van Nimwegen
34, 35 Glenn Van Nimwegen
35 (lower right) Carl Purcell
35 (right center) Joe McDonald/Tom Stack
  & Associates
36 (left) Bill Sumner
36 (right) Stephen Frink/The Waterhouse
37 (upper right) Courtesy Florida Dept. of
  Commerce/Division of Tourism
37 (lower right) Stephen Frink/The
  Waterhouse

BIG BEND
38, 39 Carr Clifton/AIIStock
40 David Muench
41 Wyman Meinzer/Natural Selection
42 (upper) Art Wolfe/AIIStock
42 (lower) Graham French/Masterfile
42, 43 Carr Clifton/AIIStock
44 Wyman Meinzer/Natural Selection
44, 45 Carr Clifton/AIIStock
45 Lindsay Hebberd/Woodfin Camp &
  Associates
46 (left) Courtesy Government of Texas
46 (right) Matt Bradley
47 (upper) David Muench
47 (lower) Courtesy University of Texas
  at Austin

GRAND CANYON
48, 49 Tom Bean
50 Liz Hymans
51 Michael Collier
52 (lower left) Bruce Forster/AIIStock
52, 53 Tom Bean
53 (lower right) Tom Bean
54 Jeff Gnass/The Stock Market
55 (top) Tom Bean
55 (lower left) Glenn Van Nimwegen
56 (upper right) Tom Bean
56 (left) Neal Mishler/Natural Selection
57 Chad Ehlers/AIIStock
58 Michael Collier
59 (top) Kerry Hayes/Masterfile
59 (bottom) Michael Collier

YELLOWSTONE
60, 61 Carr Clifton/AIIStock
62 (left) David Hiser/Photographers/Aspen
62 (right) Daryl Benson/Masterfile
64, 65 Paul Chesley/Photographers/Aspen
65 (right) Randall A. Wagner
66 David Muench
67 (left) Jeff Foott/Tom Stack & Associates
67 (right) Stephen Krasemann/AIIStock
68 (left) Phil Schofield/AIIStock
68 (right) Dennis J. Cwidak
69 (upper) Tom Bean/AIIStock
69 (lower) Paul Hurd/AIIStock

YOSEMITE
70, 71 Bill Ross/Woodfin Camp & Associates
72 (upper left) Porterfield/Chickering
72 (lower nght) Robert S. Devine
74 (lower left) James Randklev/AIIStock
74, 75 Jonathan Blair/Woodfin Camp &
  Associates
75 (lower right) Paul Hurd/AIIStock

76 Pat O'Hara/AIIStock
77 Stephen J. Krasemann/AllStock
78 (upper) David Muench
78 (lower) Bill Ross/Woodfin Camp &
  Associates
79 Pat O'Hara
80 (upper left) Hal Clason
80 (lower left) Marc Muench/AIIStock
81 (upper right) Art Wolfe/AIIStock
81 (lower right) Sugar Pine Mountain
  Railroad

OLYMPIC
82, 83 Joanne E. Lotter/Tom Stack &
  Associates
84 Michael Collier
86, 87 Chris Jones/AIIStock
87 (top) Pat O'Hara
87 (bottom) Pat O'Hara
88 Pat O'Hara
89 Craig Tuttle/The Stock Market
90 (center left) Keith D. Lazelle
90 (lower left) Keith D. Lazelle
91 (upper right) Pat O'Hara
91 (right) Pat O'Hara

DENALI
92, 93 Ron Sanford/AIIStock
94 Johnny Johnson/AIIStock
96 Charles Mauzy/AIIStock
96, 97 Ken Graham
97 Kim Heacox
98 (upper) Galen Rowell
98 (lower) Kim Heacox
99 Kim Heacox
100 Courtesy Princess Tours
101 Kim Heacox (3)

HAWAII VOLCANOES
102,103 Bob Abraham/The Stock Market
104 Thomas Nebbia/Woodfin Camp &
  Associates
105 Bob Abraham/The Stock Market
106 (left) Greg Vaughn/Tom Stack &
  Associates
106 (right) David Muench
107 Salmoiraghi/The Stock Market
108 Erwin & Peggy Bauer/Natural Selection
108,109 Bruce Forster/AIIStock
109 (lower) James Ariyoshi
110 Rita Ariyoshi
111 (upper left) Rita Ariyoshi
111 (lower right) Robert Freck/The Stock
  Market
111 (upper right) James Ariyoshi

GAZETTEER
112 Hans Strand/AIIStock
113 (top right) Tom Bean
113 (bottom left) Tom Bean
114 (top right) Art Wolfe/AIIStock
114 (bottom left) Tom Bean
115 (top) Tom Bean
115 (bottom) Tom Bean
116 Bryan Harry
117 (top) J. A. Kraulis/Masterfile
117 (bottom) Tom Bean
118 (top) Matt Bradley
118 (bottom) Ryan & Berger/AIIStock
119 (top) Tom Bean
119 (bottom) Frans Lanting/Minden Pictures
120 (top) Tom Bean
120 (bottom) Dan Budnick/Woodfin Camp
  & Associates
121 J.A. Kraulis/Masterfile
122 (left) Tom Bean
122 (right) Tom Bean
123 (top) Tom Dietrich/AIIStock
123 (bottom) Annie Griffiths/Woodfin Camp
  & Associates
124 Peter Gridley/Masterfile
125 (top) Tom Bean
125 (bottom) Tom Bean
126 (top) Will Goddard Frozen Images
126 (bottom) Annie Griffiths/Frozen Images
127 (top) Steve Kaufman/AIIStock
127 (bottom) Steve Kaufman/AIIStock
128 (top) Tom Bean
128 (bottom) Tom Bean
129 Adam Woolfitt/Woodfin Camp &
  Associates
130 Steve Kaufman/AIIStock
131 (top) Michael Collier
131 (bottom) Ric Ergenbright/AIIStock
132 (top) Tom Bean
132 (bottom) Tom Bean
133 (left) Michael Collier
133 (right) David Muench/AIIStock
134 (top) Michael Collier
134 (bottom) John Blaustein/Woodfin Camp
  & Associates
135 Tom Bean
136 (top) Tom Bean
136 (bottom) Tom Bean
137 Tom Bean
138 (top) Art Wolfe/AIIStock
139 (left) Tom Bean
139 (right) Tom Bean
140 Pat O'Hara
141 (top) Pat O'Hara
141 (bottom) Pat O'Hara

ACKNOWLEDGMENTS
Gary Barbano, Pacific Group Office, NPS, Honolulu; Lei Branco, Hawaii Visitors Bureau; Carla Hall, Montana Dept. of Commerce; Steve Kemp; Bill Laitner, Everglades NP; Linda Meyers, Division of Publications, NPS; National Park Service; John Quinley.

Cartography: Map resource base compliments of the National Park Service; shaded relief courtesy of Bill von Allmen, NPS; maps produced by Hatra Inc.

The editors would also like to thank the following: Maryse Doray, Lorraine Doré, Michel Giguère, Irene Huang, Brian Parsons, Maryo Proulx.